A ROSICRUCIAN NOTEBOOK

Willy Schrödter

A ROSICRUCIAN NOTEBOOK

The Secret Sciences Used by Members of the Order

SAMUEL WEISER, INC.

York Beach, Maine

First published in 1992 by
Samuel Weiser, Inc.
Box 612
York Beach, ME 03910

03 02 01 00 99 98
10 9 8 7 6 5 4

Library of Congress Cataloging-in-Publication Data

Schrödter, Willy, 1897–1971
    [Geheimkunste der Rosenkreuzer. English]
    A Rosicrucian notebook : the secret sciences used by
members of the order / by Willy Schrödter.
        p.   cm.
    1. Rosicrucians.   I. Title.
    BF1623.R7S4513   1992
    135'.43—dc20   92-20656
                                                    CIP

ISBN 0-87728-757-0
MV

Typeset in 11 point Baskerville

Translated into English from German by *Transcript, Ltd.*,
Wales, Great Britain.

Printed in the United States of America

The paper used in this publication meets the minimum
requirements of the American National Standard for
Permanence of Paper for Printed Library Materials
Z39.48-1984.

In nomine JESU qui nobis est omnia!

—*Amor Proxima*
The Hague, 1686

He seemeth to be a setter forth of strange gods.

—Acts 17:18

Those who were *Masters* in days of old were secretly possessed of *invisible* powers.

—Lao Tse (604 B.C.)
Tao Te Ching 15

The Rosicrucians are a people I must bring you acquainted with.

—Alexander Pope (1688–1744)
The Rape of the Lock (1712)

The sole topic of conversation is the Rosicrucians.

—Anatole France (1844–1924)
La Rôtisserie de la Reine Pédauque (1893)

There is no higher or more lasting longing than that which can never be satisfied; no one has greater enjoyment in respect of purity and reality than he who makes a voluntary renunciation. Therefore the rose-entwined cross will remain the deepest symbol of our existence!

—Dr. Ernst, M.D.
Baron Feuchtersleben (1806–1848)
Zur Diätetik der Seele

Contents

Publisher's Note

Hargrave Jennings wrote *The Rosicrucians, Their Rites and Mysteries*, published in London in 1887, after thirty-six years of study. He explained how his interest developed:

> The author began his inquiries, in the year 1850, in a spirit of the utmost disbelief; thus taught by the world's assumptions and opinions. Much of this indoctrinated preoccupation the wise man has to unlearn in his progress through life. Fogs, and prejudices, and prepossessions cleared from the author's mind as he advanced. (p. 414)

Willy Schrödter spent a lifetime studying this same subject, the Rosicrucians, out of which came this book, first published in 1954 in Germany. It is a notebook, and as such, is incomplete. We have translated the material in much the same format as it appeared in the German edition. For example, some material is footnoted and some is referenced within the text itself. Because of the extensive use of footnotes, we have left this dual method of indicated sources to make it easier for the reader.

Some credits are incomplete and vague, and they must necessarily remain that way as the author is now deceased. We have retained German titles (followed by the English translation of the title) so that readers may research sources easily. Where the German title is obviously different and we knew the correct English title, we made the necessary changes. We hope that this volume will prove helpful to students of esoteric history and to those studying the healing methods of the early Rosicrucians.

PREFACE

Be not wiser than the ancients in thine own eyes, for
They also learned from their fathers!

—Sirach (VIII:11)

In this book I am going to inquire into the strangest alleged
knowledge of the Rosicrucians. To avoid the imputation of
making it all up, I have quoted with great care all my pains-
takingly located sources of information. Due to the loss of books
during the war, many of them could be consulted only where
there is a public library. However, this shortage of materials
did not prevent me from prosecuting my inquiries.

In any case, it is certainly not true that the Rosicrucians
dabbled in "peculiar" studies. On the contrary, they were thoroughly down-to-earth people, true sociologists and philan-
thropists who, anticipating the coming overpopulation of the
world and its attendant poverty, did all they could in the food
sector, for example. Thus a certain Johannes Staricius (Dr. Johannes a Strein), the contemporary and, sad to say, personal
enemy of Jakob Böhme (1575–1624), had published details of
a meat extract in his *Ägyptischen Heldenschatz*, etc., 250 years
before Justus von Liebig (1803–1873). The first Elector of Hanover, Ernst August (1629–1698), was offered by a traveling
"natural philosopher" an infallible method for softening bones
and roasting them like meat. Thus the occultists had anticipated
the people's soup of Sir Benjamin Thompson Rumford (1753–
1814). Unfortunately, Gottfried Wilhelm Friedrich von Leibnitz (1646–1716) prevented this project from being carried out
by decrying it publicly—and then was puzzled that he could

make no contact with the Rosicrucian Order! What is more, the above-mentioned Staricius suggested "multiplying" flour in time of need by adding finely ground dried straw (chaff)— something we actually imitated in the two world wars! The Rosicrucian, Dr. Karl Franz Paullini (1643–1712) referred in his notorious "Excrement Dispensary" to the freely available, if distasteful, human (and animal) excretia as medicaments for small people; materials from which hormones are being extracted in our own day and age! In other words, he was recommending oral hormone therapy with waste substances. Another Rosicrucian brother anticipated the teaching of Iliya Ilyiitch Metchnikoff (1845–1916), according to which death originates in the intestines, and formulated a cheap tisane to combat it which still bears his name. He was the real Count Saint-Germain (1696–1784?) with his purgative Saint-Germain tea of senna leaves, elder flowers, fennel, anise, tartar and tartaric acid. Klimakos Jr., the anonymous editor of the fairly important *ABC derer echten Weysen vom Stein der Weysen* (Berlin, 1779) devoted himself to new types of fertilizer and partly anticipated the suggestions of Rudolf Steiner (1861–1925) with his "biodynamic manure"! More than 60 years ago, the above-mentioned Joseph Alexandre, Marquis Saint-Yves d'Alveydre (1842–1909), wrote a technical paper on the use of marine algae, an idea which has been translated into reality today. Tests are in progress today on the utilization of algae as food—"Algae as a sandwich spread"—in fact. These tests are being carried out under the direction of Dr. Gummert in the Carbohydrate Biological Research Station at Essen and are very promising. Particular attention ought to be paid in this connection to the so-called companions of man—the lichens, the mosses, the grasses and the stinging-nettles!

However, even the "peculiar" researches of the Rosicrucians are not simply of theoretical interest from the purely historical point of view, but are valuable as guides and suggestions, as we shall now see.

INTRODUCTION

> For we be brethren of the ROSIE CROSSE; We have
> the Mason Word and second sight.
>
> —Adamson[1]

In the *Fama*, the basic document published in 1614, the Rosicrucians claim the following abilities:

1) To be able to ward off diseases from themselves and to rejuvenate themselves;[2]

2) To be able to heal others of so-called incurable diseases (e.g., leprosy);[3]

---

[1]Adamson, Henry, Master of Arts, of Porth (Scotland), in his *Muses Threnody* (1638).

[2]The zip-fastener king, Dr. Othmar Winterhalter (born 1890) rejuvenated himself in 1950, as a matter of fact, with a radioactive tincture prepared from element 85 (Astatine). Since the Rosicrucians also relied exclusively on radioactive preparations for rejuvenation, I shall pass over the other methods for restoring youth (Bogomoletz, Bardach, etc.). The *Mainzer Anzeiger* (No. 138 dated June 17th, 1936, p. 16) published a report on "The eternal youth of Annja Czernowitsch," who lived at Uralsk on the banks of the Ural river. At the age of 50 she had the appearance of a girl of 18 and her body resisted decomposition. The presumptive cause was the radioactivity of the water. The *Mittelrheinischer Anzeiger* (Mainz-Bingen, No. 71 dated March 25th, 1941, p. 5) reported the discovery of a vein of magnetite in central Sweden which should also contain radium. "Old people who exposed themselves to its radiations maintained that they felt rejuvenated." For rainwater as the Rosicrucian "Particular," see the *Annulus Platonis* (Berlin and Leipzig, 1781, p. 80, Note).

[3]We have now (once again) got antibiotics, but the prophet Isaiah used penicillin as a cure! He used a fig plaster to recover King Hezekiah of Judah

3) The generation of a cold light resembling sunlight;[4]

4) The possession of magical mirrors, bells, hanging lamps, and chants;[5]

5) The possession of a "book" (*The Rotae Mundi*) from which everything could be learned;

6) "Making gold is a trifling matter for them and only a paragon."[6]

7) In addition, they have "some thousand better little tricks." Many of these Rosicrucian "dreams" have already come true, although many await realization.

8) In the *Confessio*, another of their basic writings (1615), they speak of further powers: clairvoyance and clairaudience;

9) Telepathy.[7]

In their basic document, *The Chemical Wedding of Christian Rosencreutz. Anno 1459* (1616, c. "Sixth Day"), they described a "blast furnace heated by sunlight reflected from mirrors, for use in chemical experiments," or to put it more accurately for manufacturing the radioactive "Stone of the Wise" (in Latin =

(727–689 B.C.) of an ulcer (II Kings 20). The famous fungal mold grew on these figs!

[4]Luminous insects are being made the subject of investigation and the active substance "Luciferin" will soon be manufctured synthetically.

[5]In the invocation of the planetary Archons, as found in *The Confessio* (c. 4).

[6]In the meantime the elements have been successfully transmuted. "Paragon" should perhaps read "parergon" here.

[7]Agrippa of Nettesheim (1486–1535) in his *Occult Philosophy* (1510, Book I, c.6), indicated fairly obviously that he had often been in telepathic communication with his teacher, the wizard abbot Johannes Trithemius (1462–1516). Paracelsus (1493–1541), one of the spiritual forerunners of Rosicrucianism, had this to say: "Magic also imparts the power of hearing someone speak on the other side of the sea. Also it enables a person in the West to converse with someone in the East. . . . in this way you may know everything that owes its existence to the imagination. . . . you may actually receive images from a thousand miles away and impress your own imaginations at the distance of a thousand miles too."

Lapis Philosophorum, or the "Philosophers' Stone"). And at the time of writing (May 1951) the world has heard the news that Argentina is building giant "Sun Reactors" in order to obtain atomic energy without Uranium 235.

Seeing that we are now talking about destructive matters, it is in order to mention that the pamphlet "Frater non Frater," in 1619, by Irenaeus Agnostus, states that each Rosicrucian carries a small device called *Cosmolothrentas*, which is capable of demolishing any and all buildings. This "atomizing apparatus in waistcoat-pocket form" is said to have been put into service during the seige of Hulst (Flanders) in 1596. The evidence particularly adduced is the alleged death of four Spanish captains, who were killed at a distance in time which makes it impossible to check the one-sided account. However there are more recent and very well-attended evidences of terrible secrets.[8]

Another instrument, the *Astronikita*, which allows the stars to be seen when the sky is overcast, so the same author avers, reminds us of the discoveries of our own day and age such as infrared photography, radar, the bolometer and electron-optical equipment now being employed for peaceful purposes.[9] Florentinus de Valentia in his *Rosa florescens* (1617) adds the burning mirrors of Archimedes (287–212 B.C.); the automata of Archytas of Tarent (430–365), Robert Bacon (1214–1294)

---

[8]An alchemist named Dupré, from the Dauphiné, demonstrated such a frightfully destructive artificial fire on the canal of Versailles and in the courtyard of the Arsenal in Paris, in the presence of King Louis XV and his military advisers, that it made the same impression from a moral point of view as the atomic bomb has made in our own day! When it was confirmed that a single person could burn up a whole city or fleet with this "devilish invention" and that water would lend fuel to the unnatural fire, the King paid enormous sums of money to the discoverer to buy his silence, as he did not wish to add to the sufferings of humanity!! (See the correspondence of Ludwig XV (Louis XV) for 1770–1782, published by Grimm.)

[9]On July 22, 1949, the head of the Danish branch of Kodak stated in Copenhagen that he himself had tried out, in the USA, an extraordinary novelty in the field of optics. This was a pair of spectacles which would enable one to see through the thickest fog and in pitch darkness. He expected that it would soon be made available in Europe. Nothing has come of it and its export must have been banned on military grounds!

and Albertus Magnus (1207–1280); the "perpetual motion"; the "everlasting fire".[10] See also the divinatory wheel of Pythagoras (580–493 B.C.); the "Squaring of the circle."[11]

Concentrating on these negative possibilities, the orthodox opponents of the RC spoke of the "pernicious magical society." (Adam Haselmeyer, "Reply to the honourable Brotherhood of the Theosophists of Rosencreutz," Cassel, 1614.) In Philadelphia in 1893, W. Keely converted a granite block into a small heap of dust in the twinkling of an eye by means of an etheric sound wave apparatus. (Boomfield Moore, "Keely and His Discoveries," London, 1893.) "The Keely Motor for atomic fission was built on the principle of fission by soundwaves." (Strauss-Surya, "Theurgic Healing Methods," Lorch. i. Württ., 1936, p. 164.) This type of apparatus is also known in India. Van der Naillen described their appearance and the experiments made with them in his "On the Heights of Himalaya." Van der Naillen was the head of an electro-technical institute in 1914 and, a Belgian by birth, knew nothing of Keely. (See *Zentralblatt für Okkultismus*. Leipzig, 1913, p. 322, the December issue!)

When Counsellor Julius Sperber (died 1616) asserted in his *Echo from the God-illumined Fraternity* (1615, Danzig) that he had made himself a scale of archetypes in which any word in any language could be shown, he was anticipating the *Archeometer* (Greek: "prototype meter") of Joseph Aleçandre, Marquis de Saint-Yves d'Alvedre (1852–1909)![12]

And when the *Clypeum Veritatis* (1618) already named "Notary" of the Brotherhood, *Irenaeus Agnostus*, dreamed of pills (even giving a formula for them) by means of which one could survive for five months without food and drink, we recognize

---

[10]Either the inextinguishable fire known to Dupré (see footnote 8) or the so-called "ever-burning lamps," as were kept in Rosencreutz's mausoleum and burned from 1484 until 1604 and can still be seen in a Leiden museum.

[11]This is always being "discovered" even today. At the time of writing (mid-May, 1951) for example, Jean Burger, a retired pit manager of rue Chemin-de-fer, Stiring-Wendel (Moselle), France, has just published a "solution" in the fortnightly magazine, *Neues Europa* (Stuttgart, No. 10, May 15, 1951).

[12]Sperber knew even more than the papal Marquis: "I have also prepared a basic scheme of different musical phrases and one for human faces." The latter is an exercise in typology.

a forerunner of the infusions used by Dr. Elmers, M.D. "as long ago as" 1933 in the hospitals of St. Louis (Missouri).

Karl Kiesewetter (1854–1895), whose great-grandfather[13] was himself a Rosicrucian, shall have the last word:

> The possibility can never be ruled out that there were still *genuine* Rosicrucians alive at the turn of the present century. However, I hardly imagine that any collection of the Order's papers matching that assembled by my grandfather can have survived.
>
> And even if, because of the strict rules of the Order, the historical material in these documents is meager, that means more space for the practical side of things and, above all, for the countless astounding occult arts of the Rosicrucians.[14]

Nevertheless, students of the subject are convinced that *even today genuine* Rosicrucians[15] are living among us and that they possess remarkable stores of technical knowledge, as can be seen in the following excerpt from a piece of research:

> When the existence of manned flying saucers has been finally admitted, consideration will be given to the fact that in past centuries there were societies like the gen-

---

[13]This great-grandfather on his mother's side was Johann Salomo Haussen (born in 1729 in Weissenfels), a mining inspector, who was initiated into the Rosicrucian Order in Amsterdam by Tobias Schulze around 1760. He became Imperator in 1769 and led the activities of the Order until 1792. On the occasion of a fire at the Kiesewetter home in Meinungen in 1874, some valuable manuscripts perished in the flames together with the Imperator's seal he had inherited from his great-grandfather.

[14]In his article "The Rosicrucians," published in *Magische Blätter* (Leipzig, Vol. 22; December 1922, p. 377). In the previous issue, No. 21 of November 1922, p. 34, he says, interestingly enough, "In the years from 1764 to 1802, my great-grandfather, with unremitting industry, copied out the main contents of the archives and library of the Order, and this very comprehensive handwritten stock of books is even now in my possession."

[15]Paul Sédir (Y von Leloup, 1871–1926) writes in his *Mystic Forces and the Conduct of Life* (Bihorel-les-Rouen, 1923, p. 224) concerning such modern Rosicrucians: ". . . These descendants of Theban colleges, who wander over the face of the globe in modern guise like true cosmopolitans and, in the 17th century, were called Rosicrucians . . ."

uine Rosicrucians on Earth which regarded the entire solar system as the field of their practical activities.[16]

We shall now lift the veil, as far as may be useful and possible, from some of those "countless, astounding occult secrets as known to the secret scientific societies of Germany."

—Willy Schrödter

---

[16]Erich Halik in his report, "The results of scientific Austrian studies on the phenomenon of the so-called 'Flying Saucers' " (p. 4), which was filed in the Austrian State Archives, Vienna I, Minoritenplatz I in June, 1951. See also the relevant article in *Man and Fate* (Villach, II: 19 and 20)! entitled "The Phenomenon of 'Flying Saucers.' "

THE SECRETS OF THE ROSICRUCIANS

O quanta sunt, quod nescitis!

(Oh, how much there still is which you do not know!)

—*(Hermetic ABC of the Philosopher's Stone)*
Berlin, 1779, Vol. III, p. 6

The primary avowed objects of the Rosicrucian Brotherhood were—in imitation of Matthew 10:3—according to paragraph one of their manifesto (in the *Fama* of 1614) to heal the sick without charge, and to serve their neighbor and thereby to serve God (Matthew 25:40). It is possible to recognize these *Erga* (Greek: "main issues") on which such stress was laid behind all the *Parerga* (Greek: "trivialities") which were rumored of them or admitted by them:

- The elixir of life, *radicale Tonicum "Aour potabile,"* drinkable light; falsely known as *Aurum potabile* or drinkable gold.

- The production of synthetic gold and silver by means of the *Lapis Philosophorum*, Philosopher's Stone or "Stone of the Wise."

- The manufacture of synthetic pearls and precious stones; the removal of flaws from diamonds.

- "Ever burning lamps."

- The sympathetic "Lamp of Life" (*Hē Lychnia*).

- Their atomizing apparatus *Cosmolothrentas*.[1]

- *Astronikita*, their telescope working beyond the range of visible light, which enabled the stars to be seen in spite of cloudy skies.[2]

- *Perpetuum mobile*, perpetual motion, derived from the rotation of the earth and also called *Mundum minutum*.

- Their clink-stone (phonolite) "AMMA,"in which A. Colot sees a crystal detector (TSF).[3]

- Plant and animal phoenixes (palingenesis).

- Homunculi.

- Magical mirrors, rings, pendulums and "some thousand other better trifles" (*Fama*).

Karl Kiesewetter (1854–1895), whose great-grandfather was a Rosicrucian Imperator and had bequeathed him a unique collection of the Order's documents, had this to say: "Even if, because of the strict rules of the Order, the historical material in these documents is meager, that only means more space for the practical side of things and what is so astounding to read is the account of the countless occult arts of the Rosicrucians."[4]

---

[1]Irenaeus Agnostus: "Frater non Frater" (1619); also *Cosmolothreuta*.
[2]Even then.
[3]Ludwig Huna (1872–1945), *Bartholomäusnacht*, Leipzig, 1932, pp. 195–196; Pierre Geyraud, *Les Sociétés secrètes de Paris*, Paris, 1938, p. 32.
[4]"Die Rosenkreuzer" in *Magische Blätter* (Leipzig, Vol. 12; Dec. 1922, p. 377).

THE LIFE LIGHT!

Then with a loud report
His apparatus burst. . . .

—Goethe
The Treasure Seeker

I wrote about this in my *Vom Hundertsten ins Tausendste* [*Small Talk*], Freiburg i.Br., 1940/1941, p. 52, 53: What the old Hermeticists taught and practiced was not all superstitious nonsense. These people were ahead of their time and were therefore decried as sorcerers. Hence *the wizardry of yesterday is often the science of tomorrow.* Think, for instance, of hypnotism and suggestion, by means of which 90 percent of all "occult wonders" can be explained.

One example is Albert, Count of Bollstadt (1193–1280), called *Albertus Magnus* or *Doctor universalis* on account of his universal knowledge.[1]

"Because of his chemical and mechanical knowledge, Albertus Magnus was suspected of being a wizard" (Brockhaus). It was only because he was a bishop that he escaped being burned at the stake. One of his students in Cologne was another "luminary of the Church" of aristocrtic stock: Thomas Aquinas

---

[1]Albertus Magnus forms an example of the correctness of my contention. In the winter of 1249 in Cologne, in the frozen cloister garden, he hypnotized King Wilhelm of Holland and his retinue to behold a magical feast set in the midst of luxuriant flowers! (Schrödter; op. cit., p. 65–66). The "great rabbi" Jehuda Löw ben Bezalel (1513–1609) entertained Kaiser Rudolph II and his courtiers at his residence in Prague in much the same way in 1592.

(1225–1274), the *Doctor angelicus*, with whom he formed a deep friendship. The two of them were in sympathetic rapport through the so-called "Life Light," so that each of them was able to know the other's current state of health from the changing condition of his blood in the "Philosophic Egg" of the retort. These Life Lights were much in vogue with the old wise men of those days. A certain Burggravius wrote a book on them called *De Lampadis vitae* around 1500. I felt inclined to dismiss the Life Light lock, stock and barrel, until the following reference to "Blood Donors and Telepathy" in a medical journal gave me pause for thought:

> When the blood donor Georg Lee of Copenhagen perceived that the patient for whom he had given his blood on the day before had died, he felt, so he said, a sharp pricking pain in the arm from which the blood had been taken about the time he supposed the patient to have died. Indeed, he also remembered two former occasions on which he had experienced this pain and, as it was such a rare occurrence, he had been anxious to get to the bottom of it. So, when he felt it again, he noted the exact time, and next day was able to establish that the patient had died. In thirty transfusions, there were seven cases of death in which he was able to ascertain the fact with certainty by some form of telepathy. So far, I have been unable to account for this.[2]

If we turn now to an old textbook we shall see how to make *a lamp of life and death from human blood*.[3]

Ernst Burggraf has this to say in his Life-Wick (*Elichnium Vitae*). Prepare a lantern or lamp from distilled or drained human blood which has been cleaned of all mucus; then feed this blood and maintain the flame with nothing else but oil and,

---

[2]While being unable to offer an "explanation" (one cannot explain everything), I have given parallels in my above-mentioned book, which I recommend to all those who want to "look into things." Publisher's Note: The book to which the author refers is not available in English.

[3]Förster Eberhard Heinrich Fischer's *Albertus Magnus der Andere und Wahre* (Albertus Magnus in fact and fiction) Altona, 1790, p. 106–107.

using an asbestos or other nonflammable wick, continue to do so for as long as the person lives out of whose blood the lamp has been made. Once this lamp or light has been lit (according to our author), it burns steadily as long as the individual breathes from whose blood the lamp was prepared, and goes out in the very hour, minute and second in which he expires. You should also know that when the flame is light and clear, tall and still, the same person experiences no hardship of mind or body. However, when it behaves differently, and flickers or wavers uncertainly backward and forward or rises in spurts, or is lower than usual, or cloudy, or similarly impaired, this is a certain sign of anguish, depression or other adversity. For, because of its inherent astral link and natural sympathy with the human body (because this blood is sustained by the blood of the man himself and the essence of that blood also sustains his physical life), it reflects the individual's condition and circumstances, whether they be bad or good.

Thus Burggraf, in the work cited, also went on to tell the story of a Strassburg student who had made such a lamp from his blood, having drawn the latter from his veins in Spring and Autumn and once, when he had a high fever, the flame in this lamp rose and fell with the fever, and went out at the very instant the patient died.[4]

The Scottish physician, Dr. William Maxwell, M.D. (1619–1669) in his *De Medicina magnetica* (1679) wrote: "There is a connection formed of spirit or rays between the body and its excretia, even when the latter is very far removed from it. The same relationship exists between the body and members which have been separated from it, including the blood." (6th maxim).

From this we get the Life Lamp; which indicates the state of health by its changes of hue, announcing death by spontaneously going out. And this is the origin of that blood salt of the same color as the light of the lamp (I. Buch, chapter 7).

The landgravial physician, and member of the Gold and Rosicrucian Brotherhood, Dr. Rudolph Johann Friedrich

---

[4]The full title of J.E. Burggraf's book is *Biolychnium, seu lucerna cum vita ejus, cui accensa est mystice videns iugiter, cum morte ejusdem expirans, omnesque affectus graviores prodens*, 1629.

Schmidt, of Hamburg, who lived from 1702 to 1761, dedicated the following love poem to the Baroness Eleonore von K. . . . :

> My gem, my lovely child,
> My angel, my delight,
> I saw how on thy breast
> The snow lay soft and white.
>
> It rises fair to see
> And fills my heart with hope;
> Oh give my eager hand
> A sleigh-ride down that slope!

When the Baroness K. died, the "Life Lamp," which Dr. Schmidt had made from her blood and had been keeping by him, exploded![5]

DISCUSSION

> Make the most of life, *because the light still shines*!
>
> —Usteri-Naegeli (1793)

Reports of "Life Lamps" figure in many of the old "knowledge Books." There must surely be some truth in them. The aristocratic physician, Dr. Rudolph Johann Friedrich Schmidt (1702–1761) conducted the experiment in Hamburg in his own day and age. I have no information about later attempts.

An earlier instance is given by the Scottish doctor, William Maxwell (1619–1669) in his *Three Books of Magnetic Healing* (1678); he repeats it from Dr. Joh. Bapt. van Helmont (1577–1644): "A citizen of Brussels," he said, "lost his nose in a fight. He went to the surgeon Tagliacozzo in Bologna, so that the latter could sew it on again. But as he was unwilling to have his own arm cut, he paid a porter to allow a nose to be cut out of his arm. Shortly afterward, some thirteen months after the man returned to his own country from Brussels, the substitute nose suddenly grew cold and a few days later fell off. Further

---

[5]Dr. Ferdinand Maack, M.D. (1861–1930), "Twice born" (Leipzig, 1912).

investigation of this unexpected occurrence revealed that the porter had died at the very moment when the nose became cold. Several eyewitnesses are still living in Brussels. This is van Helmont's story. I myself have heard something similar from a medical friend of mine which he solemnly swore he had seen with his own eyes."

Maxwell sees here crystal clear confirmation of his theory of healing at a distance (*Medicina diastitica* of the philosopher physician Andreas Tenzel, 1629).

This action at a distance between an object and its part is the rationale of the so-called "sympathetic cure."

At this point, I think I should refer the reader to an excellent little book, which is still procurable today, *Das magische Heilverfahren* [*Magical Therapy*], by Dr. G.A. Amann (Konstanz, Hamburg, 1950), in order to save myself endless explanations. This small book contains the fruit of much experience and is worth its weight in gold. In this connection, Sir Kenelm Digby's "sympathetic powder," also described by Amann, is deserving of special mention. Digby lived from 1603 to 1665. The old volume *Sympathie und Zaubermedizin* [*Sympathy and Magical Medicine*] by Oskar Ganser (Leipzig, 1921) is almost unobtainable nowadays, to say nothing of G.F. Most's *Sympathetische Mittel* [*Sympathetic Medicine*] (Rostock, 1842). Arthur Schopenhauer (1788–1860) attached the greatest importance to it. A similar remedy was the so-called weapon salve, which was so highly recommended by the old authors.[6]

I will offer some further analogies here. Ferdinand Santanelli, one-time professor of medicine at Naples, had this to say in his *Geheimen Philosophie oder magisch-magnetischen Wissenschaft* [*Occult Philosophy or Magical-Magnetic Science*] (1723): "How comes it (and I ask this question to make the apparent remoteness of some magical operations more understandable) that Spanish wine for example, after being shipped here to Naples, responds to the climatic conditions of its country of origin and is troubled when the vines blossom in Spain but not

---

[6]Mysterious ointments still exist today. At the end of April, 1951, a Persian peasant from Yazd demonstrated to doctors in Teheran a herbal ointment smelling of camphor which healed severe burns in under ten minutes!! They are still trying to fathom it!

when they blossom in Naples?" Johann Wolfgang von Goethe corroborates the belief in: "When the vines come out in flower The wine stirs in the vat."

But let us ask a modern parapsychologist and doctor! In his *Die Wiedergeburt des Magischen* [*The Rebirth of Magic*] Leipzig, 1933, p. 57), Dr. Walther Kröner, says:

> But even in the vegetable kingdom there is something like a generic soul and telepathy. How can we account for the fact that many types of trees, like the poplar for instance, which are taken as cuttings from a parent stock, die in unison with the plant from which they came when that dies? Or that an artificially cultivated variety of flower will disappear all over the world at one and the same time, as happened to the famous France-Rose? Consider, too, the group soul, shared life and common death of individuals who are separated in space and have never been united. We know that certain varieties of southern wine start to ferment and "sound" in the vat in the very same night in which the vines from which they come burst into bloom. It is immaterial how far removed the vat is from the place where the grapes were picked. What mysterious, magical contact exists here between the plant and its distant fruit juice?

Now, blood is a very special juice!! (See Goethe, *Faust*, Part I.) It is reasonably safe to assume that it will exhibit even more intimate relationships. And finally, there is one form of *plant telepathy* that anyone can study for themselves—if they are unable or unwilling to carry out tests on claret (wine).

On September 11, 1949, the local broadcasting station for Beromünster in Switzerland read from its "post box" as follows: a lady had been trying to remove fast fruit stains from some washing but had been unsuccessful after four attempts. An old woman advised her to wait until the pears were in flower and then simply hang the stained washing in the sun. The lady did not believe in this recipe because she had often bleached the piece of laundry. Nevertheless, she conscientiously carried out the old wife's instructions and lo and behold! to her great astonishment, and equally great joy, the stains disappeared! I exchanged letters on the subject with the deliberately anonymous Hamburg Hermeticist "AME," immortalized by Gustav Meyrink (1868–1932) as "Baron Müller" in his *Der Engel vom westlichen Fenster*. He wrote to me on October 3, 1949: "I am not unacquainted with the mutual relationship between fruit stains and the washing. This is a well-known fact in the Harz region. When as children we had soiled the white tablecloth with raspberry or bilberry juice, our mother treated the wash exactly as described by the old lady in Switzerland.

A Westphalian dentist who knows about the "electromagnetic return-flow connection" as he terms the "sympathetic contact," bears it in mind in his practice and uses "Paracelsus vulnerary powder" (Digby's Powder), reported on March 20, 1952, on yet another unaccountable interrelationship: "I use this action of the return-flow to explain, for example, how hypersensitive people always get a feeling of heat or even a headache on the day their washing is done. Thus someone who has thoughtlessly thrown away his hair combings may find that he suffers for it if the birds use it in building their nests, because birds have a considerably higher blood temperature than that of the human body."

BLOOD TELEGRAPHY

Blood is a very special juice!

—Goethe, *Faust* (I)

This secret is mentioned in a good many Hermetic writings. For example, the Rosicrucian, Dr. Johannes Staricius had this to say when describing his "weapon salve."[1] "Anyone who has read something of the *Steganologia*[2] and is conversant with it, already has an inkling of how one man can communicate with another over a distance of four miles.[3] This is brought about by the *sympathia sanguinis ex vulnere effusi cum sanguine in eo retento* (the sympathy of the blood shed from any wound with the blood retained in it).[4] Here is the method as quoted by Kieser[5] from Bartholin:[6]

---

[1] For the sympathetic healing of a wound, the weapon which had caused it was anointed instead of the wound itself. See also: The Distant Action of the Blood!

[2] From the Greek: *steganos* = hidden, and *logos* = knowledge; hence the meaning is "secret knowledge." In other words, a message delivered in an out-of-the-way manner. The title of a book published in 1608 by the "wizard abbot" Trithemius (1462–1516).

[3] Just before this, Staricius was talking about 40 miles! The 4 (four) here must surely be a mistake.

[4] *Geheimnisvoller Heldenschatz* etc. (Cologne and Weimar, 1750, p. 327. [*Description of the weapon salve in its most satisfactory form*], First edition, 1697.

[5] Prof. Dietrich Georg Kieser, M.D. (1779–1862) in his *Archiv für den Thierischen Magnetismus* (Leipzig, 1821, Vol. 8, Part 3, pp. 154–155; *Wechselwirkung in Distanz* [*Mutual Action at a Distance*] (Kieser, 1779–1862).

[6] Thomas Bartholin (1616–1680) in *Afhandling om Sygdommes Overplantning*,

The first person scratches his left arm with the point of a knife until he draws blood and wipes away the blood with a sponge. The second person makes a similar cut in his ring-finger and lets a drop of blood fall from it into the wound of the first person. Both cuts are then bound up until the wounds are completely healed. After this, the second person cuts his arm and the first cuts himself in the finger and after a drop of blood has been allowed to fall from the finger cut into the arm cut, the two wounds are bandaged as before until they are fully healed. Now when one of these individuals, however far away he may be from the other, sticks a needle into the scar of the healed wound, the other feels the same prick at the same time. A prearranged code is agreed as to the meaning of the first, second, and third prick, etc., and in this way either of them is able to communicate his state of health and other circumstances to the other whenever he wishes.

Similar instructions are to be found in Papus.[7] A modification is the use of "magical-magnetic papers and cloths" in "blood telegraphy."

"Much is said about the 'magical-magnetic paper' in old books on sympathetic magic. Two friends who want to keep in touch when far apart exchange specimens of their blood, which they submit to magical fermentation in paper."[8] "The intention

---

etc. [*A Treatise on the Transplanting of Disease, etc.*] (Copenhagen, 1794, Sebastian Pope).

[7]Papus, Dr. Gérard Encausse, (1865–1916) in his *Traité méthodique de Magie pratique* [*Systematic Treatise on Practical Magic*] (Paris, 1937, p. 430). [*The Sympathetic Alphabet.*]

[8]The possibility of telepathic communication as a result of blood mixing must be the forgotten basis of the so-called "blood brotherhood" of primitive races and of the 9th Grade of the Freemasons. It is the binding together of two astral bodies (from which we get the expression "bonds of friendship")! My opinion on this point is strengthened by the words of that occult master, G. Gurdjieff: "You know, for example, how various nations have the custom of BLOOD BROTHERHOOD. Two or more individuals mix their blood in the same vessel and drink from it. They are afterwards regarded as blood

is to transmit information over long distances by pricking the paper with a needle in a system rather like the Morse code."[9] "When it is planned to use blood in a 'magical-magnetic paper' or cloth, to relay one's thoughts to far distant places, an open vessel must be taken (for the fermentation process) and the blood must be dried on a warm sunny day, but in the shade. The rule must always be observed that our materials are to be fermented not destroyed."[10]

Blood telegraphy is very similar to skin telegraphy.

A passage occurs in the writings of Johann Baptista von Helmont (1577–1644) which describes a sort of *Skin Telegraphy*, where, if I remember rightly, it is called a "magical alphabet." We are told that two individuals who are fond of one another write down the letters of the alphabet on their skin with indelible ink and then undertake a skin transplant. Even if they have to separate, they can conduct a mutual conversation. What is needed is for one of them to touch a letter with his finger on the grafted skin, whereupon the other person will feel an itching sensation in the corresponding place. In this way it is possible to converse with mutually spelled out words.[11]

The Scottish physician, Dr. William Maxwell (1619–1669) had this to say in his *De Medicina magnetica* (Francof. 1679): "There is a link of spirits or radiation between the body and the excrement voided from it, even when the excrement is very

---

brothers. However, the origin of this usage lies deeper. In the beginning, this was a magical ceremony, in order to form a union between 'astral bodies'. . . . And then, you see, some peoples believe that once this link has been formed between 'astral bodies' it can only be broken by death." (See *Life Lights!*) P. D. Ouspensky, *In Search of the Miraculous* (Innsbruck, no date: p. 141).

[9]E. W. Clarence, *Sympathie, Mumia, Amulette, okk. Kräfte der Edelsteine und Metalle* [*Sympathy, mumia, amulets, occult powers of the precious stones and metals*] (Berlin-Pankow, 1927, Part II, p. 235 footnote).

[10]Prof. Ferdinand Santanelli (Naples), *Occult Philosophy or Magical-Magnetic Science* (1723), chapter 13, "Magical Fermentation". The Latin title is *Philosophia recondita, sive magicae magneticae mumialis scientiae explanatio* (Coloniae, 1723).

[11]Ernst Hentges: "Ein neues Rätsel" in *Zentralblatt für Okkultismus* (Leipzig, 1914, January, p. 359 ff.).

far removed from the body. Exactly the same relationship exists with parts (including the blood) which have been separated from the body (6th. maxim).

"This is the basis of that extraordinary natural wonder in which someone can make known his desires to a friend in the furthest ends of the earth by means of blood, spirit and flesh; a secret which ought not to be revealed to the unworthy rabble (Book I; chapter 7)."

DISCUSSION

Whether it is possible to set up a consistent means of communication in the manner described would be for qualified investigators to determine.

There seems to be a distinct possibility that Life Lamps would work for keeping partners informed of each other's state of health, as may be seen from the case of the Copenhagen blood donor Georg Lee.

The action at a distance between an object and its parts turns here on the principle of so-called "sympathy." A large amount of material can be culled from the chapter on "The Powder of Sympathy" in *Die Ausscheidung des Empfindungsvermögens* (Leipzig, 1909) by Albert de Rochas d'Aiglun (1837–1914).

Captain E. Fonville at Rollencourt (Pas de Calais) has used the *Poudre de Sympathie du Chevalier Digby* (Sir Digby's sympathy powder) since 1936 on hundreds of people, including himself, with the *greatest success* and has given a full account of it in 1950 in "Revue Internationale de Radiesthésie" (Mettet, Belgium).

In addition, I have received other reports on healing by means of sympathy which have been sent to me by genuine individuals. And even if "Life lamps" and "the blood telegraph" are nothing more than exaggerations of the sympathetic action at a distance, many people may take a useful hint from the reported method of sympathetic healing.

THE PERPETUAL LAMP

The fire in the Rosicrucian lamps is the pure elemental principle.

—Edward Bulwer (1803–1873)
Zanoni

I am an everlasting lamp
And burn without respite;
My wick and oil are God,
My spirit holds the light.

—Angelus Silesius
(1624–1677)

The *Fama* (1614) relates that, at the opening of the tomb of Christian Rosencreutz in 1604, "although the sun never shone in this vault, nevertheless it was illuminated with another sun, which had learned this from the sun and was situated in the upper part in the center of the ceiling." It is said that this lamp gradually went out after it had been exposed.[1]

---

[1]My friend Ludwig Huna (1872–1945) depicted this in his *St. Bartholomew's Night* (Leipzig, 1932, p. 195 ff.), which showed a subterranean Rosicrucian temple in front of the Nesle tower in Paris. Tr. note: The German has *Tore de Nesle* or "gate" of Nesle but this is apparently in error for the French *Tour* or "tower" of Nesle. As a matter of fact, Gabriel Naudé (1600–1653) claims that the Rosicrucians used to forgather in the Paris catacombs (*Avis á la France sur les frères de la Rose-Croix*, 1623) [*Disclosures to France concerning the brethren of the Rosy Cross*].

Licetus, a famous medieval physician of Rapallo, is thought to be the first to describe these lamps, which were prepared by the ancients by means of some occult art. They were filled with an oil which was never consumed and were designed for burial chambers. Even if the oil did get used up, the lamps were replenished from the smoke. The wicks were of asbestos and so were incombustible. The story goes that, during the reign of Pope Paul III (1534–1549), a grave was opened in Rome in 1534 in which the lamp suspended over a well-preserved body was still burning. Allegedly, the corpse was that of Tullia (who died in 45 B.C.), the daughter of Marcus Tullius Cicero (106–43 B.C.). As soon as the lamp and the body had been brought into the light of day, the former went out and the latter crumbled to dust.

Another writer gives a more exact account of the matter:

> In the middle of the 16th century, a grave was discovered near the Appian Way. Inside there was the body of a young maiden, floating in some unknown fluid. She had blonde hair caught together in a gold circlet and looked as fresh as if she were still alive. At the feet of the corpse was a burning lamp which did not go out until air was admitted. Some inscriptions indicated that the body had been there for 1500 years and it was conjectured that the body was that of Tullia, Cicero's daughter. It was brought to Rome and put on display in the Capitol, where people flocked to see it. When the foolish citizens began to venerate it as a saint, the Pope, who had a hundred means at his disposal for preventing such worship by idiots, could think of nothing better than to have this priceless piece of antiquity thrown into the Tiber.[2]

The "daemonic knight," Heinrich Cornelius Agrippa von Nettesheim (1486–1535), M.D. and Judge of the Prerogative Court—the "Kiesewetter of his century"—had this to say on the subject: "Finally, there are inextinguishable fire, oil that is not consumed by burning and *everlasting lamps*, which cannot be extinguished either by wind, water or in any other way; which would

---

[2] J. A. S. Collin de Plancy, *Dictionnaire Infernal* (Paris, 1818, Vol. I, p. 302, 303).

be quite unbelievable were it not for the world-famous lamp that once burned in the temple of Venus with an asbestos wick which, once it was properly lit, never went out."[3] According to Sédir:

> The secret of preparing everlasting lamps is ascribed to the Rosicrucians, and was also possessed by the Romans so it would appear. The secret consisted in the manufacture by hermetic art of a certain golden oil which supplied the wick with all the necessary materials for combination while, at the same time, ceaselessly renewing them. Antiquarian investigations mention several such lamps. Two were discovered in the reign of Henry VIII (1491–1547) at the time of the Dissolution of the Monasteries in England (ca. 1533–1539); they had been burning since the fourth century, in other words for about twelve hundred years. They are being kept at Leyden museum, Holland. Compare M. Balley "φιλσδορος," 2nd Edition, 1731.[4]

Spunda reports on an "everlasting light" like this in the monastery of Vatopädi, Mount Athos[5] and Peuckert (born in 1895) says, "In Trebnitz, burning lamps were found in pagan tombs."[6]

There is a small work in existence called *Zwei ewige, unauslöschliche, brennende, zeitliche Lichter*, by Trithemius, abbot of Sponheim. It is printed in *Aureum Vellus [The Golden Fleece]* (Rorschach, 1598, I, c, p. 159) and in the German *Teatrum Chemicum* [The Chemical Theater] by Freidrich Roth-Scholtzen (Nuremberg, 1730, Vol. II, p. 613 ff.).

The (wholly impracticable) formula was allegedly copied by the pseudo-alchemist Bartholomäus Korndörffer from one of the followers of the "wizard abbot" Trithemius (Johannes Heidenberg aus Trittenheim a.d. Mosel; 1462–1516), to whom

---

[3]*Geheime Philosphie [Occult Philosophy]* (Berlin, 1921, Vol. I, p. 81).
[4]Paul Sédir (= Yvon Leloup, 1871–1926) in *Histoire et Doctrines des Rose-Croix [The History and Teachings of the Rosicrucians]*, (Bihorel-les-Rouen, 1932, p. 292). Cf. also Hargrave Jennings, *The Rosicrucians* (Berlin, 1912, chapter 3, "Everburning Lamps")!
[5]Dr. Franz Spunda (Vienna), *Der heilige Berg Athos [Holy Mount Athos]* (Leipzig, 1928, p. 169).
[6]Will-Erich Peuckert, *Schlesische Sagen* [Silesian legends] (Jena, 1924, p. 305).

were ascribed all imaginable arts and who was certainly practiced in some of them at least. The story went that the abbot
of Sponheim had produced these perpetually burning lamps
for the Emperor Maximilian I (1493–1519), for which he was
paid 6,000 crowns (cf. Ziegelbauer; l.c. p. 231). However that
may be, Trithemius was held in high esteem by the emperor
and was even appointed court-chaplain. Helena Petrovna Blavatsky (1831–1891) repeated the *useless* instructions quite seriously in her *Isis Unveiled* (1875).

For the sake of lovers of curiosities, we may as well provide
a recipe from an old "recipe book."[7]

> Kaiser Maximilian gave the abbot of Sponheim, Tri-
> themius, 6,000 crowns for this arcanum. The true
> mode of preparation is as follows.
>
> Take:
>
> > 1½ oz. flowers of sulphur
> > 1 oz. burnt alum
>
> and place them in a subliming pot after a thorough
> mixing. Place a similar pot mouth to mouth with this
> and seal the join well with potter's cement. The pot
> with the mixture inside is set on a coal fire so that it
> becomes red-hot. In this way the sulphur is sublimed,
> and ascends to the upper pot as a vapor to be deposited
> there as a fixed mass. When one is certain that every-
> thing has sublimed and the lower pot has been red-
> hot for approximately one hour, the apparatus is re-
> moved from the fire and allowed to cool. The upper
> pot is then broken open, and the sublimed fixed mass
> is taken out to be pulverized in a mortar. Half as much
> pure borax by weight is added to the resultant powder
> and the whole is then reduced to a similar powder in
> the mortar. This powder is placed in a shallow glass
> or porcelain basin and is covered with the most highly

---

[7]*Wunderquelle oder die enthüllten Geheimnisse der Natur* [*Wonder Sources or the Unveiled Secrets of Nature*] (Schaffhausen, 1846, p. 3, Formula 5, "The method of making a light or lamp which does not go out but practically burns for-ever.").

rectified spirit of wine (ethyl alcohol). The basin is now placed on hot ashes, held over a coal fire in a small caldron, and the spirit is allowed to evaporate slowly. When the mass runs like a thick oil, a little of it is removed and laid on a red-hot sheet of copper. Now if the mass melts like wax without smoking, it is ready; but, if it still smokes, more spirit must be poured into the basin and evaporated as before, and the process is to be repeated until the samples no longer emit smoke when tested. The product is then ready.

A wick is now made, about 2 inches long and as thick as the biggest piece of quill. The material used is asbestos or white fibrous gypsum (steatite) bound with silk thread. The prepared mass is then placed in a strong glass made for the purpose, the wick is inserted and the preparation is left standing for 24 hours in hot sand. The wick is then pulled up and a sufficiently large lamp chimney is made for it so that it is only slightly exposed at the top and the perpetually burning sulphur mass pours onto it, and the glass is placed in hot sand until the sulphur mass melts and collects around the wick. Finally, the lamp which has been prepared in this way is lit with a light and placed in a place where it will not be disturbed. It will then go on burning without ever going out.

The glow worm shows the way to the Perpetual Lamp! The Rosicrucians have surely said this, too. Their axiom is: copy Nature—I will work in the same way as she works!

Telegraph director C. Loog[8] professes to see a reference to the "cold light" of the future in one of the quatrains of the "Prophecies of Maistre Michel Nostradamus" (1503–1566), a form of lighting in which the maximum candle power and the minimum evolution of heat are both ensured, as found in glow worms and fireflies, especially in the tropics.

If we turn to the "Brockhaus" Encyclopaedia under the heading Click beetles (*Schnellkäfer*) we read, "To the click beetles

---

[8]C. Loog, *Die Weissagungen des Nostradamus* [*The Prophecies of Nostradamus*] (1921).

(Elateridae) also belong the luminous fireflies (*Cucujo, Pypro-phorus*) native to tropical America; the most well-known being the West Indian *P. noctilucus L.* used by the native population for lights when the larvae are in the roots of the sugar cane."

The Japanese researcher Nakamura succeeded in finding in 1939 a culture medium which prolongs the life of the luminous marine microorganisms to half a year while intensifying the strength of the light they emit. These faintly luminous microorganisms had previously had a life of just some ten days![9] This light is not only adapted to (long exposure) photography, but will provide sufficient light for reading purposes. The light that the bacteria produce by a special process of oxidation is cold. It is the most economical light in the world because there is practically no heat loss. It is intended to use these living lamps in munition stores and explosives factories in order to obviate the risk of fires and explosions.

"However, the most astonishing aspect of the discovery is that animals were using bacterial lamps long before human beings did so. The marine creatures deep down in the ocean are lit up, but their source of light is borrowed.[10] They are full of foreign organisms in the form of the light bacteria, which they house for the sake of their cold light. This is how the cuttle-fish, for example, illuminates the darkness far under the sea."[11]

The luminous biological material found in the firefly and in certain bacteria (a chemical known as *luciferin*) cries out to be analyzed and manufactured synthetically with a view to the exploitation of the exceptionally long combustion time which is obviously involved, since there is almost no heat loss such as is found in all other types of lighting.

The writings of an adept that were published in 1782 mention, among other magical effects of the Philosopher's Stone, that "a perpetual light can be made from the white liquor of the white stone, if a little thereof is put in a crystal vessel, fed along a thread (wick) of very fine gold thread and ignited by the sun." According to G.W. Surya (August 23, 1873—January 3, 1949):

---

[9]"Stuttgarter Illustrierte" of October 29, 1939.
[10]Not always! (W. Schrödter).
[11]*Koralle*, Berlin (No. 14, April 7, 1940).

It has been said that 'perpetual lamps' of this sort have been discovered *still burning* in ancient Roman tombs. Obviously, this would amount to a scientific marvel. It could hardly be a straightforward process of combustion, for otherwise the white liquor—which takes the place of oil—would eventually be consumed and, in any case, a flame cannot go on burning without oxygen. Perhaps the light was produced by electricity or by some radioactive action which is at present unknown to us, for it is entirely possible that the energy for feeding this 'flame' was generated by atomic decay, which would make it more understandable that these 'perpetual lamps of the Rosicrucians' could 'burn' in airtight crypts. Thus, it is only modern physics which has given us the possible explanation of these 'perpetual lamps,' and it is easy to see why they were formerly designated works of 'magic.'[12]

DISCUSSION

Thus research into luminescence, carried out by many learned men, has discovered powers in the vegetable kingdom which are similar to the effects of big electric arc lamps in regard to ultraradiation.

—Dr. G.A. Amann
Sympathy, p. 24

I believe in the "perpetual lamps" of the Rosicrucians and, what is more, I believe it is possible to recognize their nature from incidental remarks in old documents.

No normal lamps could burn for a year, let alone for centuries, in airless tombs and vaults using an ordinary fuel such as oil, even if their wicks were in fact made with incombustible asbestos. They would go out for lack of oxygen. Therefore the luminous bodies concerned did not need atmospheric air. Such

---

[12]*Hermetische Medizin, Stein der Weisen, Lebenselixiere* [*Hermetic Medicine, the Philosopher's Stone, Elixirs of Life*] (Berlin-Pankow, 1923, p. 303).

lamps as the latter would evolve no (unnecessary) heat, but would be cold lights or luminescent lights based on the illuminating medium luciferin of the firefly.

And why should the old chemists not have been able to isolate this illuminating medium, quite apart from being able to synthesize it? They must have learned about cold light from the flying creatures, because the motto of the old masters of wisdom was, Copy Nature, copy Nature; as she works, I shall work too!

We could deceive ourselves by too smug an approach to the chemical and physical knowledge of earlier ages! There are definite traces of a knowledge of organic and inorganic chemistry in Plutarch's *Life of Alexander* (chapter 29), in the *Histories* of Herodotus (Book VII, 74), in Seneca's *Natural Questions* (Book III, chapter 25), in Pliny the Elder's *Natural History* (Book XXX, chapter 16). A manuscript written by one of the monks of Mount Athos, Ponselenus by name, discloses the early use of chemistry for photography and supports it by reference to old Ionian authors.[13]

Since we are dealing with the subject of light in this section, we shall take the opportunity of giving an example of the physical science of the Middle Ages from V. Sauval, *Antiquités de Paris* [Paris Antiquities] (Paris, 1724).

> Ca. 1250, the Rabbi Jechiele, an initiate into occult arts, was persecuted both by the rabble and by his fellow savants for using magical preparations. They complained that he had a lamp which emitted a dazzling light. It lit up automatically at the appointed hour and shone in his window like a star of the first magnitude. What is more, as his enemies were attacking his front door, beside themselves with curiosity, he touched a peg within his reach and a lively blue-colored spark crackled, to the distress of the people in front, who had hold of the door knocker. Thrown to the ground by some unknown force, they lay writhing with cries of pain. The hooligans joined forces and, holding each

---

[13]This fact was brought to light through the proceedings of Josef Nicéphore Niepce (1765–1833) and Louis Jacques Mandé Daguerre (1789–1851).

other by the hand, made several attempts to use the enchanted knocker but they were all served in the same way without discovering how it was done. The initiate was summoned to appear before the king (Louis IX; 1215–1270) in order to explain his "sorceries." It appears that his explanations were satisfactory, for far from being prosecuted, he was subsequently the recipient of high favors but, at the same time, he was forbidden to publish his secrets.

He was certainly successful in preserving his mystery, because it was not until 1812 that the arc lamp (as I think it must have been) was rediscovered by Sir Humphrey Davy (1778–1829). The Qabbalist Jechiele must have generated the current by means of galvanic elements such as were found in the "house of magic" (!) in the vicinity of Bagdad in 1943. It was estimated that these went back to sometime between 300 B.C. and A.D. 300. Galvanic electricity was discovered once more around 1790 by Luigi Galvani (1737–1798) and Count Alessandro Volta (1745–1827).

In addition to the "perpetual lamps," so-called "wonder lamps" play a fairly prominent role in the old knowledge books. For instance, they occupy much of the forty-ninth chapter of the first book of Agrippa's *Occult Philosophy*:

Also there are made artificially some Lights, by Lamps, Torches, Candles, and such like, of some certain things, and liquors opportunely chosen, according to the rule of the Stars, and composed among themselves according to their congruity, which when they be lighted and shine alone, are wont to produce some wonderfull and Celestial effects, which men many times wonder at.

After the above author has discussed various remarkable lights of this character and their preparation, he concludes by saying, "Of such like Torches, Lamps, doth Hermes speak more of, also Plato, and Chyrannides, and of the latter writers Albertus in a certain Treatise of this particular thing."

To the "Universal Doctor" (1193–1280) are ascribed (under the names "Great Albert" and "Little Albert") those once popular Wonder Books which in reality go back, after considerable distortion in the process of copying and translation, to very ancient Chaldean, Egyptian, Arabic and Greek sources. In Paris, with its "Place Maubert" (Magister Albert) and in France generally, *Le Grand et le Petit Albert* are nothing more than "grimoires."[14]

The concept of magic lamps has persisted to modern times. Here are two amusing examples: "To impersonate a blackamoor" advises an anonymous work of drawing-room magic recently published, "the performer soaks a rush wick for some length of time in jet-black ink. In a totally darkened chamber (dark room), the performer places the prepared wick in a perfectly ordinary lamp and fills it with perfectly ordinary oil. When it is lit, the natural white complexion of the European assumes the coloration of a black person."

Joe Labero gives the following recipe for a "Spirit Lamp." "Some cooking salt and flowers of sulphur are placed in porcelain dish and stirred in alcohol until they are dissolved. A lampwick is dipped in the solution and then lit. The lamp so made is taken into a dark room. An amazing and horrible result will be seen. The people who are sitting or standing nearby will seem to have faces of a ghastly blue with cheek-bones outlined like those in a skull and deep-sunken eyes." (*Wundermänner, ich enthülle eure Geheimnisse!* [*Miracle men I shall reveal your secrets*] Berlin, 1933.) This type of thing was very popular years ago and still is; however, in the Renaissance it was especially in vogue and formed a special division of "Natural Magic."

This is defined by the celebrated Casper Schott (1608–1666) in his *Magia universalis naturae et artis* (1657) as follows: "By Natural Magic I mean a certain secret knowledge of the mysteries of nature, by which, when a person has discovered the nature, the properties, the hidden powers, the sympathies and antipathies of individual things, he can produce certain effects which seem to be odd or even wonderful to those who are unacquainted with their causes."

---

[14]In this connection, the well-known Qabbalist Eliphas Levi-Zohéd (Abbé Constant) had this to say: "As soon as they have been measured against scientific authority it would be a mistake to reject the instructions in the 'grimoires' (magic books) without exception."

TELEPATHY
AND MAGNETIC DIALS

> Our solar plexus in the pit of the stomach is a receiving
> station for wireless telegraphy over which we can re-
> ceive all sorts of thought-telegrams.
>
> —Karl Ludwig Schleich (1859–1922)

Number 70 in a collection of transmutation reports[1] is "A Hermetic History of Jesse Abraham and Salomon Teelsu, translated
into German from a Dutch Document." This document is dated
January 30, 1731, and was written by the amenuensis of the
Hamburg Qabbalist and Rosicrucian[2] Benjamin Jesse (1642–
1730). It tells of the death and legacy of Benjamin Jesse[3] which
went to his two cousins, Abraham Jesse and Salomon Teelsu,
who lived in Switzerland, and consisted of magical instruments,

---

[1]Siegmund Heinrich Güldenfalk (His Hghness the Chief Commissioner for
Hesse-Darmstadt): *A Collection of more than one hundred Veracious Transmutation
Reports, etc.* (Frankfurt a.M. and Leipzig, by Joh. Gg. Fleischer, 1784, pp. 193–
204).

[2]"He was a Jew by birth but a Christian in religion. He recognized that Jesus
was the Savior of the world. He did so both publically and privately and was
a man of exemplary faith who gave a lot to charity by stealth and set great
store by chastity in the single state. He was deeply versed in the art of medicine
and healed incurable diseases."

[3]The original papers were in the Hamburg "Johanneum." A Hermetic friend
in Hamburg instituted his own inquiries into Benjamin Jesse. Initially he met
with some success but was not able to follow it up because the Ministry for
Jewish Affairs made difficulties, as they doubted that his investigations were
solely scientific. (From a private communication addressed to me on April 3,
1942.)

"Books of Knowledge," the "red lion" and alchemically produced gold bars.

After the death in the Hanseatic port of the theurgist, "I then, as I had promised, wrote to inform his cousins in Switzerland of the event. However, the following day I received a letter from one of them asking me whether my master was alive or dead, just as if he had been listening in on what had been going on in our part of the world. This puzzled me at the time, but I shall indicate in what follows how such a thing can happen, i.e., *by the use of a special instrument or technique*."

When the heirs entered the room sealed by the deceased, on the day after their arrival in Hamburg, "I saw a well-made ebony cupboard. What is more, I saw another cupboard hanging over this one and in it was a special instrument, a type of clockwork, which had a hand or pointer. However, instead of the hour numbers, there were the letters of the alphabet. Mr. Jesse said that this instrument worked in exactly the same way as one which he had in Switzerland and that it had been used by the deceased to announce his impending death. This was why Mr. Jesse wrote his letter to me the day after my master's death, because he had surmised it from the behavior of his own instrument, especially when the pointer stood still and the instrument no longer moved."

Now, in *The Great and Little Albert* ascribed to Albertus Magnus, a remarkable telegraph is described which may reveal to us the principle of Jesse's instrument. The passage reads as follows: "A wonderful secret for making a '*sympathetic dial*' for instantaneous communication with a distant friend."[4] Here is my unabridged translation from the original French text:

> Have two boxes made of fine steel (plate)—similar to the usual receptacles for mariner's compasses—and let

---

[4]*Les Admirables Secrets de Magie Naturelle du Grand-Albert et du Petit-Albert. Conforme aux meilleurs éditions de ces Grimoirs publiés autrefois chez les Héritiers de BERINGOS Fratres á l'enseigne d'Agrippa, á Lyon.* (Paris, no date, Albin Michel, pp. 168–170). [*The Admirable Secrets of Natural Magic of the Great Albert and the Little Albert.* According to the best editions of these Grimoires previously published by the heirs of the BERINGOS Fratres at the sign of Agrippa, at Lyons.]

them be of the same weight, the same size and the same appearance and have a fairly large border which can be decorated all the way round with the letters of the alphabet. Both will have a pivot set in their inner base plates on which a hand can be placed, as in an ordinary clockface. It is important to insure that the receptacles are clean and polished. Then a piece of loadstone is selected from several fine and good specimens; a piece with white veining on the south-seeking pole. This longest and straightest piece is cut into two sections as accurately as possible, so as to make two indicator needles for your two boxes; both pointers must be of the same weight and thickness and must be evenly balanced on their pivots on a hole bored in their sides.

When everything has been prepared, give one of the boxes to the friend with whom you wish to correspond and appoint a given hour in the day or week. Of course, one must be in one's chamber a quarter, a half, or whole hour before the set time, must place the pointer on its pivot *and keep it under observation during the whole period.*

A cross or some other mark must stand at the beginning of the alphabet so that the partner can see, when the needle points to it, that you want to begin transmitting a message. For the pointer must move of its own accord after your distant friend has set it at the beginning mark. Now turn one of the pointers to a letter and, at the same instant, the other pointer will automatically make an identical movement to the same letter owing to the link between them. The reply is transmitted in the same way and, at the close of transmission, the pointer is turned back to the beginning mark.

After use, the pointer is removed from the box and each are separately wrapped in cotton wool and put away in a wooden case, special care being taken to keep them free from rust.[5]

---

[5]Cf. the apparatus described by Lord Lytton (1803–1873) in his *The House of*

It may be assumed that the Rosicrucians knew that it is also possible to "telegraph" or rather "telepathize" by means of the siderial pendulum—the rotating divining rod—(Julie Kniese). Further to the case of the Rosicrucian Jew, Jesse, "We have the striking example of a young Jewess who was the daughter of a rabbi in the Eger ghetto, a wise Qabbalist. She showed women how to answer many otherwise insoluble questions by means of a small gold ring suspended by a hair taken from her own auburn locks."[6]

This type of pendulum telegraphy is also much in vogue today: "Other pendulists place a sheet with the letters of the alphabet on their desks and claim that by means of their pendulums they can pick up messages transmitted to them by a partner using a second ring swinging over an identical sheet of letters."[7]

A very experienced French radiesthesist who is still alive states, "In the summer of 1935, the dowsing association of Marsan instituted a direct link between two stations which were more than one hundred kilometers distant from one another. Each station took it in turns to be sender and receiver and a regular conversation was carried out with the help of pendulums."[8]

On April 1, 1951, a high-grade Hamburg Hermeticist wrote to me on this subject as follows, "Telegraphy with the aid of a pendulum is not new to me. As long as some 30 years ago,

---

the Black Magicians (Dresden, 1923, p. 92), which might also have been a means of communication. "We discovered in the forced open compartment a very remarkable apparatus which was meticulously arranged. There rested on a small, thin book, as flat as a plate, a glass bowl filled with a pungent liquid on which there floated a sort of compass with a needle, which swung round rapidly. However, instead of the usual signs, there were seven remarkable symbols at the compass points, not dissimilar to those used by the astrologers to represent the planets."

[6]F.V. Schöffel, *Hexen von einst und heute* [*Witches of the past and present*] (Bamburg, 1931–1932, p. 24).

[7]Dr. Jules Regnault, *Biodynamique et Radiations* (Paris, 1936, pp. 267, 268). Tr. note: Reference to the original text provides the following interesting piece of information not quoted by our German author, "They could even decipher in this way a message sent in their absence, several hours earlier."

[8]René Lacroix-á-l'Henri, *Theories et Procédés Radiesthésiques* (Paris, 1942, p. 127).

one of my acquaintances, the Qabbalist Franz Buchmann (Berlin-Charlottenburg) practiced this art. He frequently telegraphed from Berlin to Southern Germany with great accuracy and wrote articles on his experiments for Zillmann's *Metaphysischen Rundschau* [*Metaphysical Review*] before the World War."

In private life, Buhmann was chief accountant at Spandau waterworks. He wrote under the pen name Naga the *Schlüssel zu den 72 Gottesnamen der Kabbala* [*A key to the 72 names of God in the Qabala*] (Leipzig, 1925). He manufactured a medicine which was a quick cure for malaria, for instance. This was a Qabbalistic remedy, formulated *with the help of the siderial pendulum* to contain 123 herbs harmonically adjusted to one another. There were 123 components because the numerical value of the name *Shaddai* is 123. Buchmann exported a lot of it to the tropics. It had other good effects, too. (From a private communication "AME" February 22, 1949.) Surya, in his *Hermetische Medizin* [*Hermetic Medicine*] (Berlin-Pankow, 1923, pp. 313 ff.), refers to Buchmann's green and yellow elixir of life, "Pranoidin." The green is the above-mentioned Shaddai!

A certain Arthur Usthal wrote an observation on "New discoveries with the pendulum" in the *Zentralblatt für Okkultismus* (Leipzig, February, 1919) in connection with "pendular telegraphy," which at this point ought to be rescued from undeserved oblivion: "The most incredible feature of the subject is that a 'telephone connection' sought by nothing more than mental 'dialing' should succeed with persons completely unknown to me, of whose existence I had had not the least inkling until the moment of contact. All I had to do was to utter some name at random, and then concentrate on the person concerned in thought while whispering their name suggestively several times, and the contact was made."

I myself got to know a lady telepathist in Mainz around 1922 who made contact with her test subjects when she knew their Christian names only, although she could operate only at certain times durng the Moon's cycle. However, hers were record performances for someone with natural gifts!

I am conversant with a third kind of "telepathy with special equipment," of which I shall not speak. It does not involve subjective influences (as in the pendulum) and so eliminates error. There is also thought transference *without* material aids,

automatic spelling instrument "Hesperus Additor." This piece of apparatus worked on much the same principle as that of Benjamin Jesse.

I have now changed my mind about what I said earlier and will also reveal the third type of "telepathy with equipment," in order to afford as much practical advice as possible. The method in question is that used in tests performed by professor Allex as reported by C.P. van Rossem in 1933. He placed female snails on the white squares of a chessboard, and did the same thing with male snails in another room. He then pushed all the females on to the black squares and the males in the other room followed the movement of the females, slowly but surely. Whether the females were moved over two, three or four squares, the males promptly crawled to the squares indicated to them by the females. Tests run between Paris and Marseilles over 497 miles have given the same results!

Von Rossem (sic) writes that the flow of "affinity," as Allex calls it, is so reliable that it can be used for the purposes of telegraphy! Richet explains this phenomenon by "cryptaesthesia," Sudre by "metognomy," Myers by selaesthesia, Allex, as already stated, by "affinity" and, while clever men are using names to try and cover their ignorance, the snails are laughing up their sleeves!

ROSICRUCIAN OPTICS

> At that time, by means of two solar microscopes or
> reflectors, which were a wonderful new discovery of
> mine, I disintegrated and so projected invisible beams
> of light into the sky. Where they met, they became
> visible and formed the bright disk.
>
> —the optician, Cervenka, in *Dr. Lederer*, a novel by
> Gustav Meyrink (1868–1932)

Hofrat Karl von Eckartshausen (1752–1803)—"this pre-
eminent disciple of the Rosy Cross"—Sédir calls him in his
Mystische Nächte [*Mystical Nights*] (Munich, 1783, 4th Night):

> In optics, my Brother, inconceivable things still lie hid-
> den, undreamt of by our physicists. Just think of the
> concave mirror! But all this is only a hint that ought
> to lead the researcher to higher truths.

The basic Rosicrucian document *Fama* of 1614 speaks of
"mirrors of manifold virtues," meaning nothing more or less
than "magic mirrors"—earth mirrors for treasure-seeking,
mirrors for seeing at a distance, etc. In the *Spiritual Diary* of
the Order's (second) founder's *Chemical Wedding of Christian
Rosencreutz Ao. 1459* (1916), a *"Sun Reflector = Blast Furnace"*
for chemical experiments is described on the "Sixth Day." A
gilded, polished sphere filled with liquid hung by a strong
chain in the center of the mirror room. All the mirrors (after
the blinds which covered them had been rolled up) concentrated the sun's reflection on the sphere which was soon in-
tensely hot.

I have dealt with the "Utilization of Solar Energy" (by means of mirrors) elsewhere,[1] and will simply confine myself to remarking here that the Arabs, who are the most skillful workers in enamel in the Near East, make use of burning mirrors in order to fuse the enamel and for chemical processes generally. This idea of a sun-reflector oven, which was unusual for Europe at the time when the *Chemical Wedding* was published, points once more to the Arabian origin (or rather to the transmission by Arabian adepts) of the Fraternitas Rosae Crucis, as maintained as long ago as 1618 by its opponent Eusebius Christianus Crucifer (a pseudonym) in his *Kurtzen Beschreibung der Newen* (sic) *Arabischen und Morischen Fraternitet* [*A Brief Description of the New Arabian and Moorish Fraternity*].

Kiesewetter[2] is even able to report that, at the time of the publication of the four fundamental Rosicrucian documents, not only were ordinary mirrors in use to generate high temperatures, but regular *concave mirrors*:

Even theologians were members of the Rosicrucians; men like Johann Arndt (1555–1621), the famous author of the *Wahren Christentum* (1609) who, in 1599, wrote a Rosicrucian work entitled *Zweytes Silentium Dei* which I have in my possession. The preparation of the *Lapis Philosophorum* [Philosophers' Stone] without artificial fire, but only by the heat of the sun concentrated by an arrangement of *concave mirrors*, is taught in this manuscript. Let the value of the instructions be as great or small as it may, what *is* of scientific importance is that *the Rosicrucians knew about concave mirrors a century before Tschirnhausen* which, taken all in all, were quite as effective as the famous instrument of this Saxon Philosopher of the period of *Augustus the Strong*.[3]

---

[1]Willy Schrödter: *Vom Hundertste ins Tausendste* (Freiburg i. Br. 1940–1941); Willy Schrödter: *Streifzug ins Ungewohnte* (Freiburg i. Br., 1949) [*One Thing and Another*, and *A Venture into the Unusual*].
[2]Karl Kiesewetter (1854–1895): "The Rosicrucians," in *Magische Blätter* [Magical Papers] (Leipzig, November 1922, Vol. 11, p. 344).
[3]Ehrenfried Walter von Tschirnhaus (erroneously known as Tschirnhausen), mathematician and philosopher, born April 10, 1651, at Gut Kieslingswalde (O. Laus), who died October 11, 1708 at Dresden. He built the first glassworks

The idea put forward by Johann Arndt (1555–1621) in his *Zweyten Silentium Dei* (1599) of making the Philosphers' Stone without artificial fire, merely by using powerful lenses (sic) to concentrate the sun's rays, led to his rehabilitation in 1922.

A distingushed Dutch Theosophist and reputed Rosicrucian[4] had this to say:

> The vitality of the physical body is to be found in the etheric body. If the latter can be strengthened, health and a long life are obtained. And absorbing condensed ether is the most convenient way of achieving both. Our experts have failed to make it to this very day and therefore imagine that the thing is impossible. However, the impossibilities of today are the realities of tomorrow. When Roger Bacon wrote in his *Opus Major* the prophecy that one day horseless carriages would travel more quickly than any other vehicle, he was thought to be a sorcerer and the Inquisition threw him into prison. When Sir Isaac Newton repeated the same prophecy several hundred years later, Voltaire made merry at his expense; but history has brilliantly justified the two first-named! This encourages me to say something about the elixir of long life, impossible as it may seem.

> The ether is set in motion by the rays of the sun. Whoever succeeds in diffracting and concentrating the sun's rays by means of mirrors and lenses, can generate certain waves in the ether; and he who knows how to unite the energy of the elemental fire with that of the Ignis Essentialis (the essence of fire) will be able to observe the very slow but very sure formation of fluid drops which are without peer for a host of diseases!

---

in Saxony and manufactured a frit which was very like porcelain in appearance, so preparing the way for Joh. Friedr. Böttger (1682–1719).

[4]Frater Syntheticus in *Meinung und Wirklichkeit* [*Concept and Reality*] published in the Dutch fortnightly periodical *Eenheid* (March 16 and March 23, 1922), reproduced from Fr. Witteman's *Histoire des Rose Croix (History of the Rosicrucians]* (Paris, 1925, p. 187–188).

He will prove the truth of the old alchemical maxim:
Scias enim summum artis secretum in ignis consistere![5]

When the offspring of Count Karl von Heimhausen and Annemarie Eckart, the beautiful daughter of his castle steward, declared in 1788 that "many mysterious things still lie concealed" in optics, it should be remembered that he did so long after the discovery and utilization of the microscope and telescope, so that, presumably, he must have been referring to something else which is "undreamt of by our physicists." The latter may at times have dreamt of seeing smaller or further than before, but what are those other mysterious things? Could that "mechanical tube" (yet to be invented!) have been meant, which would "discover the nobler and more gifted things that hover in the illimitable air"[6]—the "microbes of the Astral Plane", the etheric cosmic intelligences, beings invisible to normal sight?

The imperial captain and knight, Henry Cornelius Agrippa von Nettesheim (1456–1535) who, when he was only 20, founded a society in Paris for the study of occult sciences and, at 24, had prepared the first draft of his epoch-making *Occulta Philosphia* [*Occult Philosophy*] (published in 1533), wrote as follows.

> And it is well-known, if in a dark place where there is no light but by the coming in of a beam of the Sun somewhere through a litle (sic) hole, a white paper, or plain looking-glass be set up against that light, that there may be seen upon them, whatsoever things are done without, being shined upon by the Sun (Vol. I, chapter 6).

This was an anticipation of Giambattista della Porta's (1541–1615) invention, the *camera obscura!*[7] This Neapolitan

---

[5]"Know then, the chief secret of the Art resides in fire!"

[6]Lord Edward Bulwer (Lytton) 1803–1873), *Zanoni* (IV, 4).

[7]Porta first described it in the Naples edition of 1558, in Book 4, chapter 2. However, sixteen years earlier, in 1542, the astrologer Erasmus Reinholdus had depicted the apparatus in his edition of the *Theoricae novae planetarum* of Purbach which came out at Wittenberg. He had already used it in 1540 to observe the solar eclipse. Leonardo da Vinci (1452–1519) also knew the

nobleman had already published his famous *Magia naturalis* at age 15 (1556) and in 1560 established in his native city a "Society for Investigating the Secrets of Nature," which was promptly dissolved on the orders of Pope Paul V (1605–1621)!

In the second volume of his *Occult Philosophy*, the "demonic knight" takes a retrospective glance at the optical wonder of antiquity: "And I know how to make reciprocal glasses, in which the Sun shining, all things which were illustrated by the raies thereof are apparently seen many miles off" (chapter 1).

Agrippa states this even more emphatically later on: ". . . especially in glasses. And I knew how to make by them wonderful things, in which anyone might see whatsoever he pleased at a long distance" (Vol. II, chapter 23, last sentence). *A precursor of the reflecting telescope of 1671 invented by Sir Isaac Newton (1643–1727)!*

Lehmann[8] is of the same opinion: "A *reflecting telescope* is obviously being described here. If the mirror is not mounted in a tube, one will generally speaking see in the telescope only those things which are directly illuminated by the sun. Agrippa's description is so accurate that, in my view, he had undoubtedly handled a reflecting telescope, primitive though its form may have been, and had done so one-and-a-half centuries before Newton invented it in 1671." (It might be worth adding here that in 1950 a *reflecting microscope without lenses* was developed by Dr. Hans Hartmann of the "people's" Zeiss Works in Jena. It is intended to put the microscope into regular production and to exhibit it at the annual Leipzig Fair: From a German Press Agency report.)

---

apparatus. It is mentioned in the Commentary on Vitruvius as well, written by the duke of Milan's architect, Cesare Caesariano (died 1542). This Commentary was published at Como in 1521. It gave the name of the inventor as the Benedictine monk Don Paphnutio (Dom Panunce) "Monastico Architecto of Sanoto Benedicto" [the monastic architect of the Benedictine Order].

[8]Prof. Alfred Lehmann, Copenhagen (1858–1921) in his *Aberglaube und Zauberei* [*Superstition and Sorcery*] (Stuttgart, 1925, p. 210 footnote). It is entirely possible that Agrippa von Nettesheim was also acquainted with optical lenses (in addition to optical mirrors), for the Druids had known them in even earlier times. They had polished lenses from crystal or glass of up to 1½ inches diameter, known today as "Druids' buttons." (From Karl Kiesewetter: *Der Occultismus des Altertums*, Leipzig, 1896, p. 860).

But what is to be made of the following statement by this man who was so many centuries ahead of his time?

And there is another sleight, or trick yet more wonderful. If anyone shall take images artificially painted, or written letters, and in a clear night set them against the beams of the full Moon, whose resemblances being multiplyed in the Aire, and caught upward, and reflected back together with the beams of the Moon, any other man that is privy to the thing, at a long distance sees, reads, and knows them in the very compass, and Circle of the Moon (Book I, chapter 6).

The late captain (since 1512) of the Emperor Maximilian I (1493–1519), who was knighted for bravery on the field of battle against the Venetians, was anxious of course to employ this optical secret for military purposes: "Which art of declaring secrets is indeed very profitable for Towns, and Cities that are besieged, being a thing which Pythagoras (580–493 B.C.) long since did often do, and which is not unknown to some in these dayes, *I will not except myself.*"

One of those to whom the technique was "not unknown" must have been the "wizard abbot" Johannes Trithemius (1462–1516), his teacher at Würzburg, with whom he was in telepathic communication, as he mentions in the same chapter shortly before describing the above experiment.

Plancy[9] also knew about Agrippa's "moon projections." "When Francis I (1515–1547) was at war with Charles V (1519–1556), a magician kept the Parisians informed of what was happening in Milan, by writing the news from this town on a convex mirror and exposing it to the Moon in such a way that the Parisians could read in the starry sky what the distant mirror had written on it." Colett de Plancy quoted a certain Aporta as his authority, but unfortunately I am unable to trace him. He ends by saying, "Alas! This beautiful secret has been lost—like so many more!"

---

[9]Jacques Albin Simon Collet de Plancy (1793–1881) in his *Dictionaire Infernal* (Paris, 1817, Vol. II, p. 75; under "Mirrors").

If one is to believe the statements of Professor V. Raman in the Indian *Astrological Magazine*, the ancient Indians made an absolutely incredible use of optics.[10]

He starts by pointing out that *Vimanas* [Machines flying in the air] are mentioned in the *Mahabharatha* and *Ramayana*. "Of course these references could be dismissed as fantasies. But I remember that for thousands of years there has stood in India a tall pillar which has been a source of wonder to generations. It is made of a metallic alloy which is still unknown to modern technology and the striking thing is that this metal does not rust. Now our own metallurgy has had the ability to produce rust-free metals only relatively recently."

A Maharishi Bharadwaja writes in the chapter entitled "Vimanadhi" in his book *Yantrasarwaswami* about the construction and operation of aircraft. He states that he compiled his work after painstaking study of the writings of Shounaka, Narayana, Garga, etc. He mentioned eight types of *Vimanas*. Each of these machines was driven by a specific process of energy exchange. From the reports made by the great sages, we are led to believe that these aircraft were fitted with different *lenses*, lenses of special construction, which made it possible to reflect various components in the solar energy and to harness them, so that the machine was enabled to rise from the earth and soar through the air—in other words, to fly. Sakatayana Rishi, in his *Loha Tantram*, gives yet another description of *Manis*[11] (lenses), which were made from certain types of glass and acted as a sort of mirror with the special property of absorbing or discharging certain forces of sunlight according to requirements. Modern scientists talk of cosmic rays. Thirteen different sorts of lenses were employed and their composition was accurately known.

---

[10]*Flugschiffe in vorgeschichtlicher Zeit [Prehistoric Flying-machines]* translated by A.M. Grimm (born February 4, 1892) in *Mensch und Schicksal [Man and Fate]* (Villach, No. 22 dated February 1, pp. 3–7).

[11]The secret sect of the Cathars in 13th century Romania possessed a mysterious sacred object which they called *Mani* and an associated sacred rite—the *Mani-sola*—about which nothing is definitely known. The *Mani* is said to be a star fallen from Heaven, a strange gem, a "Holy Grail"; but might it not have been a lens for collecting the solar ether (Korschelt), the *Mani*? And might not *Manisola* have been irradiation with this Mani to a liturgical accompaniment?

DISCUSSION

The first thing which ought to be mentioned is that in the burying-places of Libya and in the ruins of Niniveh, plano-convex lenses have been found, and a green-black obsidian concave mirror has been discovered in Esmeralda (Ecuador); all of which are believed to go back to the Proto-Egyptians (the Atlanteans). It may be that the Babylonians and Druids were enabled to make such exact measurements of the stars by the use of lens systems and telescopic tubes. The Chinese employed lenses of rock-crystal long before Galileo Galilei (1564–1642) and even today they have spectacles made of the same material. (I shall refrain from giving references for this as they would occupy too much space). Putting it in a nutshell, Saint-Yves d'Alveydre takes the view that, "As far as optics is concerned the learned societies (of Antiquity) were already in possession of all our instruments, such as mirrors, concave, convex and conic lenses, prisms, dark chambers, microscopes and tele-scopes."

I have no explanation to offer for the *Moon Projection* of which the "demonic knight" Cornelius Agrippa spoke with such assurance. The uninitiated can only make the trite remark that when the moonbeams fall on us it is obviously possible to reflect them back again.

Finally, in regard to the ancient Indian aircraft driven by solar energy which has been collected by means of lenses, Raman is not alone in crediting them with this invention. The Anglo-Saxon (sic) savant, James Churchward discovered and translated 120 old Indian inscriptions which he suggested might be some twenty-thousand years old (!) and told the story of a continent called Mu which had been swallowed up by the sea about eleven-thousand years earlier. The forty-six million white inhabitants who perished in the inundation must have reached a high level of technology.

> Evidence in my possession suggests that, ten thousand years before our era, the Indian armies possessed flying machines with a carrying capacity of up to twenty soldiers at a time. These machines were propelled by engines of almost unbelievable simplicity, making use of natural forces for which present-day science is

looking once more. I have in my hands data enabling me to say that the Indian general, Ramschandra flew from the island of Ceylon to Northern India in one of these constructions. These aircraft were also sent to bomb towns in time of war. Gun-powder was also known and fire-arms were employed. This degree of civilization was seen in the Hindu Kingdom of the Ramanaga dynasty.[12]

Guideo von List (1848–1919) has also described *Atlantean* aircraft.[13]

In order to include something of practical value in this section, I shall conclude by touching upon the direct and indirect use of concave mirrors and of lenses in medicine. In regard to their direct use, we learn from the writings of Prof. Joh. Fr. Osiander, M.D. (Göttingen, 1826), that he employed or recommended them for colds in the head and cataracts. At the turn of the century, lieutenant-colonel M. Mehl, in his *Sonnentherapie* [*Sun Therapy*] (Oranienburg bei Berlin, published by Fritz Koslowsky), advocated the use of burning-glasses for lupus, skin cancer, lumps, eruptions, and other skin diseases. In the advertisement for his booklet, which is unfortunately now out of print, we are told "the author was the first to achieve a fundamental and permanent cure of the most frightful and allegedly incurable skin diseases with the rays of the sun and an ordinary magnifying glass. Anyone can avail themselves of this method to secure the prompt disappearance of simple skin troubles (spots, warts, etc.)." In other words, he used concentrated sunlight!

Sad to say, this forerunner of Niels Ryberg Finsen (1860–1904) has been treated with undeserved neglect, while the Dane received the Nobel Prize in 1903 for his *Phototherapy*!

The Austrian "father-figure" among mediums, Jakob Lorber (1800–1864), exposed simple products like cooking salt to sunlight and turned them into remedies by this "dynamizing." According to the little volume, *Die Heilkraft des Sonnenlichtes* [*The*

---

[12]Walter Holstein, "Has the Atlantis Riddle been solved?" in *Wochenschau* (Vol. 27, 1934), p. 18.

[13]*Die Bilderschrift* [*Hieroglyphics*] (Berlin-Lankwitz, 1910), p. 27.

Healing Properties of Sunlight] (Bietigheim i. Württ., undated, Neu-Salems-Verlag) such remedies can be made by anybody. However, anyone who is not prepared to take the trouble to do this can obtain the improved materials from Gg. P. Sponsel, Ochsenfurt/Main.

About thirty years ago, Karl Kessler went further in his Freiburg (Breisgau) laboratory "Kajoka" and manufactured his "Solar Energy Remedies" by placing the materials under specially designed and colored glass covers and under a large magnifying glass, which could also analyze the spectrum into its colors, with solar illumination above. Kessler claimed that he had discovered how to fix the solar substance or electromagnetic sun power and thus to have guaranteed the long-lasting radiation and effect of his remedies. The old dowser, Friedrich August Frank Glahn (1865–1941), from whose *Pendelbücherei* (Vol. IV; p. 83–85) [*Pendulum Library*] I am taking these facts, gave his approval to Kessler's products. At the time of writing, K.J. Kessler is engaged in the manufacture and distribution of his "Humina" chemical and pharmaceutical products.

Here is another, but non-medical, point of interest: Prof. Karl Christian Wolfart (1778–1832) used to write under the regular heading, "Things that surprise us and things that don't" in *Jahrbücher für den Lebensmagnetismus oder Neues Askläpieion* (Leipzig, 1820; Vol. 3, p. 179) [*Annals of Animal Magnetism or the New Æsculapius*]:

> It is no longer any cause for wonder that the concave mirror should warm, heat and even cause things to burst into flame by means of a phantom image of the sun or its reflected glow, nor even that a concentration of coldness can be focused from a block of ice by means of a concave mirror.

A chemist friend of mine has tried the latter experiment several times without result. Perhaps others will be more successful![14]

---

[14]Tr. Note: Apart from its cooling effect on the atmosphere by convection, the block of ice is radiating less heat to us than we are radiating to it, and therefore it is cold to us. It is not radiating rays of coldness, as there is no

Dr. Ernst Busse, a dentist from Halle, Westphalia, elaborated the idea of using lenses for curative purposes when he wrote to me December 9, 1952. He claimed "that it should be possible, by inserting such glass lenses into the ears, to introduce a steady beam of concentrated light into the inner ear and so obtain a good and quick healing of abscesses in the middle ear or of deafness. The idea occurred to me on seeing a recent report that a specialist had inhibited suppuration in the middle ear by the introduction of sunlight which had been collected and concentrated with a lens. Why should not simple daylight, if it is continuously concentrated in this way, not have a better and persistent remedial action, if a somewhat milder one?"

As far as daylight is concerned, a French engineer in a London apartment house used mirrors to throw indirect sunshine on the white ceilings. This was a form of hygiene, although what we should try to do is to bring in building regulations which will make the construction of such gloomy living quarters impossible in the first place.

In my opinion, artificial sunlight could be supplied to the whole organism (and perhaps might favorably influence lung diseases and skin affections in this way), if the patient were to be irradiated both front and back by concave mirrors the height of a person, provided, of course, they were not focused too sharply. I am inclined to think that the healing of wounds could also be accelerated by this means.[15]

On the whole, mirrors conceal many secrets. I think, for instance of the "spiritist mirror phenomenon" of my friend Franz Vincenz Schöffel (born October 3, 1884) and of the "mirror magnetism" of Heinrich Jürgens.

I remember how mad people look reflected in those distorting mirrors at fairgrounds, and how an American

---

such thing. All that is happening is that the heat exchange is in its favor and, on balance, it is gaining and we are losing heat. Hence the action of the mirror in concentrating such heat rays as the ice manages to emit must have a slightly warming effect, so that the concentration of rays making up the image of the ice block would be marginally warmer than their surroundings, although still cold to us.

[15]It is difficult to come up with anything really new. After writing the above, I found the idea in *Kiesers Archiv* (Leipzig, 1822, Vol. XI, Item 2, p. 46).

millionaire used this effect to drive his unloved fiancée insane in 1944. But, above all, I think of that clever remark by August Strindberg (1847–1912) in his *A New Blue-Book* (Munich, 1920, p. 689) in the section entitled "Energy gain":

> When the sun is reflected in a mirror, its reflection gives more warmth than the sun itself. But if I cut the mirror in twenty pieces, I get twenty times more warmth, enough to set a house on fire. The energy source here is inexplicable and the gain cannot be due to the negligible amount of work performed in cutting up the mirror. George Louis Leclerc Graf von Busson (1707–1788) took a great number of plane mirrors and arranged them in a concave frame so that they all came to a focus. With this equipment he melted gold in the sunlight, while the sun itself scarcely melted butter. That is an unheard of energy gain without any increase in work; it proves the possibility of perpetual motion.[16]

To which we shall add only this: the melting point of gold is 1063° and that of butter is 32°.

---

[16]Tr. Note: Strindberg fails to see here that merely by raising the potential of the available energy we do not increase its *quantity*; we are only concentrating our resources upon a smaller area. There is no intrinsic gain in energy as he supposes, nor do we have here a proof of perpetual motion.

ROSICRUCIAN SPIRITUAL HEALING

> They brought forth the sick into the streets, and laid
> them on beds and couches, that at the least the *shadow*
> of Peter passing by might overshadow some of them.

> —Acts of the Apostles, 5:15

Today we know that nervous diseases can be mentally caused
and (with the exception of bone fractures) organic troubles can
also originate in the mind. One speaks of psychosomatic diseases, in which the soul (Greek, *psyche*) and body (Greek, *soma*)
are seen to be a unit. Obviously, psychosomatic diseases can be
healed only if we start with the soul or spirit.

*Psychosomatic diseases arise from some defect in the master plan
of the "I".* Pre-selection comes into operation here. Angelus Silesius (1624–1677) sings:

> Vor jedem steht ein Bild
>   des, was er werden soll;
> Solang er dies nicht ist
>   Ist nicht sein *Friede* voll

> (A vision have we each
>   Of what our lives should be;
> Until that state we reach,
>   Full *peace* we cannot see.)

With deeper intention, the Lord Jesus Christ greeted his
followers with the words, "Peace be with you!" This was also
the form of farewell intoned by the Hellenic neophytes in the

darkness of the temple of initiation. Mongolian shepherds still salute each other with, "Is there peace in your soul?" (*Mendu sai beino?*) instead of with the superficial "How do you do?" Whenever anyone is perfectly happy (for the time being), he will say that he feels as if he were in Heaven. Thus a feeling of happiness could be called "The Kingdom of Heaven"; this being a state on earth not a place (Luke 17: 21)! As the Apostle Paul said, "The kingdom of God is . . . righteousness and peace and joy in the Holy Ghost" (Romans 14: 17), and "Rejoice!" the reiterated exhortation of our Lord, was also how the Essenes (a secret Jewish sect of his times) used to greet one another. Nor should we forget the sensible advice used as a greeting in the Tyrol, "Take it easy now!"

That the fevered existence of today leads to cardiac troubles, circulatory disorders, gastric disturbances (both nervous and organic) and diseases of the thyroid gland, not to mention the general "nervousness" among people, is common knowledge. *A lack of peace = a shortage of time = the loss of health!* Needless to say, the Rosicrucians allowed themselves sufficient time to experience a sense of peace and, since they were so saturated with it, they enjoyed superabundant health (*plusquamperfect*) and "infected" their suffering fellow men with health, so to speak, triggering self-healing (the *Archaeus*) in the sick person. *"Ben Salem"* (= Sons of Peace) is what the would-be occultist, Carl von Eckartshausen (1752–1803) called them. The *Confessio*, one of their basic documents, dated 1615, expresses it so invitingly: "Would it not be something worth having to be able to live each hour as if you had been alive since the creation of the world and would live there until the end of time?" "Lessing the Wise" (1729–1781) had reached the same conclusion: "What have I then to neglect? Is not the whole of eternity mine?" (*Erziehung des Menschengeschengeschlechtes* [*The Education of Mankind*] p. 100). "If you want to help people, the Spirit and the Truth will lead and guide you!" said Paracelsus, and added this thought for our deepest contemplation, "Love is the basis of the healing art" (*Spitalbuch* [*The Infirmary Book*] p. 58).

A sentiment which has the agreement of Hans Heinrich Ehrler, who writes in his *Briefe aus mein Kloster* [*Letters from my Cloister*] (Lorch, i. Württ., 1931): "I believe that a man can become so good and loving that he can heal the sick," and goes on to relate one of his own experiences of the power of a loving thought.

Nyoka, crown prince of the "Empire of the Snakes" (in Tanganyika) told F.C. Carnachon, "The snake men have been charged by Limdini, the great shepherd, to keep his children happy and healthy. To be a snake man one must first and foremost have kind thoughts and a heart full of pure truth" (*Das Kaiserreich der Schlangen* [*The Kingdom of the Snakes*] Erlen-bach-Zürich, 1934, pp. 27–28).

One who has love in his heart, is "God-filled" so to speak. Not only do his hands possess the power of healing (by the laying on of hands) but the whole man is turned into the "Stone" (of the Wise). Merely stepping into the aura (the shadow) of the consecrated one exerts an influence, soothes, alleviates and eventually heals. Paracelsus understood this too: "True self-consciousness is attended by a spiritual power which is transmitted from the doctor to his patient if the former possesses it. *By this means, the presence of the doctor in itself will do more good to the sick man than any medicine.*" And he adds an explanation that could well have been given by the heliotherapist Carl Huter (1851–1912): "For the etheric vibrations penetrate the human etheric body and in doing so can convert his inharmonious vibrations into harmonious ones." Cornelius Agrippa, who belonged to the same school of thought (that of the Trithemius), knew of course, that, "Neither is another's body less subjected to another's mind then (sic) to another's body. *Upon this account they say, that a man by his affection, and habit only, may act upon another*" [*Occult Philosophy*, Book I, chapter 65]. "And it is verified amongst Physitians, that a strong belief, and an undoubted hope, and love towards the Physitian, and medicine, conduce much to health, yea more sometimes than the medicine itself" (Book I, chapter 66).

In our own day and age, the Berlin doctor Josef Gemassmer M.D., healed with this type of *"meditative resonance." To my mind it is a total and radical therapy!*[1] The person who feels that he has

---

[1]The expression "Meditative Resonance" is well chosen! "If two pianos are standing in adjacent rooms and a note is struck on one of them, the string

lost contact with the "Supreme Power" must turn to his neighbor. As Jean Paul (1763–1825) so aptly says, "When a man is no longer his own friend, he goes to his brother who still is, that he may gently advise and restore him." Petrus Blesenius was not wrong when he said, "No remedy is better for man than his fellow-man," a pronouncement which should not be restricted to the imparting of vital force from one individual to another by healing magnetism!

I believe I have said enough to show that the Rosicrucians knew about spiritual healing. And if they knew it, they must have used it, for "to him that knoweth to do good, and doeth it not, to him it is sin" (James 4:17). Then again, they were able to employ spiritual healing because of their spiritual lives. Admittedly, they have bequeathed no method to us; all they have done is to indicate its source to us, to which I must now turn in framing my next remarks!

The human being is tripartite—body, soul and spirit. This teaching is called trichotomy. Master Duan says in his *Lehre vom dreifachen Ich* [*The Doctrine of the Threefold "I"*]: "The first I is an unreal I; the second is the true I; the third is the godlike I within the true I, the soul of the soul. In nature, the first I is the mortal I of the body, the second is the soul, the third is the essential spiritual existence."

The difference between soul and spirit is made plain by Michail Jurjewitsch Lermontow (1814–1841): "Two beings live in my breast. The first lives in the full sense of the word; the other observes and passes judgment on the first" (*Ein Held unserer Zeir* [*A Hero of Our Time*].

Fundamentally, the soul is the attention that can be paid at will to the body or to the spirit. *"Or" not "and"!!* The spirit is the "Debit" (the target), the soul is the "Credit" (the present state of development). If the soul constantly turns to the spirit, follows and amalgamates with it, it will share its perfection and become full of wisdom, power, and peace, while gaining release from pain, disease, change, and mortality. The soul is the bride

---

of the same pitch in the other will be set vibrating." Thus wrote the spiritual healer Horatio W. Dresser (Epston) in his *Methods and Problems of Spiritual Healing* (Jena, 1902, p. 21).

who must unite with the king's son, or spirit, in the "Chemical Wedding" (Matthew 22:1–14). As we hear from Schlesien's Aeolian Harp:

> Die Braut des ew'gen Gottes
> kann jede Seele werden
> wenn sie nur seinem Geist
> sich unterwirft auf Erden.

> To be the heavenly bride
> has every soul the worth,
> If but its spirit now
> is humble here on earth.

Unfortunately this is true only in the rarest instances. Much more often the soul settles down with the body, indentifies with it and so shares its limitations. It shares its afflictions, or, in other words, becomes sick.

One can agree with the challenging assertion of the Munich University Professor, Joh. Nep. von Ringeis (1785–1880): *"Sin is the mother of disease."*

Etymologically speaking, to sin is to *sondern* or "to separate," to live for oneself and to keep what one has for oneself. "We are constantly wishing that someone would come or that something would happen and this continual discontent occasions an equally continual squandering of energy" (Dresser, p. 18). The tendency to separate runs counter to the common spirit (the "mystical Vine of Christ"). "If a man abide not in me, he is cast forth as a branch" (John 15: 6). In modern terms, Ricarda Huch (1867–1950) put it like this, "If self-consciousness outweighs God-consciousness, that is to say the living power of the feelings on which we are based, we become ill" (*Der Sinn der Hl. Schrift* [*The Meaning of Holy Scripture*] Leipzig, 1919, pp. 5, 6.) It is the law of cause and effect which Jesus called "righteousness" (Matthew 6: 33).

"Every disease starts as a psychosis," says Dr. Sheldon Leavit M.D. (born 1848) in *Wege zur Höhe* [*Ways to the Heights*] (Stuttgart, 1909, p. 239). First there is the sinful thought, and this is followed by a depletion of the body's energy system, although its warning signals (symptoms) are usually ignored!

According to the law of least resistance, the diseased state expresses itself in various ways in each individual body. In one it will manifest as liver disease, in a second as eye trouble and in a third as nervous exhaustion, and perhaps in each case the mental root cause will be worry. "Where there are illness and worry, there is always an excessive self-consciousness" (Dresser, p. 24). The road to healing is summed up in the single word *metanoia* (Greek: "repentance"). "Repent ye!" was the whole teaching of the Baptist (Matthew 3:2) and was incorporated in Jesus' own message (Matthew 4:17) who singled John out for the highest praise (Matthew 11:11). "To lose oneself in order the better to find oneself is actually the quintessence of the healing process" (Dresser, p. 24). Jesus expressed this key thought of his teaching in the words: "Whosoever will save his life shall lose it; but whosoever shall lose his life for my sake and the gospel's, the same shall save it" (Mark 8:35). "Death is avoided by the man who braves it, and strikes down the faint-hearted," said Darius III. Both Kodomannus and Job learned that "the thing which I greatly feared is come upon me, and that which I was afraid of is come unto me" (Job 3:25).

Friedrich Stanger (1855–1934), who was able to help many in his "Ark of Refuge" at Möttlingen, gave this guiding principle to those who came to see him: "Become smaller." At other times he used to remark, "You must desire to become nothing, not always be striving to become number one! Then place your nothingness or naught behind the number one that no longer belongs to you, and you—who are now nothing in yourself—will form part of something really big." I was astonished and delighted to read on a subsequent occasion a very similar statement by "our brother who is resting in God," Angelus Silesius:

> Die Nichts die Kreatur
> wenn sichs Gott vorgesetzt
> Gilt nichts; stehts hinter ihm
> Dann wird es erst geschätzt.

> Wie all und jede Zahl
> Ohn Eines nicht bestehn
> So müssen die Geschöpf
> Ohn Gott, die Eins, vergehn.

The creature's little naught,
   When God it stands before,
Is nothing still; but set
   Behind, becomes a mighty
store.

As numbers one and all
   But for the first would fail,
So too in God, the One,
   We live and in His life prevail.

"The key to the whole operation of spiritual healing is the concentration of the thoughts on another center or region of consciousness, so that the recuperative power can have an un-restricted field of play" (Dresser, p. 30). This "*displacement of the center of gravity of the attention*" or, as it may also be termed, "this re-location of feeling," in short—this distraction—is the secret mode of working of many sympathetic remedies! (See the chapter on manipulations.) Looked at in its true light, scratching oneself is a diversion which overwhelms the first small discom-fort of the sting or bite. Arthur Schopenhauer (1788–1860) tells us of an offender who endured the rack without com-plaining by bearing in mind that unless he did so he would consign himself to the worse torment of burning at the stake. It was this sort of distraction that Saint Paul had in mind when he said, "Forgetting those things which are behind, and reach-ing forth unto those things which are before, I press towards the mark for the prize of the high calling of God in Christ Jesus" (Philippians 3:13–14).

Christ and His almighty power was the main objective. Dorothea Trudel (1813–1862), the faith healer of Männedorf (in Switzerland), gave this advice, "Do not look at your suffering but to the Lord the Victor!" That self-forgetfulness can remove even severe pains (at least temporarily) is shown by the example of the wounded warrior who is only aware of his injuries when the battle is over. Dr. William Baker-Fahnestock (ca. 1880) taught that one can achieve a willed, continual self-forgetfulness in his long-forgotten book *Statuvolence* ("willed state," from the Latin *status* and *volo*). Saints and sorcerers of all parts of the world knew this fact thousands of years before he did. Here are two examples of fairly recent date.

The saintly Marquis de Renty, when in obvious bodily pain, was asked whether he did not suffer and replied, *"I feel nothing, for I do not pay any attention to it,"* and then he went on to say, "The love of God is bearing everything, his servant nothing," by which we may understand him to mean that God's servant feels nothing because his thoughts (by which he becomes conscious of anything) are concentrated on HIM. The latest Indian prophet, Sri Ramakrishna Paramahamsa (1833–1886) once entered a state of *samadhi* ("statuvolence") by fervent contemplation of the Highest Being and was accidentally burned by the fire on the sacrificial altar. On coming out of his trance half an hour later, he was badly scorched. The Greek word for trance is *ecstasis* from *"ex"* and *"histanai,"* meaning to cause to stand outside of (oneself): the astral body stands outside the physical body, or rather has stepped outside it, and so the power of sensation is withdrawn from the latter (Rochas). Hence, he who masters this "royal art" shall not taste death. Incidentally, he can commit suicide at any time by projecting his astral body and cutting the "silver cord." This was done by the Chinese hermit, Ma-Ming-Tsun, in order to escape from his persecutors, and the secret remnant of the Cathars in the South of France still practice it today! The Gnostics alleged that Jesus did the same at his crucifixion. However, he did not avail himself of "spiritual local anaesthesia" by dispatching his spirit to some distant place, but suffered just as much human agony as any of the crucified slaves whose gibbets lined the Roman roads.

We may say then, that displacement of the center of interest is the secret of the "art." It is achieved by entertaining a so-called "superior idea." The most superior idea is God. "My Father . . . is greater than all" (John 10:29). It can and must be attained in one of two ways. The first of these is prayer. Prayer is based on the fact that "God is a Spirit: and they that worship him must worship him in spirit and in truth" (John 4: 24). Now we can only pray in the spirit when our ego keeps silent. "As soon as we count ourselves as nothing, God, who never leaves an unfilled space, will flow into us" (Madame Guyon, 1648–1717). This is the metaphysical counterpart to the physical law that "nature abhors a vacuum" or *horro vacui*. The inscription in Father Rosencreutz's Mausoleum, *Nequaquam vacuum* (by no means void) has the same import. All good things are potentially present; all we need do is make ourselves receptive. "Open thy mouth wide, and I will fill it!" (Psalm 81: 10). Someone who had been seriously ill with tuberculosis was asked how he had cured himelf, to which he replied, "First of all I made myself perfectly calm and then set the greater power of God over against the smaller power of the disease." God pledges Himself to help us if only we are willing to let Him.

"He is not like a carpenter," says Meister Eckhart (1260–1327), "moving round from one job to another, but is like the sun, which always shines when the sky is clear."

The second way involves our neighbor. For serving him is a service to God. "Inasmuch as ye have done it unto one of the least of these my brethren, ye have done it unto me" (Matthew 24:40). The Indians call this sort of mutual obligation with God (Latin, *re-ligio*) "Karma-Yoga" and Jesus said of this "Yoke" (i.e., Yoga) that it was easy and that by taking it upon them, men would find rest for their souls (Matthew 11: 29–30). Baron von Feuchtersleben, M.D. (1806–1849) reached the same conclusion: "He who would preserve body and soul in perfect health must early on take some share in the concerns of his fellows" (*Zur Diätetik der Seele* [*Dietetics of the Soul*], 1838). With this agrees the philosopher Elisar von Kupffer (Elisarion, born 1872):

> Bist Du betrübt, so tröste
>   Den, der noch ärmer ist.
> Du selbst bist der Erlöste
>   Wenn er sein Leid vergisst.

> If troubled, comfort give
>   To him who's poorer yet,
> And you yourself will share
>   The power to forget.

Nevertheless, whoever has become so impoverished that he can no longer make contact with the higher powers must apply to his neighbor. I have already quoted the beautiful saying of Jean Paul in this connection, so will add a quotation from

Dresser: "The healer is not in himself the almighty factor, but only the willing instrument of the higher power. What he tries to do is to be open and free in spirit and then to induce the selfsame condition in the sick person" (p. 13). This is to pray "in spirit and in truth"! Disease (as has already been said) is a summons to think and to change one's ways, for God wishes to convey an important truth to the patient through suffering. And this is where the spiritual healer has to face the most crucial issue, "What is the Almighty Will seeking to bring about in this particular phase of the stricken person's life? In what way will this purpose pose problems? Where is the seat of the trouble? What can be done to remove it?" (Dresser, p. 27). "What is the place of the illness in the person's life? What does God want him to do?" (Dresser, p. 38). Spiritual healing is a total therapy, a radical treatment. Since there is only a *single* root, there is no need to diagnose the symptoms. "The acute sensitivity of the healer can recognize the true nature of his patient's disease by merely reading his spiritual atmosphere and, like any first impressions, it uncovers what otherwise might remain hidden" (Dresser, p. 45). The whole method can be summarized as follows: "The healer addresses no questions to the sick person and allows no recital of his symptoms, a recital which would only serve to reinforce the concern, anxiety, and mental image of the disease. All attention must be focused on the end in view. One must think of how the patient has to be in good health, harmonious, restful, and strong. One must hold the thought of his true health more strongly than he can retain his false thought" (Dresser, pp. 12, 15, 16).

However, this certainly does not mean gaining an ascendency by will power and imagination! We need to be compassionate! "And it grieved him, he wept, he groaned within himself, he was troubled in spirit," are all expressions used of Jesus. This feeling of compassion, of sympathy and love ("Love is seeing someone as God intended them to be"—H. von Hattungsberg) forges the link to God as only it can do and this link acts like a transformer that strengthens the weak currents we send out to our fellow human beings.

The healer must represent the sufferer and do for that person what he or she should—but no longer can—eliminate self-centered thoughts and immerse in a feeling of unlimited goodwill in an atmosphere of silence and, if need be, with the laying on of hands.

> Ich will—anstatt an mich zu denken—
> Ins Meer der Liebe mich versenken.

> Instead of thinking of myself and me
> I'll lose my being in Love's mighty sea.

DISCUSSION

Various books of magic written in the Middle Ages professed reliance on the Holy Ghost; for example the *Clavicula Salomonis et Theosophia Pneumatica; das ist: die wahrhaftige Erkenntnis Gottes, seiner sichtbaren und unsichtbaren Geschöpfe, die heilige Geist-Kunst genannt* [*The Clavicle of Solomon and Theosophia Pneumatica*; i.e., *the true knowledge of God and of his visible and invisible creatures, called the doctrine of the Holy Ghost*], which was published in 1686 at Wesel by the bookseller Andreas Luppius, who was frequently prosecuted for the dissemination of magical texts.

Personally, I prefer a reference to the power of the Holy Spirit to the modern terms of psychosomatic therapy and meditative resonance, when speaking of the health-giving radiation from those ultra-vital people who are filled with inner peace. And in this I side with the wise men of the Middle Ages, who were well aware of these radiations. I feel I can justify my preference from the teaching of Meister Eckhart (1260–1327) and the Jewish Qabala concerning the "Divine Spark."

I began this chapter with the proposition that: "Psychosomatic diseases arise from some defect in the masterplan of the ego." This is a slight variation on the dictum stated by Dr. H. Vorwahl: "Wrong-doing is a departure from the ground-plan of the ego." Instead of wrong-doing, one could say "sin" in the sense of a departure from what one should become. In this (and of course in a somewhat narrower sense) Professor Johann Nepomuk Ringeis, M.D. (1785–1880) dared to speak in his uncompromising way of "disease caused by sin."

Another and equally good way of expressing this idea comes from the well-known biologist, parapsychologist, and iatrosophist, Dr. Herbert Fritsche (born June 14, 1911): "Illness is an invitation to stop and think and change one's ways."

This is the *metanoia* (Greek for repentance) of John the Baptist and of Jesus Christ.

Even Friedrich Nietzsche (1844–1900) had something to say on the subject:

> That hidden and imperious thing for which it takes us a long time to find a name, until at last it reveals itself as our Task in Life, that tyrant within us, takes a terrible revenge for each attempt we make to avoid or escape from it, for each premature decision, for each identification with something that is none of our business, for otherwise respectable activities if they divert us from our main concern—yes, even for each virtue which would keep us from the stern call of our personal duty. Disease is the response whenever we doubt our vocation, whenever we begin to make things easier for ourselves. How strange and, at the same time, frightening it is that we obtain more relief the more we atone! If we would regain our health, we have no choice: we must shoulder a heavier burden than we shouldered before.

The Rosicrucian "Tyrsan," Francis Bacon, Lord Verulam (1561–1626) once said, "Magic is practical metaphysics." One might just as well say: "Theurgy is practical mysticism."

Nevertheless, mysticism is superior to all forms of magic and Johannes Müller (Elmau) was right when he remarked: *"The highest privilege attainable by man is to become an instrument of God!"*

HEALING BY
TRANSPLANTATION

Everything in the universe is animate and alive. All is
the product of a common life force and the Producer
is never cut off from the product.

—Plotinus (204–270)

The royal alchemist, Emperor Rudolph II (1552–1612) had
Dr. Michel Maier as his personal physician and elevated him to
titular Count Palatine. After the demise of the "German
Hermes Trismegistos," the "Schleich of his century" entered
the service of that Rosicrucian enthusiast August Moritz (1572–
1622), the sage of Hessen-Cassel. In 1620, Maier introduced
the "Societas Germaniae" (Latin for German Society), as he
called the Rosicrucian Brotherhood to veil its real identity, into
England, where he found a formidable promoter. This was the
polyhistor Robert Fludd (Latin: Robertus de Fluctibus) (1574–
1637), who was renowned equally as a physician, anatomist,
philosopher, physicist, chemist, mathematician and mechanic.
It was Fludd, not Evangelista Torricelli (1608–1647), who invented the barometer (*Hist. utriusque cosmi*, Vol. I). The man
who was nicknamed the "Seeker" had already developed the
bicycle. He published a defense of the Rosicrucians—*Apologia
compendiaria Fraternitatem de Rosea Cruce, etc.* (Leyden, 1616) and
was chiefly interested in amalgamating Neoplatonism, the Qabala, and Christianity.

This astrologer, magician, and chiromancer with a European reputation related in *Philosophia Mosaica* (Gouda, 1638),
his most notable book as far as we are concerned, how a certain

Johannes Pharamundus had cured gout without leaving any residual effects, and cured it by means of transplantation.

"This doctor of medicine took toenail parings and hairs from the legs of the gouty individual and put them in a hole which had been drilled as far as the pith in the trunk of an oak and, after plugging the hole with a piece of the same wood, he covered the place all over with cow-dung. If the disease did not recur within the space of a quarter of a year, he judged that the oak possessed enough power to draw all the evil into itself" (Book II).

"The famous Rosicrucian, Dr. Robert Fludd, taught that the secret of the transplantation of disease lay in a fine agent which he termed *mumia*. It was this *mumia*, for example, which enabled a dog to recognize its master. Fludd recommended different plants for the different diseases for transplantation purposes."![1]

According to a contemporary commentator,[2] care must be taken to enrich this *mumia* with sweat, blood, hairs, or particles of skin detached by scratching. This improvement of the *mumia* is unnecessary however in the case of gout. All that is required as a vehicle for the transference is the nail parings and hairs from the legs of the sufferer, as already mentioned.

Now for some practical details. On February 5, 1900, Mr. Harden, a member of the Academy of Science at Bucharest and former keeper of the Royal Romanian Archives, wrote as follows to the researcher, Albert de Rochas:

> I must inform you of a very important and thoroughly checked fact. I could have told you about it three years ago, but waited until I was reasonably sure of success. My wife has been a martyr to gout since 1890. The doctors contented themselves until 1894 with repeating the words, "It's the gout," to her, adding smoothly, "you have to expect this sort of thing at your age," but found no remedy. It was just at that time that you sent

[1]An article which appeared under the nom de plume "Malret" in *Magische Blätter* [*Magical Papers*] (Leipzig, July/August, 1921, p. 243 ff). The article was entitled "Occult Transplantation of Disease," and was based on Rochas.
[2]The Abbé de Vallemont (August 29, 1578), *Occult Physics* (1693, chapter 9).

me your book on transference of feeling and, on page 143[3] I came across the case given by Fludd: "Take the toenail parings and the hairs from the legs of the gouty individual and put them in a hole which has been drilled down to the pith in the trunk of an oak and, after plugging the hole with a piece of the same wood, cover the place all over with cow-dung! I took my wife to a country-house near Campina, where oak trees were growing and followed Fludd's instructions to the letter. . . . A week later my wife no longer felt any pain. After three months she was completely healed and even her deformed finger had begun to return to its proper shape. This continued until the year 1899, when she felt renewed twinges of gout. We then went through the same procedure using another oak tree and my wife felt fine from the next morning on. (Rochas, pp. 13–14.)

An old remedy for gout was bryony (*Bryonia alba L.*). Ganser (p. 37) and Amann (p. 63; 3) both refer to it. White bryony is an extremely interesting plant from the point of view of folklore. Its poisonous root was used as a substitute for mandrake. A countess of Westerburg cured some 2,000 people in Rosicrucian times by the arcane use of bryony (Surya). It was the Rosicrucian plant *par excellence*: "The old Rosicrucians relied on it a lot for healing" (Surya). The *Clypeum veritatis* of Irenaeus Agnostus C.W. of February 21, 1618 praised it. So did an alleged itinerant Rosicrucian brother, if we are to believe the town physician of Wetzlar, Dr. Georg Molther, who brought out two books with long-winded Latin titles in 1616 and 1621. In an investigation initiated at the University of Marburg in 1619 for the study of Rosicrucian practices, a certain Philipp Homberger, of the same university, stated that he had recommended bryony root to his tutor, Philipp Homagius, as a remedy for hypochondria (Peuckert).[4] The plant has not had enough study done

---

[3]Page 184 ff of the German translation from the fifth French edition of *Die Ausscheidung des Empfindungsvermögens* [*The Transference of the Faculty of Sensibility*] (Leipzig, 1909).

[4]"What makes the Fraternity so noteworthy is their wonderful Knowledge of all sources of the healing art. They do not operate with magical powers but

on it. It is poisonous too. *I would caution readers not to experiment with it.*

Finally, here are the subdivisions of transplantation (according to Ganser):

a) Insemination;
b) Implantation;
c) Imposition;
d) Approximation;
e) Fecundation (fertilizaiton);
f) Irrigation.

The *Book of Sirach* (chapter 8, verse 11) advises us not to overestimate our own knowledge or to underestimate that of our ancestors! To give but one example, there is the case of penicillin, discovered in 1928 by Professor Alexander Fleming. Hermetic physicians made a lot of fuss about "skull moss," which was "moss" found on whitened skulls. John Parkinson recommended it in his *Theatrum Botanicum* (1640) as an application for wounds. It contained *Penicillium notatum*, from which the antibiotic is obtained.

Prof. Theodor Billroth, M.D. (1829–1894) treated a woman with breast cancer without success in 1867. One day she presented herself to him as cured. She had followed the instructions in an old herbal and used a plaster of figs cooked in milk. The figs carried mold spores.

But long before this, the prophet Isaiah had cured King Hezekiah (717–699 B.C.) of his boil (a very severe swelling, probably involving the lymphatic glands, which threatened the king's life) by means of a fig plaster (II. Kings 22: 1–7).

DISCUSSION

Everything is controlled by sympathy and antipathy.

—Empedocles (492–432 B.C.)

---

with medicinal herbs." (MS report on the origins and characteristics of the true Rosicrucians, by J. v. D.).

Mr. Harden could hardly be called a nonentity. He was an educated man of science with highly developed critical faculties, who allowed several years to elapse until he could establish that his results were trouble-free. His final account, which included a notice on the relapse, commands our belief. There would be nothing to lose in trying the remedy, since it could never do any harm.

Rochas cites another authority for the action of the sympathetic method of healing, an authority whose scientific credentials are impeccable. He is Mr. von der Naillen, the founder and former director of the famous engineering school in San Francisco.

> He was laying a railway track in California and one of the workers gave himself a deep wound in the leg while chopping down a tree. The injury was quickly bound up to stanch the bleeding. One of those present advised that the first piece of cloth that had been soaked with the blood should be taken instantly to a neighboring doctor who was named the *Sympathy Doctor* and performed wonderful cures from a distance. It was done as he suggested and, after the doctor had been given the blood-stained cloth, he took a big earth-borer, made a hole in a *vigorous* oak tree, put the cloth in the bottom of this and closed up the hole with a piece of gristle, which he hammered in with heavy blows. Observers were astonished to find that the wound started to heal rapidly from that moment in a completely abnormal fashion! (pp. xiv–xv).

It should be noted that a *powerful* oak was chosen. Weak trees and other types of tree are not used in this illness.[5]

---

[5]Trans. note: Thus we read in *Medicina Diastatica—A Mumiall Treatise* abstracted from Paracelsus by Andrea Tentzelius and translated by Ferdinando Parkhurst, London, 1653: "And it must also as carefully be observed, that the fruit or tree into which the disease is transplanted, do not grow up too suddenly and rankly, (which often happens) for such superfluous vegetation is dangerous, and hurtful for the member: This may appear by the example of Hair, which is often transplanted into a Willow, that it may grow the faster, nor is it without success; but when they are left in it beyond the proper time, being not cut down nor burned, that over rank and moist *vegetation* oftentimes

Critical, academic friends of mine have conducted very careful tests with sympathetic medicine, including some with small children who are not suggestible.

The Abbé de Vallemont already reported long before, "that a man who was suffering from gout could be freed from it by a dog that attracted it to itself by sleeping in its master's bed. The unfortunate animal then had the gout intermittently in the same way as his master before him" (p. 367). However, this really belongs to another section (Animal Magnetism) and of course it is to be rejected from a moral point of view!

Strictly speaking, this is no way to treat vegetables either, because plants are also living things and can be made drunk, drugged, poisoned, etc. Therefore the responsible sympathetic practitioner will adopt the same standards of behavior as the noble "Healer of Plaisance" in Paris, who has been so beautifully described by Teddy Legrand in his *Guerisseurs, Mages et Sorciers* [*Healers, Mages and Diviners*] (Paris, 1933).

---

proveth hurtfull to the brain and eyes, especially to the latter; which is also dangerous to any afflicted or troubled with Phthisick and Feavers (while they happily think themselves secure;). . . ."

ISOPATHY OR
HOMEOPATHIC HEALING

Follow Nature! Follow Nature! As she works so will I
work!

—Old Rosicrucian Motto

Whereas the basis of homoeopathy is "likes are cured by likes,"
the basis of isopathy is "likes are cured or expelled by likes."
What that "like" is we shall see. (*Ison* = "like" in Greek.) This
idea is found embryonically in Hippocrates (430–377 B.C.); it
was justified by the researches of Louis Pasteur (1822–1895)
and the vaccines are its latest offshoots.[1]

This is how Agrippa von Nettesheim (1486–1535) expresses its axiom: "And it is well known amongst Physitians,
that brain helps the brain, and lungs, the lungs."[2] Agrippa seems
to be thinking of "animal Ison," at best he leaves the question
of whether it is animal or human open.

However, Paracelsus (1493–1541) rejects this crude form
of treatment with the animal Ison in no uncertain terms. He
calls for "auto-isopathy," or treatment with the organ specific
in the form of a secretion from the patient's own body: "from
which it follows that the prescription must be so framed that
member is applied to member,[3] so that each acts on its coun-

---

[1]The ancient Chinese used to put the crusts from pockmarks in the noses of
healthy children in order to protect them against smallpox (Ad. Reitz: *Schöp-
ferkräfte der Chemie* Stuttgart, 1939, p. 185) [*The Creative Powers of Chemistry*].
[2]*Occult Philosophy*, Book I, chapter 15.
[3]Who is not reminded of the ninth century "Merseburg spell": "Bone to bone,
blood to blood, limb to limb"? Or of Mephistopheles (Arabic *Mustafil* = "I

terpart: heart to heart, lungs to lungs, spleen to spleen. Not the spleens of cows nor the brains of pigs to the brain of man but the brain that is the external brain of man."[4]

Prof. Gustav Jäger (1832–1917) had this to say about the third member of the Triumvirate—Fludd: "I pick up a periodical which has been lying unopened on my desk for several days and read this, 'In 1638, or 252 years ago, the celebrated English anatomist, Robert Fludd wrote in his *Philosophia Moysaica—sputum rejectum a pulmonico post debitam praeparationem curat phthisin* (the sputum expectorated by a consumptive will, if suitably prepared, cure phthisis), *and in fact it is mentioned as something very well known.*"

How was isopathy practiced in the Middle Ages? What was the *debita praeparatio* (suitable preparation) made from the sputum of someone suffering from pulmonary consumption, which was used to cure the disease? Fludd does not tell us, but not for the same reason that Prof. Robert Koch, M.D. (1843–1910) shrank from stating his mode of preparing Tuberculin.[5] Fludd

---

bring herewith" i.e., "serving spirit") in Goethe's *Faust* (Part II; verse 6336–7; the Reclam edition):

> Zu Gleichem Gleiches, was auch einer litt
> Fuss heilte Fuss
> So ist's mit allen Gliedern.

> Like to like, whatever's wrong,
> Foot heals foot
> And so with all the members.

[4]*Labyrinthus Medicorum*, chapter IX, paragraph 43. The following newspaper report is worth reprinting as a grisly curiosity relating to the criminal procurement of an "Ison": "Farmers discovered, in the vicinity of Kormorn, a male corpse with the skull completely smashed. The murderer was the shoemaker's assistant Krepesar, a nephew of the victim. He confessed to having killed his uncle with an axe, *in order to use the brains of the dead man for curing an illness.* The murderer was suffering from cerebral atrophy and imagined that he would regain his health if he could be injected with *brain extract.*" (*Offentl. Anzeiger f.d. Kreis Kreuznach,* [*Reversion to the Darkness of the Middle Ages,* a report from Budapest] No. 165, July 17, 1943, p. 2.)
[5]Tuberculin (Kochin), "A metabolic product of the tuberculosis bacilli, prepared by Robert Koch from meat broth cultures of the tuberculosis bacillus with glycerine. . . . its healing value has often been called in question and is only provisional. . . . old tuberculin, prepared from the glyerine broth culture of the tuberculosis bacillus by evaporation and filtration, and new Tuberculin

thought his method was too well-known to require description. This follows from the fact that for stone in the kidney or bladder he gives the "neceessary mode of preparation" without more ado as *calcination* (reducing to ashes), and by no means as an exceptional case. Anybody who takes the trouble to look at old folk remedies or leafs through ancient leech-books, will invariably find not simply the isopathic remedies but the *burning* of human, animal and plant tissues to ashes and the use of these ashes as a medicament.[6] What did this represent if not another form of *attenuation* or *potentizing* of the medicine?

Dr. Samuel Hahnemann (1755–1843), who rediscovered the procedure of attenuation, introduced the methods of trituration with milk sugar and shaking up with spirits of wine, whereas the isopaths and homoeopaths of earlier centuries had prepared their potencies (i.e., the attenuated substances) by burning the original materials to ashes.

But burning them to ashes destroyed the specific animal or vegetable materials which were thought to be curative, since these are completely combustible substances, and all that was left was the "universal matter" as they called it, that is to say, the universally found earthy and incombustible substance!

---

made of mechanically pulverized and lixiviated tuberculosis bacilli." (Brockhaus Encyclopedia.)

[6]"In view of this, perhaps those isopathic practitioners are in the right who slowly evaporated the urine of the patient, for example, triturated the residue with milk sugar to the 30th potency and then administered this (homoeopathic) potency to the patient—without telling him what he was being given. To a certain extent the urine is a quintessence of all the excretory products of the body. For this reason, many of the body's diseases may be diagnosed from the urine. This isopathy with the solid constituents of the urine represents a universal isopathy so to speak. Another example of this would be the attempt to make a specific remedy for some individual by potentizing a drop of his blood. What is more, the modern school of medicine is turning to the isopathic principle, too. One has only to think of hormone therapy, autohaemotherapy etc." This observation comes from Surya's *Homoeopathy, Isopathy, Biochemistry, Iatrochemistry and Electrohomoeopathy* (Berlin-Pankow, 1923 p. 143, fn).

An academic iatrochemist, a graduate dentist from Westphalia, astounded me in a letter of March 25, 1952 with the idea of combating the "putrefying" disease, cancer, by incinerating a specimen from the tumor and using the "cancer ashes" as a remedy. The ancient Chinese used incinerated human placenta made up into pills to accelerate birth (Henry Frichet).

Use your noses, honorable testers! Do not the ashes of the beech tree smell of beech, those of the fir of fir, the ashes of flesh like the flesh of the animal from which they came, just as the homoeopathic potencies of Hahnemann retain the odors of the original substances even in very high attenuations?[7]

DISCUSSION

The destruction of the disease by itself, using its own disease material, is called *Isopathy*.

—Oskar Ganser (1921)

Isopathy is one of the oldest methods of healing. I take my motto from the Rosicrucians: let us copy nature. As she works, so will I.

Now isopathy is a practice that is true to nature—hence it is Rosicrucian practice. "What is seen by the man who lives close to nature? All those animals that devor poisonous creatures such as snakes, scorpions, bees, wasps, and so on, are bitten and stung by them, as for example the hedgehog, the ichneumon, the snake eagle, the secretary bird and bee-eater; yet it makes no difference to them however much they are strung or bitten, they are immune to the poison. This man who lives close to nature observes that the snake-killer catches the poisonous reptile, is bitten by it, then eats it and suffers no harm in spite of the bite. He is accordingly struck by the simple, straightforward idea, 'If I am bitten by some creature, I should eat it in the same way as the hedgehog or mongoose does, and then perhaps the bite will not poison me.' He acts upon it and—*probatum est*" (Jäger).

The venom is almost completely neutralized in the stomach and the small residue that manages to pass from the intestines into the lymphatic system becomes as "homoeopathically" attenuated in the intestines as if it had been reduced to ash. *The above section is no introduction to isopathy*. It will merely substantiate

---

[7]Prof. Gustav Jäger, *Gleich und ähnlich. Notschrei eines misshandlten Naturgsetzes* [*Equal and Similar: A Cry of Distress from an Abused Natural Law*] (Stuttgart, 1891).

its existence and its development by the occult physicians of the Renaissance.

Sury claims that two things must be observed in isopathy *whatever happens*:

1) One must take only the body's own products (its auto-ison)!

2) If a disease product is used as such an auto-ison, it must only be in the potencies 30 to 200.

For example, in his issue for December 1890, Jäger proposed that a medicament should be prepared by diluting the aqueous extract from a patient's *own* sputum.

I will just say this: a form of healing which, like isopathy, has survived from Adam so to speak, in folk medicine, with the Gipsies, in love-spells and partly in sympathetic cures right down to the present day, cannot be shrugged off by our "qualified" doctors. Here is an everyday proof of the effectiveness of isopathy. For a hangover one drinks a small drop of exactly the same alcoholic liquor to which one is indebted for it; this is called "taking a hair of the dog that bit you." If, in addition to the immediately apparent relief of pain, there is vomiting, bowel action, the passing of wind, or heavy perspiration, then the ison is behaving as a regular antidote!

Dr. Puller Stöcker reported in the *Medical Press* in 1951 that the injection of alcohol has an immediate sobering effect on people who are very drunk!

MAGNETIC HEALING

The doctrine of magnetism was studied with particular
fondness by the Rosicrucians, who were the Freemasons of that era.

—Trömner[1]

If, initially, I feel compelled to draw support from a number
of authors in this section, it is because I do not wish to give
the impression that I am putting forward a theory of my own;
and I have been obliged to quote these authors because their
works have been long out of print and are to be found only in
large libraries, if at all. Now, since this book is written for the
general public, I have to bear in mind that many of my readers
would have difficulty in referring to the original Rosicrucian
sources.

When Max Retschlag (Leipzig) suggested that "In the dark
Middle Ages, this form of healing was confined to the *occult
physicians* until Paracelsus made it the basis of his new system
of therapeutics,"[2] he surely knew that the latter was himself an
occult physician?! Besides, the Middle Ages were not nearly so
benighted as was being stated as recently as 1924. In Germany,
the years 1933–1945 were scarcely more enlightened.

It is true, however, that only the occult physicians used this
type of healing. Healing magnetism has been secret knowledge

---

[1]Dr. E. Trömner: *Hypnotismus und Suggestion* [*Hypnotism and Suggestion*] (Leipzig, 1908, p. 8).
[2]*Die Heilkunst der Geheimwissenschaft* [*The Healing Art in Occult Science*] (Leipzig,
1924, p. 127).

from time immemorial. It was a priestly prerogative in ancient Egypt and was taught in the lodges of the Essenes, who were forerunners of the Rosicrucians. The word "lodge" is quite in order here, for in 1897 A. Kohn (Pressburg) demonstrated that "the Essenes were the Freemasons of antiquity"! Thus healing magnetism was secret knowledge, like the *Medicina Diastatica* [*Distant Treatment*] of Dr. Andreas Tenzell (Jena, 1629).

And so a hermetically minded lady who was unable to obtain any of it for gold, offered what she had that was more costly (Lenglet du Fresnoy).

It is not out of place to mention healing magnetism in the same breath as the sympathetic treatments of Tenzell, for the old occult physicians did not content themselves with postulating "human magnetism," but regarded the latter as emanations from the Universal Magnetism, which we meet later on in the guise of Mesmer's universal fluid! The evidence is as follows.

> The first germ of this theory (of "animal magnetism" as it was originally called) is found in Paracelsus' use of the old doctrine of the mutual attraction between things of the same kind. Anything which, in his opinion, exerted an attraction he called a *magnet. The peculiar treatment of disease with sympathetic remedies is a direct derivative of this theory.* Paracelsus' theory was developed by J.B. van Helmont and Richard Fludd and formed into a system. . . . but Franz Anton Mesmer was its chief exponent.[3]

Lehmann overlooks William Maxwell here, the friend of Fludd, who anticipated Mesmer in the task of systematization rather well, even to the extent of putting his teaching in the form of aphorisms!

Because it is so important, let us lend renewed support to Lehmann's opinion: "In his (Paracelsus') writings is first found the term *Magnetismus* used in the sense of the later doctrines of Mesmerism. According to Paracelsus, the universe is filled with a magnetic force, which is also found in the human body in consequence of a transference from the stars (as a siderial

---

[3]Prof. Alfred Lehmann (1856–1921), *Aberglaube und Zauberei* [*Superstition and Sorcery*] (Leipzig, 1924; p. 127).

entity). *The human being is nourished not only in the obvious sense through food but by the magnetic power distributed throughout nature.* A mutual attraction exists between the stars and the human body. Paracelsus also referred to the mutual influence of one person upon another."[4]

Mention should be made here of Mesmer's book *De influxu planetarum* [*The Influx from the Planets*] and so-called pranic nourishment, or feeding on a fine essence contained in the air, which is sufficient for the refined bodies of Indian and Christian holy men, so experience has shown (e.g., Nikolaus v.d. Flue, 1417–1437). However, this is outside the scope of our present investigation!

According to Trömner, Paracelsus (and Fludd after him) distinguished two sorts of magnetism: "In his opinion . . . human beings in particular have two sorts of magnetism in them, a healthy and an unhealthy kind. The healing of diseases takes place when the magnetism of a healthy person draws that of the ill person to itself and paralyses or cancels it."[5] This looks like an anticipation of the "infection with health" of Carl Buttenstedt! (ca. 1890). And also of the necessity for the magnetist to free himself from the harmful Od picked up from the patient. Paracelsus had this to say about magico-magnetic healing:

> Just as the ordinary magnet attracts iron, so man is a magnet and draws other men to him. Hidden magnetic forces lie concealed in all things, in plants, medicinal herbs, the bodies of animals and the bodies of human beings. We ought always to remember, therefore, his (i.e., God's) unfathomable wisdom, in giving us in ourselves as many powers as heaven and earth possess. From true self-consciousness there springs a spiritual force which can be transferred from the doctor to the sick person, provided the physician possesses it. *In this way, the doctor's presence does more good to the patient by itself than any medicine.* For the etheric vibrations impinge on the human ether and can so change the inharmonic human vibrations into harmonic ones.

---

[4]Dr. L. Loewenfeld: *Der Hypnotismus* [*Hypnotism*] (Wiesbaden, 1901, p. 5).
[5]Trömner, *op. cit.*, p. 7.

The all-penetrating magnetic fluid was called *magnal* by Parcelsus (1493–1541), but it was more frequently termed *spiritus mundi* (in the macrocosm), *spiritus vitae* (in the microcosm of mankind) and was analogous to the *spiritus vitalis* of William Maxwell (1619–1669) and to the Universal fluid of Dr. Anton Mesmer (1733–1815). Was Paracelsus a Rosicrucian?

The basic Rosicrucian document *the Fama* (first published in Cassel in 1614) does in fact read, "Such a one likewise hath Theophrastus been in vocation and callings, although he was none of our Fraternity." Nevertheless, in reality, the "Luther of Medicine" was a Rosicrucian of the Rosicrucians, although, to use the language of the *Fama*, he possessed both his own "sharp ingenium" and a "knowledge understanding . . . of nature," as evidenced in his reissued theosophical writings, once more available.

Even Prof. Andreas Libau (Libavius, 1540–1616), the adversary of the Rosicrucians and Rector of the Collegium Casimir of Coburg, repeated as the *general* opinion of his time that Rosicrucianism was Paracelsian in origin![6]

"The Ober-Lausitz Scientific Society possesses three manuscripts, containing the theological dissertations of Paracelsus. They are copies going back to the second half of the 16th century and belong to the circle of friends of Johannes Montanus[7] the protagonist of Paracelsus. Presumably they were made from originals in his possession."[8]

In the Görlitz manuscript, *Ex Libro de Martyrio Christi*, Paracelsus reveals his Rosicrucian initiation with the words:

---

[6]"If Paracelsus had never lived, the Brotherhood would never have materialized and the Arabian and Moorish sorcerers would not have exported their folly to Germany." *D.O.M.A.: Wolmeinendes Bedencken von der FAMA und Confession der Brüderschaft dehs Rosen Creutzes* [*D.O.M.A.: A Sympathetic Consideration of the FAMA and Confession of the Fraternity of the Rosy Cross*] (Frankfurt a.M., 1616).

[7]"In Hirschberg under the Giant Mountains dwelt Johann Schultheiss or Johannes Schultetus Montanus, who had accumulated a stupendous hoard of Paracelsian manuscripts. He journeyed everywhere looking for them with unremitting zeal, industry and devotion. It was rumored that his copies approached the originals in value and that he possessed the theological writings too" (Will-Erich Peuckert: *The Rosicrucians*, Jena, 1928, p. 254). Montanus lived ca. 1600.

[8]E. Wolfram. *Der esoterische Christ Paracelsus* (Leipzig, 1920, p. 14).

Der *Orden der Kreuzer*
steht nicht in äusserlichen Waffen,
sondern im Worte Gottes und feurigen Zungen.

The Order of the Crucians
relies not on outward weapons
but on the Word of God and tongues of fire.

What is more, the protracted introduction to his book *Para-granum* ends:

Ich wirdt *Monarchia,*
und mein wirdt die Monarchey seyn
und ich führe die Monarchey.

I shall be monarch,
and mine the monarchy shall be
and as monarch shall I rule.

On substituting the Latin *Imperator* for the word of Greek derivation, *monarch*, we get the title of the chief of the Rosicrucian Order . . .

The evidence for the order membership of the Brussels scientist and physician Johann Baptista van Helmont (1577–1644) is as follows:

1) He was admitted to the *Rosicrucian Order* in Bavaria, writes Alphons Leroy, professor at the University of Liège, in the *Biographie Nationale [National Biography].*[9]

2) "In 1630, Mecheln carried out the process for that great savant and pansophist Helmont, because he was an alchemist and Rosicrucian."[10]

In his most important publication, *De magnetica vulnerum curatione* (Paris, 1621) we read:

---

[9]Fr. Wittemans. *Historie des Rose-Croix [History of the Rosicrucians]* (Paris, 1925, p. 26).
[10]Peuckert, op. cit., p. 171.

Magnetism, which now flourishes everywhere, possesses nothing new other than its appellation, nor is
there anything paradoxical about it save to those who
scoff at everything and ascribe to Satan whatever they
do not understand (para. 11).

Magnetism, too, is a celestial property, unaffected by
distance and its influence is similar to the astral (para.
40).

All things contain a particular kind of firmament in
their *Ens seminale* by means of which that which is above
associates with that which is below according to the law
of friendship and harmony, and from this association
can be abstracted the magnetism and the forces found
everywhere in the things (para. 61).

*What I mean by magnetism here is, for lack of a better word,
the universally prevailing yet variable influence of sublunary
things and an occult adaptation through which two things
which are absent from one another act on one another by
attraction, impulsion and repulsion* (para. 62).

Robert Fludd (1574–1637), the most famous Rosicrucian
of the 17th century, described in his *Philosphia Mosis* "two sorts
of magnetism, a spiritual and a physical."[11]
There is no doubt about Fludd's membership of the Rosicrucians, so there is no need to do more than mention it here.[12]
One need only think of his defense of the Rosicrucians in Book
4 of the *Summa Bonum* (Frankfurt am Main, 1629). His "Lodge
name" was Rudolf Ortreb. And as far as the "two sorts of magnetism" are concerned, reference may be made to the summary
in the relevant section of his *Philosphia Moysaica* (Gouda, 1638)
as follows:

Man, as the microcosm, possesses the properties of all
things including those of magnets. He is endowed with
magnetic power (virtus magnetica microcosmica), which

---

[11]Trömner, op. cit., p. 8.
[12]Karl Kiesewetter (1865–1895), *Geschichte des neueren Occultismus* [*A History of
Modern Occultism*] Leipzig, 1909, pp. 129, 263, 264.

is subject to the same laws in the small world as it is in the great world. Man is polar and has polar attractive and repulsive magnetism. He has two poles like the earth, from which circulates a north and south, an attractive and repulsive magnetism. The backbone in man is like the earth's equator and divides him into two 'hemispheres' with opposite magnetism. His left-hand side corresponds to the southern hemisphere and its magnetism is passive, while his right-hand side corresponds to the northern hemisphere and its magnetism is active.

When two human beings approach one another, their magnetism is either active or passive. In sympathy and attraction the bodily radiation travels from the center to the periphery. Should the magnetic radiations of the two individuals interpenetrate and mingle, there is an affinity between them; if, on the other hand, the radiations are broken and thrown back, there is a negative magnetism and aversion, because where there is antipathy the radiations retreat from the periphery to the center.[13]

Fludd's most important adherent in Britain was the Scottish physician, William Maxwell (1619–1669), whose only surviving book is *De Medicina Magnetica Libri tres etc.* (Francofurt, 1679). In the Author's Foreword to the philosophical reader, grateful mention is made of "the noble knight and learned gentleman, Edmund Staford of Stafordsberg in Ireland, the earnest friend of occult philosophy and rich possessor of philosophic secrets."

And R. H. Vincent said, "It is worthy of notice that theories of magnetism gain in power and precision with each succeeding author. . . . Maxwell's 'Spiritus vitalis' is already well-developed and is in fact the true precursor of Mesmer's 'universal fluid.' "[14]

In view of its importance, further light should perhaps be shed on Maxwell's "Mesmeric" concept, but from a somewhat

---

[13]Kiesewetter's version, op. cit., p. 280, 281, from the *Phil. Moys.*, Fol. 113, 114.

[14]R. Harry Vincent: *Die Elemente des Hypnotismus* [*The Elements of Hypnotism*] (Berlin, 1911, p. 18).

different angle—not that of the magnetizing of one person by another but that of sympathetic cures as he explained in his various publications.

He believed that radiations in which the soul is actively present flow from each body. In his opinion, these radiations possess a vital spirit through which the soul operates. Since even the excrement from animal bodies contains part of this vital spirit, Maxwell attributed a positive effect to it and used it for curing diseases (sympathetic cures). Diseases were also thought to be removed by transferring them to animals or plants. Thus Maxwell was already entertaining the idea of a common vital spirit (*spiritus vitalis*), by which all bodies are interconnected,[15] an idea which recurs in the general Fluidum of Mesmer.[16] All this is immediately apparent from a perusal of Maxwell's three small volumes: "Long before Mesmer, he outlined a theory of magnetism in a series of aphorisms annexed to his treatise.[17] There is *no doubt that at the end of the 18th century, Mesmer borrowed his theory of Magnetism from Maxwell*."[18]

It is certainly true that "When Dr. Anton Mesmer first came to Germany, he found the ground prepared by the Rosicrucians, who had eagerly applied themselves to the study and practice of the occult sciences, had performed cures etc."[19]

What is more, Mesmer was also himself a Rosicrucian of the later school:

1) In 1786 Mesmer became "Imperator" of the Gold-und Rosenkreuzer at Vienna;[20]

---

[15]"The Platonic Ring and the chain of Homer are nothing more than the disposition of things which divine Providence created for service, a regular and so to speak interlinked chain of sympathy." Thus the Paracelsist Oswald Croll (died 1609) in *Basilica Chymica* (Ffm., 1624).

[16]Moll, op. cit., pp. 5–6.

[17]In his dissertation of 1766 *De influxu planetarum in corpus humanum*, Mesmer lists 27 aphoristic theses as a framework for his system.

[18]Dr. August F. Ludwig, *Geschichte der okk. (Metapsych.) Forschung von der Antike bis zur Gegenwart* [*A History of Occult Research from Antiquity to the Present Day*], Pfullingen (Württ.), 1922, p. 53.

[19]A.J. Riko: *Handbuch zur Ausübung des Magnetismus* [*Handbook on the Practice of Magnetism*] (Leipzig, 1904), pp. 4, 5.

[20]Wittemans, op. cit., p. 125.

2) The Rosicrucian Count, Saint-Germain, joined Mesmer in Vienna in the study of animal magnetism;[21]

3) Mesmer took part in 1785 in the great Masonic Conference at Paris, together with Lavater, St. Martin, Wöllner, von Gleichen, Cagliostro and Saint-Germain.[22]

The following is an excerpt from a Hermetic document of 1604, that is to say, from the time when the *Fama* and *Confessio* were already being circulated in manuscript, because it already contains the ideas of Mesmer's "Universal Fluid."

> The wise know of three sorts of gold. The first is an astral sort, whose center is in the sun, the rays of which impart light to all the surrounding stars and also to our own sphere and earth; it is a fiery substance and always fills the whole universe in an incessant ebb and flow (owing to the movements of the sun and stars) by the emission of solar particles. It pervades everything in heaven above and in the interior of the earth. *We constantly absorb this astral gold with our breath and these astral corpuscles penetrate our bodies, which also exhale it without intermission.*[23]

All that can be said of the Rosicrucian method of magnetizing is this: "In their Order's secret documents there are complicated statements concerning various passes combined with invocations."[24]

It is not possible to tell exactly what is meant here, but it may be assumed that the Rosicrucians employed in particular,

---

[21]ibid., p. 145.

[22]Dr. Eckert: *Magazin der Beweisführer für die Verurtheilung des Freimaurerei-Ordens* [*Review of the Party Giving Evidence for the Condemantion of the Free Masons*] 1857.

[23]Eudoxus in *Der uralte Ritterkrieg* [*Time-honored Knightly Combat*] from an unknown German savant. The first edition printed at Leipzig in 1604. (Cited from *ABC vom Stein der Weisen* [*ABC of the Philosophers' Stone*] (New impression, Berlin, 1922), Part III, pp. 39–40. The "astral gold" which we are continually inhaling with our breath, is the Indian *prana*, the vapor of the Od.

[24]Rud. Thetter, engineer: *Magnetismus—das Urheilmittel* [*Magnetism—the Original Means of Healing*] (published by Julius Kittl, Leipzig-Mähr. Ostrau, n.d.), p. 15.

1) The energy of the young to sustain the old, as the young Shunamite woman embraced King David in his old age to "give him heat" (without sexual relations) (I Kings 1: 1–4);

2) "Boltzianism," in which handkerchiefs taken from the healer's body cure the sick (see Acts of the Apostles 19:12);[25]

3) The method of "measuring themselves" against the patient (Acts of the Apostles 20:10; I Kings 17:21; II Kings 4:34);

4) Collective magnetization, especially in the form of collective aspiration.

Collective manipulative magnetization was not performed by several people simultaneously making passes over one and the same subject,[26] but the laying on of hands on specific nerve ganglia either by several operators on the same subject at the same time or by forming a magnetic chain ("human column") in which only one of the operators laid on hands.

Illness comes from a deficiency, health from a sufficiency and healing power from a superfluity of the vital force,[27] which overflows from the operator to the subject according to the "law of the communicating siphon."

The first consideration of the healer who relies on vital force must therefore be to build up his vital force to full strength

[25]So called after the healing Swedish pastor Friedrich August Boltzius (1836–1910).

[26]"Hufeland had his subjects treated by two mesmerists at the same time" (Riko, op. cit., p. 33). The person referred to is Prof. Christoph Wilh. Hufeland, M.D. (1762–1836) and his method was that of "passes."

[27]Thus the author is a "Fluidist." What he says is true, provided he recognizes that the influence of suggestion is not to be discounted even in magnetic treatments. Magnetism is not the same as hypnotism! On the contrary, hypnotism depends to a great extent on the "magnetic" process of making passes with the hands (Chazarain, Décele, Durville, de Rochas, Baréty, Sidney Alrutz, Kindborg). It also depends however on: a) A fatigue which is produced artificially (by fixation); b) Outside suggestion which has become autosuggestion when independent thinking has been eliminated or reduced; c) Telepathy = "volute."

at just the right time and in this way to raise his Od to a "more than perfect" level (more than he needs for himself).

The age-old way of Yoga will achieve this.

Yoga is of two main kinds: the purely psychical Raja Yoga and the physiological Hatha Yoga. "Raja Yoga has a certain affinity with the instructions of the Orders of Christian knights."[28]

The Rosicrucian Order, too, could lay claim to be one of these. This is not the place to expatiate on its methods of meditation. Thomas a Kempis (1380–1471), Johannes Tauler (1300–1361) and Jakob Böhme (1575–1624) are represented as teachers who "follow Christ" and also as *"fons et origo"* (the source and origin) of Rosicrucian doctrines.[29] Whatever methods these were, they were certainly modelled on those of Elijah (I Kings 28: 42), of the Qabalists and of the monks on Mount Athos (*omphaloskepsis*).

> This subjective transformation is moralistic and ascetic on the one hand and has an affinity, on the other hand, with the results of those psychic exercises invented by the Indian Yogis, exercises which are still being practised today by our theosophists and anthroposophists in their so-called 'meditations' and *were being described and used as long ago as the 17th century (possibly by the Rosicrucian Nollius).*[30]

Unfortunately, I have not been able to gain access to the writings of Nollius. All I could discover concerning this doubtless interesting man is that during his life he remained true to his principles as a Rosicrucian and Hermetic physician. One of his books was entitled *System medicinae hermeticae* [*A System of Hermetic Medicine*] (1613) and he wanted to found in Hamburg a "Brotherhood of the Heavenly Wheel for the Restoration of

---

[28]Major Francis Yeats-Brown: *Ist Yoga für dich?* [*Is Yoga for You?*] (Berlin, n.d.), p. 65.

[29]Theophilus Schweighardt: *Speculum Sophicum Rhodostauroticum* [*The Mirror of Rosicrucian Wisdom*] (1618).

[30]C.F. Hartlaub: "Rosenkreuz oder der Mythos des Barock" [Rosencreutz or the Baroque Myth] (A review of the "Rosenkreuzer" of W.E. Peuckert in "Literatur-Beilage" [The Literary Supplement] of the *Frankfurter Zeitung* No. 803 of 27.10.1929; p. 4.)

Hermetic Medicine and Philosophy." When at Steinfurt in 1616 he openly took the part of the Rosicrucians, he was forced to flee to Giessen. He then made a new attempt to promote the Rosicrucian cause in his publication *Via sapientiae triunae* [*The way of triune widsom*] and, having incurred the displeasure of his university, took his leave under cover of darkness with the intention of going to Hamburg.[31]

Rosicrucian-type Hatha Yoga, or physiological self-transformation ("The Chemical Wedding") is based on "the practice of the old Turkish Freemasons," as conclusively shown by Rudolf, Baron von Sebottendorf, the engineer, Rud. Glandeck, born November 9, 1875, in his booklet of the same name.[32]

Here is a résumé of this physiological (or somatic) alchemy:

1) The index finger and thumb of the right hand form the vowels, *I*, *A*, *O*, (line, angle, circle; together comprising a wheel, in Latin *Rota*, the very ancient name of God: JAO. These three signs also denote the phallus, the vagina and the uterus.[33] Cf. the *mudras* (a series of subtle and meaningful hand gestures) employed by the Balinese *Pedanda* = priests![34]

2) *Voluntary control over the normally involuntary blood flow* is obtained by concreting the thoughts on the finger positions and simple syllables. Cf. the *"psychological exercises"* of the *"New Thought."*[35]

3) An *objectively measurable* rise in temperature is developed

[31]Peuckert (pp. 175, 176, 177, 231, 410; sub 175).

[32]Leipzig, 1924, subtitled: "The Key to the Understanding of Alchemy."

[33]Karl Weinfurter: *Der brennende Busch* [*The Burning Bush*] (Lorch Württemberg, 1930), pp. 104–105.

[34]P. de Kat Angelino: *Mudras auf Bali* [*The Mudras on Bali*] Hagen i.W., 1923. (See also *Therapeutic Mudras* by Dr. C.P. Mehra, in *Yoga Today*, Vol. 8, Nos. 8 & 9. *Tr.*)

[35]Hans Ertl: *Vollst ändiger Lehrkursus des Hypnotismus, etc.* [*A Complete Course of Lessons in Hypnotism, etc.*] (Leipzig, n.d.), p. 83 (6th edition).

in the finger which is being contemplated.[36] Cf., *"Tumo"* heat creation of the Tibetan lamas.[37]

4) This attracts a quantity of Od which is over and above the individual's own requirement, at the same time, and

5) it is systematically incorporated in the body—with the exception of the head—by means of *manipulations* performed in a downward direction.

6) In this way the invisible body (the "salt body") is fortified, loosened and finally made independent. ("The homunculus in the Philosophical Egg," i.e., the human body.)

7) During this physiological *Magnum Opus* the performer smells sulphur on the finger *"magnets"* contemplated and tastes the salt and mercury on them;

8) He also perceives (mentally) the recognized alchemical color scale of black—white—peacock's tail—green—yellow—vermilion.

This "Auto-Alchemical Processing" was first formulated in *Charam ed Din* by Sheikh Yachya, but must go back to the hermit Ben Chasi who was the "spiritual master" of Mohammed (570–632) and was of Indian origin!

This "autogenous training" is termed *Ilm el Miftach* (= "The science of the key") and those who practice it are called *"Beni el Miftach"* (= "Sons of the Key"). Closely related watchwords are, among others, "key," "rose," and "stone." The "Science of the Key" was also called the "Science of the balance" by the Arabs, or *"Ilm el Nizan."* There is also *"Ilm el Quimiya,"* *"The Science of Chemistry."* It is a time-honored heritage *and makes its appearance in Venice around* A.D. *900.*[38]

Venice has been acknowledged from of old as a home of occult arts and place of origin of the "Venetians" in Germany, to whom we owe the saying, "Germany is blind, Nuremberg

---

[36]Dr. A. Severin-Köln: *Die Autosuggestion etc.* [*Autosuggestion, etc.*] (Pfullingen: Württemberg., n.d. *Baum-Verlag*), p. 17.
[37]Alexandra David-Neel: *Saint and Sorcerer* (Leipzig, 1932).
[38]Sebottendorf, op. cit., p. 45.

sees with one eye, but Venice sees with both eyes." This city of the Doges was said to have a "School of Magic" in the Middle Ages and even Pater Johann Adalbert Hahn (1750–1825), the wizard of the Ore Mountains (the Erzgebirge) in Saxony, called his hocus-pocus *"artem venetianam"*![39]

The Arabist Artephius (ca. 1150), whom many called *Artefi* and took to be an Arab, taught us the art of "calling down spirits" in his *Clavis Majoris Sapientiae [The Key of Higher Wisdom]*[40] and mentions the following forms into which the spirit willingly pours itself: *I, V, X, O* through *L*. Here we have the *I* and the *O; V* and *X* are two forms of the *A*, the so-called peak which is formed when the thumb is not spread open in a full right angle. The *L* signifies a setsquare.[41]

The word *"Clavis"* (= Key) indicates, according to Artephius' sources the "Science of the Key"!

Victor Masséne d'Essling published in Paris and Florence in 1907 four volumes entitled *Etudes sur l'art de la gravure sur bois à Venise; Les Livres á figures vénétiens de la fin du 15° et du commencement du 16° siècle [Studies in the Art of Wood Engraving at Venice: Books with Venetian woodcuts from the late 15th and early 16th Centuries]*, in which may be seen a series of illustrations with the typical *I, A, O*, finger positions of the secret Middle Eastern lore which had been brought to Venice.

Dr. Michel Maier, Imperial Knight, (1568–1622) seems—judging from his *Themis aurea (Golden Themis)*—to have cultivated the art of "making letters" too, as did J.B. Kerning (Krebs, 1774–1851), Karl Weinfurter (died February 1942) and Peryt Shou (born April 22, 1873): "The knowledge of the arcanum must be the key! I shall give you the secret: d. wmml. zii. v. sggqqhka. x.—unlock it, if you can!"

It may be worth mentioning in this connection that a contemporary American has built a complete method of relaxation around the letter *Z* (Lafit).

---

[39]Dr. Johann Endt: *Sagen und Sahwänke a.d. Erzgebirge [Legends and Drolleries from the Ore Mountains]* (Reichenberg, 1925), p. 21.

[40]*Clavis Majoris Sapientiae* = "Key of the Higher Wisdom." The first Latin edition appeared in Paris in 1609, the second was printed in Frankfurt in 1614 and a German translation was published in Nuremberg in 1717.

[41]Sebottendorf, op. cit., p. 28.

DISCUSSION

> The day will come when animal magnetism will be the ornament of academic science and physicians will employ the procedures they now condemn.
>
> —du Potet (1796–1881)

"Nowadays, anyone who denies the effectiveness of magnetism should be regarded not as a sceptic but as an ignoramus." This dictum sums up the position neatly and it came from the pen of none other than Arthur Schopenhauer (1778–1860).

In our own day and age, the effects of animal magnetism are no longer called in question but they are ascribed to hypnotism or to suggestion (a common accompaniment of any form of healing). As if babies, animals and plants could be hypnotized or influenced by suggestion!

However, anyone who has experienced the "healing current" either as a donor or as a recipient, will require no long-winded argument to convince him of its reality. Besides, there are numerous differences between hypnotism and magnetism, although it is not my intention to list them here, as I have already done so in some detail elsewhere.[42]

Healing magnetism is a royal art with which everyone ought to be familiar, first of all in theory and then in practice; although the layman should confine himself to easy domestic cases.

I have just said that "everyone" ought to be familiar with magnetism, but, of course, not everyone will display the same aptitude or efficiency in this as in anything else. Besides, Surya found that many magnetizers were particularly good at curing certain diseases. For example, where one was very good with eye troubles, another specialized in nervous disorders and a third in gastric complaints, etc. In the same way, the Catholic Church has found that certain saints can be invoked for certain diseases (from a private letter dated October 17, 1942).

---

[42]Among the textbooks on the subject which are currently obtainable (in 1954) are: 1) Rudolf Thetter's *Magnetismus—das Urheilmittel* [*Magnetism—the Original Means of Healing*] (Vienna 1951). 2) Egon M. Hein's *Atomare Heilkräfte* [*Atomic Healing Power*] (Vienna, 1951). 3) Ph. W. Kramer: *Der Heilmagnetismus* [*Healing Magnetism*] (Lorch i.W., 1931).

A further restriction is mentioned by the Hamburg hermeticist "AME," whom I have quoted so often already. He says, "If the healer and patient are not in harmony with one another (+ and −), any benefit will be transitory, because the Od, the transmitted energy, has no inherent or permanent link with the patient and evanesces after a certain time. The accumulator must then be repeatedly recharged and refilled" (from a private letter of July, 1943).

Carl Buttenstedt believes he has evidence that even the dead have been restored to life by "collective magnetizing" (a special form to which I have drawn attention).[43] Professor Oskar Korschelt confirms this.[44] This was at the turn of the century. (I must digress here to remark that the so-called "Black Masses" were not always orgies, but sessions of collective magnetization with heterosexual (mixed) partners with the object of intensifying the odic radiations.)

Mention will be made of only one case of resurrection in an earlier age, one that took place in 1758. This is because the previous successful use of this strange method induced the famous physicist, René Antoine Ferchault de Réaumer (1683–1757), to recommend it in no uncertain terms in a work published in 1740.[45] Almost unknown but highly effective modes of application are the *biomagnetic vortex* of a certain Bernhard Richter ("Berica"; died August 11, 1923) and the *rotation magnetism* which I have treated of elsewhere for the first time.

The evangelical treatment of magnetism can serve as a stepping stone to people who prefer natural remedies which will help them on their way to becoming Magnetic Magicians.[46]

---

[43]*Die Übertragung der Nervenkraft: Ansteckung durch Gesundheit* [*The Transmission of Nervous Force—Infection with Health*], published by the author, Berlin-Rüdersdorf (n.d., pp. 32, 104, 105).

[44]Willy Schrödter: *Ausflug ins Wundersame* [*An Excursion into the Supernatural*] (Freiburg i. Brsg., 1939, p. 113).

[45]Ibid., p. 111.

[46]Baron du Potet, *Die entschleierte Magie* [*Magic Unveiled*] (Leipzig 1925); his full name was Jean de Sennevoy Baron du Potet (April 12, 1796–July 1, 1881). He also wrote a compilation from various unnamed authors entitled *Die Mysterien der Magnetomagie* [*The Mysteries of Magnetic Magic*] (Weimar, 1854).

I myself have constantly used healing magnetism in my family circle with gratifying results; especially aspiration (breathing out) on the pit of the stomach, which revives those who have fainted within a matter of seconds. It is just as the personal physician to the King of Saxony, Prof. Karl Gustav Carus, M.D. (1789–1869) said, "Even the untrained observer will appreciate that the breath of a loved one affects us quite differently from the equally warm and damp vapor emitted by a kettle" (*Über Lebensmagnetismus etc.* [*Animal Magnetism*] Basel, 1925, p. 105).

Ezekiel wrote, "Thus saith the Lord God; come from the four winds, O breath, and breathe upon these slain, that they may live" (37:9), and, so anticipated the Korschelt revelation of *collective aspiration!*

I have traced the numerous variations of healing magnetism in every age and among all races and hope to be able to reveal what is worthwhile in my findings.

Now as far as enrichment with Od is concerned ("supercharging oneself"), the rule applies: "Practice makes perfect." Or, "Increase the power gradually like a bar magnet to which ever greater weights are entrusted" (Meyrink).

Now here is a little-known secret: magnets become stronger when they are exposed to the rays of the sun. And this is what the magnetists do, too, when they are better-informed than usual.

Here is a quick review of the historical development of the subject. In an Egyptian sarcophagus in the Louvre at Paris there is the image of an extremely attractive goddess with her body extended, her hands raised above her head and (this is significant) her fingers, which are lying close together, stretched forward. Between the yearning arms are symbols of the sun; hence the goddess is attracting the solar od *and doing so at sunrise,* because only then can she stretch her palms straight out in front of her. Later on she must form an arch upward, and this is important, as we shall see!

The Indians have known a similar technique for thousands of years: *Suryamanaskar* (= obeisance to the sun); it forms a part of *Laya-Yoga*. And they were themselves anticipated by the monkeys! "The lemurs, too, adopt a sun-worshipping attitude at times, when, like the *Laya-Yogis* of India, they turn the palms of their hands towards the daystar and remain silent and motionless. It is as if they are extracting some form of energy from the sunlight and absorbing it through the centers of their palms. The *Laya-Yogis* claim that they *draw vital energy from the sun in this way*. Since we are neither *Laya-Yogis* nor lemurs, we are hardly competent to set ourselves up as judges in this matter and ought to reserve judgment on such phenomena instead of smiling at it or, what is worse, denying it" (Dr. Herbert Fritsche, Ph.D., in *Tierseele und Schöpfungsgeheimnis* [*Animal Soul and the Secret of Creation*] Leipzig, 1940, p. 123).

The Indians call this *vital energy Surya-Prana* (= solar Od). The exercises used to extract it are performed with and without breath-control (*Pranayama*) and with or without a special salutation (*Mantram*) or secret syllable (*japam*). The body is made to assume certain positions known as *asanas*, and the fingers assume certain positions known as *mudras*. The 26-year-old Indian, Witaldas, gave a demonstration of Hatha-Yoga in Berlin in 1937, including "an exercise bestowed on us by a yogi living high in the Himalayas, an exercise which attempts *to draw down the energy of the sun*." The left leg is wound around the right leg, which bears the main weight, and the right arm entwines the left in the same way, both being bent at shoulder level and turned upward. The hands are clasped and the fingers stand up like antennae.

His compatriot, the yogi Swami Sivananda Sarasvati (= Dr. P. V. Kuppuswamy Lyer, M.D.) had this to say in 1950: "The rays of the rising sun are a veritable gift from God for the preservation of our health and the healing of our diseases."

The Chinese form of yoga known as *Tso-kung-yün-ch'i* has a purely therapeutic intention, namely to keep the body healthy, youthful and long-lived. Its textbook *Y-chin-ching* [*The Book of Muscle Restoration*] is another source of "helioreceptive postures."

We still see these poses in the monuments over the graves of Yugoslavian Bogomil initiates ("Dobri"). The apostle of the sun stands straddle-legged with his left hand on his hip and the flat of his right hand held forward with the arm bent. Above are an archer's bow and the sun and moon, as if to say, "I aim at the two eyes of Heaven." For it is not only the sun's *prana* that is drawn down but also "moon dew" and "star water." The favorite stars are the Pole Star, those in the Great Bear, Capella in the Charioteer and the "Northern Cross" or Cygnus, of which we already read in the basic Rosicrucian document *Confessio* (Cassel, 1616). "Yea, the Lord God hath already sent before certain messengers, which should testify his will, to wit, some new stars which do appear and are seen in the firmament in Serpentario and Cygno, which signify and give themselves known to everyone, that they are powerful 'signacula' of great weighty matters. So then, the secret hid writings and characters are most necessary for all such things which are found out by men."

However, if the Bogomils had done no more than indulge in wishful thinking about absorbing stellar *prana*, their fellow-believers in Romania, the Cathars, actually achieved this absorption; indeed, Jean Marqués-Rivière ascribed regular Yoga practices to the latter in *Histoire des Doctrines Ésotériques* [*A History of Estoeric Doctrines*] (Paris, 1940, p. 232).

The physiological alchemists, who derived their "art" from Venice, exploited their links with the masonic guilds to enshrine it in the great cathedrals. We find poses portraying in an obvious manner the reception of "our heavenly water which does not wash the hands" in St. Stephen's Cathedral in Vienna, in the vestibule of the minister in Freiburg (Breisgau) and in the church in Kiedrich, to mention but a few religious edifices. The expression, "heavenly water which does not wash the hands," is a way of referring to the "current" which flows through those who are charging themselves.

The Rosicrucian scholar, Hofrat, and State Archivist of Chur, Karl von Eckartshausen (1752–1803), writes in his *Aufschlüsse zur Magie aus geprüften Erfahrungen* [*An Explanation of Magic in the Light of Experience*] (Munich, 1791–1792, Vol. I, p. 188 ff), "I then raised my hands toward heaven for some time, so that my ten fingers were extended toward the sky, and in this way absorbed more *electrical* matter."

The magnetizer, Dr. Karl Bertram (of Berlin) "now and then lifted his hands above his head into the air, holding them like open shells, and stood ready to receive the Od (or life-force). I know from my own experience that this is not an imaginary aid, for I, too, take in something by this procedure, something which I instinctively try to retain by closing my hands, even though it is quite unnecessary to do this as it flows into the body automatically" (Marie Knorr-Schmidt).

Similarly, the mental specialist, Dr. Johann L. Schmitt got his patients to cup their hands so that they were three-quarters closed (the "lotus Blossom" or "Holy Grail" position). This *mudra* releases tensions and invigorates at one and the same time.

P. Johannsen, who was investigated by the engineer Fritz Grunewald (died in 1925), charged himself by making passes in the air. Hans Sterneder (born February 7, 1889) describes in his *Frühling im Dorf* [*Spring in the Village*] (Leipzig, 1929) both the assimilation of lunar Od (when the moon is waxing) and the solar *prana* (at daybreak). This "brother of the sun"[47] learned much from the gipsies, as he admits. A traveler tells the following tale about these nomads. He says that in Cairo they used to pitch their tents in the most exposed places and lay in front of them for hours at a time soaking up the blazing African sun. . . . as soon as you start to leave them they huddle round, sitting cross-legged, chatting to one another and turned to the sun. (*Voigtländers Volksbücher* [*Voigtländer's Chap-Book*] No. 23, p. 5, 22.) They behave just like cats, which are decidedly magical animals.

A magnetopath of great ability, who is also clairvoyant, told me twenty years ago that his teacher was a very ancient gipsy (reputedly 120 years old), who used to do something similar every morning at sunrise, except that he stood in his bare feet on the earth with his fingers spread out and facing the rising sun. Whenever he wished to convey his surplus vital energy to someone else, all he did was to hold his right arm high and grasp with his left hand the arm of the other person, who also stood turned to the sun with his bare feet on the ground but with his left arm hanging down. (Communicated in a private letter of January 7, 1943.)

Saorevo (born in 1882) the initiated Indian chief from the Andes who lives in exile in Unterwesterwald, calls out the words,

---

[47]Tr. note: "Sonnenbruder" usually means "tramp" but here it is put between inverted commas, apparently to show that it is being used in a somewhat different sense as translated, unless of course Sterneder was a "super-tramp" who was also an author, like W.H. Davies!

"Lua, lua, kii wai!" (Sun, sun help me anew!) each morning from the bare hill near the blockhouse he has built for himself. He performs this ritual with his face turned devoutly to the sun and his arms folded on his chest, in the same way as the medicine man who was his grandfather did.

Marie Corelli (1864–1924) writes in her *A Romance of Two Worlds*: "The confidential instructions of Heliobas for regaining health and acquiring an extra electrical charge were extremely simple and so marvelous in their simplicity that I was utterly astounded." She was referring to a Chaldean magician, living in Paris around 1870 and known as Count Casini Heliobas. This name is both a pseudonym and a codeword formed from two Greek words, *Helios* (the sun) and *bas(is)*, implying "the sun is the basis of my extraordinary powers."

In the Middle Ages they rightly exclaimed, when thinking of the solar spirit, "O arcana arcanum (O! Thou mystery of mysteries). *Arcana* is also a term applied to the 78 ancient Tarot cards (the Book of Thoth or Key of Solomon as they are sometimes called) of which we shall have something to say in the section on the *Rotae Mundi*.

But what about "Turkish Masonry?" I hear someone ask. I did all right for a little while and I succeeded in drawing sparks, which were visible to everyone in subdued daylight, by touching my left elbow with my right index finger. And then, all of a sudden I gave up, and a learned and critical friend of mine very wisely did so too.

In the form in which they have been handed down to us, the exercises seem to be incomplete and are therefore considerably dangerous. Dr. Alfred Strauss LL.D. (died in 1935), the well-known author of the profound *Theurgischen Heilmethoden* [*Theurgic Healing Methods*] (Lorch i. Württemberg, 1936), advised me against them in a detailed letter dated October 14, 1933. In the opinion of those who claim to know it, this training has entailed the death of the experimenter, and it is said to have upset one noted dowser, G. Gustav Meyrink who wrote quite candidly to his friend "AME" that he had gone down with myelophthisis (wasting away of the spinal cord) for this reason, a condition which was cured later by Hatha Yoga exercises.

It is because of this danger that I have contented myself with a summary description of the performance. It comprises thirty different forms which I have intentionally refrained from naming. Nor have I mentioned the times for the exercises. *Therefore it will be impossible for anyone to start the system.* Reference must be made to it, however, for the sake of completeness. Nevertheless, there is nothing to stop anyone making a start, for we have the perfectly simple exercises of the "worship of the rising sun," if one may call it that.

"Now there remains yet that which in short time, honor shall be likewise given to the tongue, and by the same, what before times hath been seen, heard and smelt, now finally shall be spoken and uttered forth, viz. when the world shall awake out of her heavy and drowsy sleep and with an open heart, barehead and barefoot, shall merrily and joyfully meet the now arising sun" (*Confessio*, 1616).

MAGNETIZED WATER

I will not deny that the art of magnetic healing will one day be easy. Now, however, it is in its infancy and is kept concealed in the secret cabinets of a few.

—Dr. William Maxwell (1619–1669)
De medicin. magnetica, L.II; c

In the *Archiv für den Thierischen Magnetismus* [*Archives of Animal Magnetism*] (Leipzig, 1817, Vol. I, Part Three, pp. 153, 154), one of the three editors, Prof. Dietr. Gg. *Kieser*, M.D. (1799–1862), published a note on *the use of magnetized water in the 17th century*, which will be reproduced here in its entirety as a typical Rosicrucian formula:

> The following instructions show that magnetized water had been in use very early on, although without reference to the concept of magnetism which was introduced later: Guerni Rolfincii, *Chimia in artis formam redacta, sex libris comprehensa* (Genevae, 1621–1624, Lib. III, Sect. I, Cap. VII) p. 127. *Aqua vitalis microcosmica.*[1]

---

[1]Trans. note: Translation of the Latin prescription: *Microcosmic Cordial and Vital Water*. Take mumia of a healthy man, i.e., the human sulphur! It is like this: a fasting man, who has swilled out his mouth with water, breathes with a long and powerful breath into a glass phial, and his breath is dissolved in the water on account of the "recoil" of the cold. Application: When this is done with good intent, a pure heart and prayer, then we have a potentially useful remedy in incurable diseases for those who admit that the breath is efficacious.

R/ Mumiam hominis sani i.e. ♃ humanum. Est autem illud, halitus hominis jejuni, mane ore bene aqua mundato in phialam vitream fortiter, et diu inspirando immissus, et propter αγτιπεξιξαοιγ *frigoris, in aquam solutus. USUS. Summum, si id fiat bona intentione, corde puro, precibusque devotis, habetur in morbis incurabilibus confortativum, ab illis, qui halitum censet magnam esse efficaciam.*

I have been unable to discover the source of this apparently Paracelsian form of treatment, and J.J. Manget does not include it in his list of more than 200 artificial waters; nor do A. Libavius (1560–1616) and Quercetanus (1524–1609). I understand that there are details in S.P. Hilscher's *Proclusiones de aqua vitali cordiali microcosmica* (Jena, 1739), but so far have not managed to examine a copy.

DISCUSSION

The natural universe is magnetic.

—Seb. Wirdig (1613–1687)
Nova Med. magn., Hbg., 1673

Back of everything magnetism.

—James Joyce
Ulysses, II, p. 371

The art of cure by means of magnetized water can be looked up in the three works mentioned. The generally approved method is to magnetize a glass of water with the right or left hand as the case may be. These two waters taste quite different from one another and may obviously be used as two distinct domestic medicines. This excerpt has been given only because it belongs to the history of the subject and because it may be interesting to students of out-of-the-way matters and recent books nowhere mention it.

DIGITATION

Where the poles of index finger and thumb form a magnet.

—P.M. Verlaine (1844–1896)

This is the neo-Latinism coined by Aubin Gauthier, secretary for life of the Société du Magnétisme in Paris, for a special type of magnetic treatment against the "bloody flux" (dysentery). Prosper Alpini[1] who visited Egypt in 1580 has left behind a very learned work on the healing arts of the Egyptians, *De Medicina Aegyptiorum*, in which he deals with frictions, and says that in treating dysentery gentle massage with the whole hand is followed by inserting a finger in the navel and rotating it several times: "*digitumque pluries circumvertunt*" (Book III). Cap. 14: "*De dysenteriae curatione empyrica.*"

Alpini says he has often seen people suffering from dysentery restored to health by this method (*aliquos dysentericos sanitati fuisse restitutos memini*) and this type of massage seemed so important to him (on that account) that he made up a Latin word for it in imitation of the word used by the Egyptians: "Nowadays there are very few," he says, "who can perform this circonvolution of the navel (*circonvolutionem umbilici*) correctly."[2]

If, as long ago as 1580, a French or Latin word was required for the Egyptian plan of treatment, it is clear that some such are indispensable today to designate the procedures now being envisaged.

---

[1]An Italian botanist, born in Parostica in 1553 and died in Padua in 1617.
[2]Note by Aubin Gauthier: *circumvolutio* is wrong here. The Latin should be *circumversio* or "rotatory action," whereas *circumvolutio* would be "circulatory action."

Finger magnetization takes several forms—by contact or at a distance, turning or circling motions—and each form is used in a special way and has its own characteristic effect. Therefore three-word expressions are used to name a given form of treatment, e.g., "rotary finger magnetizing" or "circulatory finger magnetizing" (i.e., curative magnetism imparted by turning the finger on its axis or by moving the finger in a circle). However, two-word expressions like "rotatory addigitation" are simpler and better.

The word "addigitation" comes from *digitus*, a finger, *agere*, to act on and *ad*, to—so it means "to act on someone or something." Nothing could be more reasonable or expressive (*Le Magnétisme Catholique* [*Catholic Magnetism*] (Brussels and Paris, 1884, pp. 177, 178).

The reference to a special magnetizing procedure used by the Egyptians in the Middle Ages gains additional interest from the fact that Christian Rosencreutz (1378–1484) might have heard of it during his return journey through Egypt some thirty years before Prosper Alpini did so!

On the other hand, he could have learned about it and, in fact, we may fairly safely assume that he did learn about it, in one of the annual scientific congresses at *Fez* (Latin: *Fessanum*), where he stayed for two years. We read in the *Fama* (1614) that "every year the Arabians and Africans do send one to another, inquiring one of another out of their arts, if haply they had found out some better things, or if experience had weakened their reasons. Yearly there came something to light, whereby the mathematics, physics and magic (for in those are they of Fez most skillful) were amended." It is curious that a *moxa cone* (Spanish: "burning cylinder") placed on the navel was an old medical treatment for an epidemic of Asiatic cholera. A piece of linen cloth the size of a handkerchief would be dipped in methylated spirit, laid over the navel, set alight and allowed to burn for 5–6 seconds. The results were said to be extremely surprising and patients who had almost been given up for dead were restored to life.[3]

---

[3]J.L. Casper: *Die Behandlung der Cholera etc.* [*The Treatment of Cholera etc.*] (Berlin, 1832).

The Rosicrucian Dr. Johannes Staricius, an acquaintance of Jakob Böhme (1575–1624), recommends in his *Geheimnis-voller Heldenschatz, etc.* [*A Treasury of Mysteries from the Heroic Age, etc.*] (1st. ed. 1695; my copy dated 1750, Cologne and Weimar) "smearing the navel with nutmeg oil" to cure dysentery! Here again, the navel acts as a fulcrum to give medicinal leverage! In addition crushed dried bilberries in wine were prescribed together with beer broth to assist the cure. Osiander[4] says that "another Egyptian folk remedy for dysentery was to rub almond oil into the abdomen, and to use a special sort of friction in the navel with an oiled finger." The accompanying footnote 4 refers to Prosper Alpini's *Medicina Aegypt.*, p. 226; "*Digito intra umbil-icum posito, ipsum pluries circumvertunt.*"

DISCUSSION

For mankind there is no better remedy than man.

—Petrus Blesenius

I have never suffered from dysentery, so I am unable to pass judgment on these special healing methods from my own experience. I do not think there would be any harm in trying them, however, should the need arise! They could only help. We must allow the possibility that they could turn out to be useful; they deserve to be rescued from oblivion on grounds quite other than their historic interest.

Here I will put on record a *country remedy for dysentery* that is still very useful. My brother-in-law, Georg Merz, was lying sick in 1945 in a prisoner-of-war camp at Le Mans (Sarthe), suffering from dysentery and loose bowels. As he was on his way to the lavatory, where he was practically living at the time, he met a fellow prisoner who asked him, "Have you still got some yellow Amy toothpaste?." "Yes," he replied, "do you want some?". "Not I," he was told, "you are the one who needs it. Squeeze out some 2 cm and take it, repeating the dose after twenty minutes, but on no account take any more. The reason

---

[4]Prof. Joh. Fr. Osiander, M.D.: *Volksheilmittel* [*Folk Remedies*] (1877).

I am telling you this is that it's full of magnesia." My brother-in-law did what he was told and the magnesia took effect just in time, when all the usual doctors' drugs had failed to stop the incessant diarrhea. I cannot guarantee that the same thing will work for anybody else though.

As a point of interest, Prosper Alpini, from whom we have quoted above, made a thorough investigation of every kind of occult phenomenon in Egypt. He relied on his own observations in the field of "sympathetic influence" and the so-called "sympathetic cures." One thing he did was to bring back home a pot of earth taken from a field not far from the Nile. He was astonished to find that the earth became lighter and darker during the year. What is more, when the soil from which it had been taken was overflowed by the Nile and grew heavier with waterlogging, the weight of the earth in Alpini's pot also increased. Then it lost weight as the waters of the Nile receded and its parent soil dried out. This would be worth investigating!

RETURNING TO LIFE

He caught her fiercely in his arms
With all the vigor young love gave,
Saying, "I still should give thee warmth
Though thou wert sent me from the grave!"

—Goethe

In an old Rosicrucian book[1] the seventh guest related the following story as the wine was passed round the royal supper-table:

In my youth I was deeply in love with a beautiful and noble maiden and she reciprocated my love, but we were unable to marry because her friends would not allow it. So she was married to a respectable fellow, who looked after her well and lovingly until she came to give birth, and then she fared so badly that many thought she had died, and so she was committed to the earth at great expense and with great sorrow. Then I said to myself, "You may not have been able to have any share in this person while she was alive, but you can embrace her in death and kiss her to your heart's content." Therefore I took my servant with me and we disinterred her by night. I opened the coffin and folded her in my arms and her heart fluttered. I found that it continued to move slightly and gradually beat more and more strongly as I warmed her until it was

---

[1] *The Chemical Wedding.*

obvious that she still lived. And so I carried her stealthily to my house and after I had restored heat to her frozen body in a costly herbal bath, I entrusted her to my mother until she was recovered from the delivery of a fine son under my mother's careful nursing. After two days, when she was still completely bewildered, I explained to her all that had happened and asked her to live with me as my wife from that time on. She objected that this would grieve her husband, who had treated her so kindly and honorably, but that she would consent if my loving claims on her were as strong as his. So, after two months (in the meantime I had had to travel elsewhere) I invited her husband to be my guest and, when I asked him among other things whether he would accept his deceased wife if she were to come home to him, he said that he would and wept aloud as he said it. At last I fetched his wife and son and told him everything that had been transacted and asked him to ratify my proposed marriage with his consent. After a prolonged argument he conceded that it would be wrong to deprive me of my rights and felt obligated to resign his wife to me, but still took issue with me over his son. At this point the young lady interrupted us and said, "I am surprised that you want to double the poor man's sorrow." Here the story-teller looked round at us and inquired if he were not entitled to his demands and, after we had discussed it, most of us allowed that he had acted within his rights. "No," he said, "I made him a gift both of his wife and his son; but tell me gentlemen, which was the greater, my virtue or his joy?"

In a book written by a professor of medicine at "the Royal Prussian Army Medical College," which came out 200 years later, we read:

The following remarkable event affords even stronger evidence for the effectiveness of animal magnetism in cases of apparent death:

Sometime in the middle of the last century in Paris, a young man was in love with the beautiful daughter of a rich citizen. Although she loved him in return, he failed to achieve the object of his love, because the obedient daughter eventually yielded to the stern command of her hard-hearted father and married someone else, a man for whom she did not care. Quietly pining over her unhappy love-affair, this pitiful woman was soon brought to childbed and from there to her coffin. She was buried within 24 hours, according to the custom of those times, and her father now repented of his stubbornness too late. Impelled by fervent and irresistible longing to look once more on the sweetheart of whom he had been bereft in life, the young man stole to the churchyard in the dark of the following night, pressed a gold coin into the hand of the sexton and got him to open the grave. As he looked at the deceased, the thought suddenly occurred to him that she was not really dead. He quickly lifted her out, forced the grave-digger to cover the coffin with earth again, threatening to murder him if he did not hold his tongue, and carried his dear lady-love to a nearby house. Here he brought her into the warm, undressed her quickly, hastily rubbed her limbs, and attempted to instill life into her with fiery kisses and a thousand warm embraces. After several hours of fruitless exertions, he heard a sigh and with that the passionately awaited life returned. Soon after this remarkable occurrence, this pair, so strangely united by the grave, journeyed in complete secrecy to England, got married there and only ventured to return after several years, in order to claim the fortune of the person who was presumed dead. There followed the most bizarre process-at-law. The first husband maintained that the wife was his, while the second argued that she was dead to her former spouse and had been restored to life solely by his own efforts. However, as the parliament seemed inclined to give her back to her first husband, the happy couple abandoned the inheritance and hastened back to England without waiting for the verdict. The records of this unusual lawsuit were to be found in the parliamentary records shortly before the Revolution.

Here is another case. The daughter of the Toulouse parliamentary president, a Miss de Lafaille fell in love with young Georges de Goran, but he was given an overseas posting with his regiment for a number of years and she married a certain Mr. Boissieux. When Goran finally returned home, he learned that his sweetheart was dead and had just been buried. During the night, he disinterred her with the help of a grave-digger whom he had bribed. He could think of nothing else but her parting words to him of long before, "Even if I were dead, your kiss would revive me." So Goran kissed her and immediately a scream escaped from the lips of the deceased—she had returned to life. The couple fled in order to avoid any molestation. A few years later, Boissieux was visiting his dead wife's grave when he met a person remarkably like her who hurried away when he stared at her. Full of misgiving, he had the grave opened and found it empty. The police investigated, legal proceedings were instituted and a court order was made for the woman to return to her husband within 24 hours. On this, the pair of lovers, who could no longer live as man and wife, poisoned themselves.[2]

We have given the above parallel cases for two reasons. One, because they are evidence for the effectiveness of "animal" magnetism on people who appear to have died and two, because

---

[2]Prof. Carl A. F. Kluge, M.D. (1782–1844), *Versuch einer Darstellung des animalischen Magnetismus als Heilmittel* [*An Attempt to Present Animal Magnetism as a Means of Cure*] (Vienna, 1815, The Second or Practical Part, pp. 438, 439; §354). Prof. Kluge cites the following sources for his narratives: 1) C.W. Hufeland: *Über die Ungewißheit des Todes* [The Uncertainty that Death has Occurred] (Weimar, 1791, p. 13 ff): 2) Adalbert Vencenz Zardas *Patriotischer Wunsch für die Wiederbelebung der todtscheinenden Menschen* [*A Public-spirited Desire for the Restoration to Life of those who Seem to have Died*] (Prague, 1797, p. 7 ff).

they show the kind of results on which the old Rosicrucians so confidently relied and also the empirical basis of their confidence.

DISCUSSION

The "total magnetism" obtained by bodily superimposition is as old as it is effective. We read that Elijah (I Kings 17:21) and Elisha (II Kings 4:34) used it in Old Testament times and that the Apostle Paul did so in New Testament times (Acts 20:10), either by stretching themselves upon or by embracing the dead person.

In addition to a full embrace (Latin: *incubation*) there are treatments where the patient is hugged round the shoulders or neck or held by the hands. Incubation is often combined with *insufflation* (or breathing into the person's mouth).

Similar to these is "Gerokomy" (from the Greek, meaning to renew the youth of the aged), also known as "Shunammitism" because King David performed it with Abishag, a Shunammite (I Kings 1:1–4); it consists of sleeping in the same bed with someone without having sexual relations with them. The old person draws strength from the young one with whom they sleep, according to a general folk tradition, and it is held that a grandmother will weaken her grandchildren if she sleeps with them.

Kallias, the Syracusian historian informs us that the African tribe of the Psyller held that the last resort in disease was for the sick person to sleep in the nude with a healthy one!

Claudius Galenus (131–200) advised that the bodies of the feeble should be covered with the bodies of vigorous young women.

In his old age, Barbarossa (1123–1190) had boys constantly applied to his hips and stomach, so Bacon, Lord Verulam (1561–1626) tells us.

Favorable results in practice have been reported by the following doctors of medicine: Capivaccio (died in 1589), Forestus (1522–1597), Borelli (1608–1678), Cohausen (1665–1750) and Boerhave (1668–1738). John of Damascus (died 760), the Christian saint, and Moses Maimonides (1135–1204), the Jewish "Plato," who are claimed by the Rosicrucians as their spiritual fathers, agree (although separated by the centuries) that the body-heat of young maidens is the best remedy for paralyses and gouty pains.

Francis Bacon, Lord Verulam (1561–1626), who has been supposed by some to be the real author of Shakespeare's plays and is the "Tyrsan" in his technosophistical Utopia *Nova Atlantis* (1624), in the same way Thomas Bartholinus (1616–1680), a bright medical luminary in Denmark's Heaven (Fromann), recommends this form of rejuvenation and Bacon in particular prescribes additional massage with balsamic substances.

Paracelsus, however, employed the Elisha method of applying the body of the healer to that of the patient in cases of insanity.

The book of magic entitled *Des Juden Abraham von Worms Buch der wahren Praktik* [*The Book of True Practice of the Jew Abraham of Worms*], published at Cologne in 1725, recommends insufflation and incubation in its instructions on how to arouse someone who has fallen into a deep swoon or death. Puyseégur (1751–1825) relates how Princess Ligne recalled her nearly dead child to life by lying on it lightly. A certain Foissac, like Dr. Desprez, successfully did the same thing with his wife.

The *Vossische Zeitung* (Berlin, No. 12) of 1773 announced: "In Montiers near Amiens, a four-year-old child was drowned in the Bresse, a small stream. He was discovered after one hour and pulled out. He was then laid on a bed. After two hours an 'expert' arrived, who restored his life by 'measuring himself' upon the child."

Rétif de la Bretonne (1754–1806) writes in his *Le Palais Royal* about the professional "Shunammites" of the 17th century. The most famous Shunammite practitioner was a Madam Janus (!) and her medical adviser was a certain Hermippus (!).

Alexandra David-Neel discusses the corpse-magic of the Tibetan Ngag-pa magicians which is performed by embracing the dead. It is called *Ro-lang* (= the rising of the dead body). Apparently, it is a ghastly dance with a corpse which has been temporarily galvanized by Od. (*Heilige und Hexer* [*Saints and Sorcerers'*] Leipzig, 1932, p. 161, 162.)

The seriousness with which the age-old method of "measuring onself" on the patient has been taken right down to modern times, is evidenced by the *Shunammite experiments in concentration camps*, as reported by Dr. Eugen Kogon (born February 2, 1903) in his *Der SS-Staat* [*The SS State*] (Berlin, 1946, p. 169, 171). According to him, there are others alive who could tell the same tale! In brief, what happened was the re-animation of "refrigerated warm-blooded animals" (a euphemism for "prisoners frozen stiff in cold baths") by putting them into bed with one or two female persons. The experiment was *successful* in two thirds of the cases.

WHAT MESMER BORROWED
FROM THE ROSICRUCIANS

When the man who, as much as or more than Galvani, has given wonderful and mysterious demonstrations of the phenomenon he has discovered, dies in neglect, an immeasurable benefit is lost to mankind.

—Lorenz Oken (1779–1851)
Mesmer, 1810

"The first great publicist of magnetic treatment was Dr. Franz Anton Mesmer (1754–1815), who (when he first appeared in Germany) *found the field prepared by the Rosicrucians*, who were zealous in the practice and study of the occult sciences and performed cures etc."[1] For "one of the main preoccupations of the Rosicrucians in their second system was magico-magnetic healing."[2]

The young Mesmer was possessed by a great desire to immerse himself in the writings of "outsiders."

"Ever given to the unusual and unaccountable, it was a favorite occupation of his to investigate the *old mystics*, whose works had been contemptuously dismissed as the products of superstition, and to study them diligently. The result was that, in his promotion in the year 1766, he published a 'dissertation on the influence of the planets on the human body.' "

---

[1] A.J. Riko: *Handbuch zur Ausübung des Magnetismus etc.* [*Handbook of Magnetic Practice*] (Leipzig, 1904, pp. 4, 5).
[2] Karl Kiesewetter: "Die Rosenkreuzer" *in Magische Blätter* ["The Rosicrucians" in *Magical Pages*] (Leipzig, Vol. 11, November, 1922, p. 346).

This is what a learned contemporary, Professor Carl Alexander Ferdinand Kluge (1782–1844) had to say about him in his *Versuch einer Darstellung des animalischen Magnetismus* [*An Attempt to Present Animal Magnetism as a Means of Cure*] (Berlin, 1815, p. 28, para. 24), from which we shall be quoting further. Kluge devotes three pages to the literature of these old mystics, mentioning Robert Fludd among others. I am in full agreement with Kluge when he goes on to say: "It is highly likely that Mesmer did not make the discovery of animal magnetism by himself but was led to it by reading the old authors of the 16th and 17th centuries, who had already expressed similar ideas" (p. 33, para. 31).

So imbued was he with the spirit of the old mystics, to borrow Kluge's expression, that Mesmer not only copied their findings but imitated their way of life as well: "After making this discovery, he became more and more secretive, concealing his tests and observations as if they were some holy mystery" (p. 38, para. 31).

Hence Dr. Karl Adolf von Eschenmayer (1768–1852) was quite justified in his assertion that, "animal magnetism has a wizard's cap on its head. Anyone who hears tell of its phenomena for the first time could easily conceive that he had been transported to the era when the Qabala, with its attendant sympathetic and magical wonder cures, infiltrated medical practice." But when Kluge continues, "he no longer made use of magnetic rods in his treatments but made his own person the sole proprietor of this force, which he already knew how to impart by means of will-power not only through personal contact but also at a distance, and so healed the most complicated diseases without saying how he did it" (p. 38, para. 31), his blame is transformed into praise before our very eyes. In other words Mesmer had meanwile realized that the success of his cures did not arise from the use of magnetic rods but were the product of his own person alone, of his own soul (Latin, *anima*). For this reason he came to prefer "animal magnetism" to the metallic kind.

Kluge speaks very significantly, in the above excerpt, of the healing of complicated diseases even at a distance.

If Mesmer was disinclined to explain how he operated, perhaps it was not so much that he feared to reveal his secrets to competitors as that he foresaw that they would be misunderstood by the medical profession. Yet, apparently, even he was not fully informed of the nature of his power. We know from some of his trustworthy contemporaries (other than Kluge) that Mesmer was possessed of astounding magnetic healing ability. It seems that he regarded it as being "electromagnetic" as we would say nowadays, because he wore beneath his shirt a tight-fitting leather tunic lined with silk in the hope of accumulating the "electric fluid." The "holy mystery" in which he shrouded his method of cure had the result that, in Paris, "Mesmer was idolized as a man full of Egyptian wisdom and as a benefactor of the human race and that his house was constantly occupied by sick people of all classes and from all parts of the country" (p. 44, para. 38). It was in Paris, too, that Mesmer "refused an annuity of 20,000 livres offered by the French Government if he would reveal his secret; his stated reason being that should his art become common knowledge it might be open to grave abuse" (p. 48, para. 42).

In my opinion, there is no need to see this refusal as a pretext; Mesmer could very well have been convinced that danger would attend popularization. Presumably, he was also reluctant to profane his art, which had descended from the age-old arcana of the temples. He therefore decided that it must remain a mystery teaching.

"For this purpose, he founded a secret society under the name of Harmony, in which he initiated into his secret and under the most sacred vows of silence those who paid the above sum" (p. 48, §42).

That even here nothing was done without money, we may attribute to human frailty—every institution costs something to run and, anyway, "the laborer is worthy of his hire"—and the accusation that, in this way, Mesmer accumulated a fortune of 150,000 German thalers is, in my opinion, entirely beside the point. If he had been commercially inclined and had accepted the offer of the French Government, he would have acquired considerably more than this!

These Sociétés de l'Harmonie (Societies of Harmony) spread over the whole of France and her colonies, with the "Mother Society" in Paris. "These associations, called themselves harmonic societies because their object was to investigate the harmony in Nature everywhere and thus to benefit mankind both physically and spiritually" (p. 53, §45).

Their object and the obligation to silence were by way of being masonic attributes and it need cause no surprise that these "societies" adopted a masonic rite.[3] And it is even less surprising when we learn that Mesmer was a member of the Gold and Rosy Cross: The famous Comte de St. Germain (Prince Rackoczi, born in 1696) studied magnetism with him in Vienna.[4]

Kaiser Joseph II of Austria (1741–1790) issued an edict in 1785 against the members of the Order of the Gold and Rosy Cross (Rosicrucians of the Second System), and in 1786 an effort was led by Mesmer to revive it. In the same year a great masonic convention was held in Paris, in which Mesmer took part, too. Saint Germain, his pupil Count Alexander Cagliostro (1743–1795), J. K. Lavater (1741–1801), Louis Claude, Marquis de Saint-Martin (1743–1803), J. Cristoph von Wöllner (1732–1800) and Count Charles-Henri von Gleichen (1735–1807) also participated[5]

Mesmer's ideal state was the typical Rosicrucian one of a kingdom of physician priests: "To him, God was transcendental and man's concept of God found expression in the sun as the central source of activity; in colorful solar festivals, in nature and in the temple, he encouraged people to express their loftiest feelings as a divine service dedicated to the highest Being. In this mesmeric Sun Kingdom, which is worked out in all its details of constitution, government and education, the physician, who holds in his hands the powers extracted from the universe, is the bearer of the divine transmission. Medicine is the highest calling in the community. The physician is not only the protector of health but is the servant of God; he is the people's priest."[6]

Goethe (1749–1832) made Mesmer's acquaintance in Constance in 1788 and enshrined his memory in the person of his

---

[3]Rudolf Tischner: *Mesmer* (Munich, 1928, p. 59).

[4]Graefer: *Kleine Wiener Memoiren* [*Minor Reminiscences of Vienna*] (1846).

[5]Dr. Eckert: *Magazin zum Beweis für die Verurtheilung des Freimaurerei-Ordens* [Treasury of Proof for the Condemnation of the Masonic Order] (1857).

[6]Karl Bittel: *The famous Dr. Mesmer of Constance* (Friedrichshafen, 1940, pp. 40–41).

"astrological physician" in the book *Wilhelm Meisters Wanderjahre* (1821). However, the extraordinary Makarie could be "Peregrina," the enigmatical student love of Eduard Möricke (1804– 1875), if—or even if not—he fell in love with her only two years after the appearance of the *Wanderjahre*!

A stone memorial has been erected to Mesmer in the beautiful Meersburg cemetery, high above the Lake of Constance at the instigation of Prof. Karl Christian Wolfart, M.D. (1778–1832). The triangular block of marble is richly adorned with Rosicrucian and Masonic symbols on all sides which are deeply engraved and were formerly gilded. On top there was a sundial and a compass to represent movement in time and space. The sundial and compass had been taken down by ill-intentioned individuals as long ago as the days of Dr. Justinus Kerners (1856). At the time of my visit in 1951 they had not been restored and the memorial was neglected.

TOUCH AND DISTANT HEALING

Many arts have been written down, a few true hand-
grips give the proof, labor makes it clear. Practice ver-
ifies things which are written and handgrips confirm
all knowledge, which is thus assimilated.

—Leonh. Thurneisser (1530–1595)

A Rosicrucian instruction book[1] contains an initiation short
story called "Parabola,"[2] which has been elucidated by the Vi-
ennese psychoanalyst Herbert Silberer.[3] In this short story its
author is admitted into the *Collegium Sapientiae* [*College of the
Wise*], otherwise known as the "Faculty" and really none other
than the Brotherhood of the Rosy Cross.

After successfully passing the grueling oral examination,
the Neophyte has to undergo a practical test, his task being to
tame the lion of the brotherhood. In the lion's den "I remembered many holds, as I had trained so diligently in this form

---

[1]The *Geheimen Figuren der Rosenkreuzer* [*The Occult Symbols of the Rosicrucians*]
is a publication written by a few of the Rosicrucian Brethren who were still
living in northern Germany (especially in Hamburg) around 1780–1790. It
has since become famous. Actually the book is entitled *Einfältig ABC-Büchlein
für junge Schüler* [*A Simple ABC book for Young Scholars*]. It has recently been
reprinted by Barsdorf, Berlin, 1920.
[2]It is found in Karl Weinfurter: *Der brennende Busch* [*The Burning Bush*] (Lorch
i. Württemberg, 1930, pp. 253–274).
[3]*Probleme der Mystik und ihrer Symbolik* [*Problems of the Mystics and their Symbolism*]
(Leipzig, 1914).

of ATHLETICS, I was also expert in natural magic . . . and seized the lion with such skill and adroitness," that he lost his life. This "skill and adroitness" in the handholds together with the word "athletics" makes us think of the Japanese *Judo*.

In fact, in his book, Dr. Martin Vogt (Munich) has produced evidence from old wrestling manuals and other traditional sources that *Ju-Jitsu* was used by our ancestors in much the same way as it is used today.[4]

To give but one example of the "nerve zones" which will be discussed later: Pascha says in his *Advice to those in the Ring*, "When your opponent has you in a hold, press him behind the ear!" A modern textbook has this to say on "defending oneself against clinches": "A. has grasped the hips of V. from the front. V. places the tips of his two thumbs behind A.'s ears and exerts strong pressure on the nerves lying in the hollows there."[5]

It is no part of Rosicrucian doctrine to cause any creature to suffer without cause. On the contrary they believe in relieving suffering. Hence, in the parable, there was a sharp dispute between the members of the Order (the Elders) and "one of them said that he must restore him (i.e., the lion) to life or he could be no member of their College."

Therefore, we have to discover whether the Rosicrucians knew of manipulations which would alleviate or remove pain and to ascertain whether or not they were masters of *magnetic healing*. This removes or eases pain, a) by the induction of a healing sleep,[6] b) by local treatment with passes.

The English alchemist and mystic, Thomas Vaughan (Eugenius Philalethes, born 1622) speaks in his writings "of the maiden (all experienced spiritists will confirm that young virgins make the best mediums)—*who is thrown into slumber by the magic hand.*"[7]

---

[4]*Alte und neue Raufkunst [Old and New Fighting Arts]* (Verlag Wilh. Limpert, Dresden, n.d.).

[5]Erich Rahn *Jiu-Jitsu, die unsichtbare Waffe [Ju-Jitsu, the Invisible Weapon]* (Berlin, 1931, p. 14).

[6]"All diseases can be cured by sleep" (Menander, 342).

[7]Marvin Faquir: "Die 'Materia prima' der Alchimisten—eine neue Entdeckung" [*The Prime Matter of the Alchemists—A New Discovery*] in *Magische Blätter* (Leipzig, Vol. 12, December, 1922, pp. 367–368).

"The Frenchman, too, d'Espagnet[8] quite often declared that *the hands of an 'alchemist' must be trained to throw the body into a trance.*"[9]

Kiesewetter (1854–1895) asserts that "one of the main studies of the Rosicrucians of the Second System was *magnetic healing.*"[10] Riko confirms this: "The first great popularizer of magnetism was Dr. Anton Mesmer (1733–1815), who, when he first visited Germany, found *the ground had been prepared by the Rosicrucians*, who zealously applied themselves to the theory and practice of the occult sciences, *performed healings, etc.*"[11]

Thetter[12] gives us details of how "in the Middle Ages, the knowledge of mystery cult treatments appears in various occult orders by some unseen route . . . there are, in their writings, *complicated instructions on different types of pass together with the appropriate forms of prayer.*"

What we have here is not simply "different types of pass" but also complicated instructions as to the special healing power of the individual fingers! As far as I am able to ascertain from the relevant literature, this refinement was criticized by two authorities (Kramer and Schröder) but approved by a third (Sédir). In order to make this rare material more widely known, it is reproduced here from Schröder: "Just as inconceivable and valueless is the theory of Mesmer's French followers, who thought to cure each given disease with a specific finger. If magnetic healing had continued in this direction, it would have become a virtuoso performance."[13]

---

[8]Jean d'Espagnet, speaker of the Bordeaux parliament and famous alchemist of the 17th century. Two instructive alchemical works.

[9]Faquir, ibid. Anton Memminger in his *Hakenkreuz und Davidstern* [*Swastika and Star of David*] (Würzburg, 1922, p. 219) had this to say: "Suggestion and hypnosis were known even to the ancient Egyptian priests, who combined astrology and magic with medicine . . . both the therapeutists in Alexandria and the Essenes in Israel threw people into a hypnotic sleep and brought them back to life from this apparent state of death."

[10]"The Rosicrucians" in *Mayische Blätter* (Leipzig, Vol. 11, November, 1922, p. 346).

[11]*Handbuch zur Ausübung des Magnetismus etc.* [*Handbook of Magnetic Practice etc.*] (Leipzig, 1904, pp. 4, 5).

[12]*Magnetismus—das Urheilmittel* [*Magnetism the Original Form of Healing*] (Leipzig, n.d., p. 15).

[13]H.R. Paul Schröder, *Die Heilmethode des Lebensmagnetismus* (Leipzig, 6th

Pastmaster Kramer has this to say:

One ridiculous method of healing lays down *the exact finger to be used when magnetic treatment is being given for the various diseases of the five sense organs*: the thumb must be used in disorders of the sense of touch, the index finger in eye troubles, the middle finger in earache and hearing problems, the ring finger in diseases of the nose and finally the little finger for anything that is wrong with the tongue—the implication is that each finger has a specific healing force stored inside it![14]

Sédir makes his "spiritual teacher" say: "Use the index finger for hepatic diseases, the middle finger for the bones, the ring finger for the heart, the little finger for the nervous system and the thumb for mental disorders."[15] He also refers

---

edition, 1898, p. 18). Dr. Jules Regnault (Toulon) gives the following example of diagnosis with the fingers for "digital" therapy, in his *Biodynamique et Radiations* [*Biodynamics and Radiations*] (Toulon, 1936, p. 120): Dowsers in France have come to the conclusion, on the basis of their observations on the sidereal pendulum, that relationships can be established between the individual fingers and the most important of the organs of the body. Regnault gives the following correspondences for the right hand in men:

  Thumb: right side of head
  Index finger: right respiratory apparatus
  Middle finger: liver
  Ring finger: right kidney
  Little finger: abdomen

For the left hand in man he gives:

  Thumb: left side of head
  Index finger: left respiratory apparatus
  Middle finger: stomach
  Ring finger: left kidney
  Little finger: abdomen
  Mount of Venus: heart

The reverse is true of women.

Regnault quotes as his source for this information, *Essais de diagnostic digital avec le pendule paramagnétique* [*Experiments with Finger Diagnosis using the Paramagnetic Pendulum*] by A. Bovis, Nice (1933).

[14]Phillipp Walburg Kramer (1815–1899) *Der Heilmagnetismus* [*Healing Magnetism*] Lorch i. Württ., 1931, p. 38).

[15]Paul Sédir (1871–1926): *Initiations* (Bihorel-les-Rouen, 1924, p. 77).

to "the spirits of the fingers," as Carus Sterne (1839–1903) did to the "Dactyls,"[16] and even employs a form of invocation!

Anyway, even if he does not give credence to special healing power for different diseases residing in the individual fingers, Kluge[17] nevertheless discovered a different healing intensity in the separate fingers, on investigation, much as the Rosicrucians always designated the thumb and index fingers as the strongest "magnets" and so must have experienced a difference in the "current strength"![18]

In Rosencreutz's time, the Brotherhood of the *Saludadores* (Healers) in Spain "touched the place affected *with a predetermined number of strokes made in a certain manner*, and it is said that they were very often successful in healing chronic diseases in this way, drawing fragments of metal from wounds, etc." (Kiesewetter). They were still exercising their old skills under the name of *Saludados* in the south of France later than 1891. However, the Rosicrucians had not only various passes for imparting the healing current but also others for receiving the cosmic magnetic flow, in order to supercharge themselves with it.

Baron Rudolf von Sebottendorf (born 1875) sees the "key to the understanding of Alchemy" in the "practice of the old Turkish Freemasonry."[19] By this is meant the alchemicalizing of the human body (The Philosophical Egg), the consolidation and rendering independent of the subtle body so that it becomes the "glorified rose" (Phoenix arising from the ashes).

---

[16]*Daktylomantie [Dactylomancy]* (Weimar, 1862, p. 176).
[17]Carl Alexander Ferdinand Kluge *Versuch einer Darstellung des animalischen Magnetismus als Heilmittel [An Attempt to Present Animal Magnetism as a Curative Agent]* (Berlin, 1815).
[18]Cf. this verse by Paul Verlaine (1844–1896):

> *Où le pouce et l'auriculaire*
> *Donnent les poles de l'aimant.*

> Where the thumb and little finger
> The poles of the magnet supply.

[19]Sebottendorf: *Die Praxis der alten türkischen Freimaurerei [The Practice of Old Turkish Freemasonry]* (Leipzig, 1924).

"In oriental masonry the Work is known as "the Science of the Key" or *Ilm el Miftach*, and the masons quite often refer to themselves as *Beni el Mim* or "Sons of the Key" (p. 17).

"The Science of the Key is also called the Science of the Scales in Arabic, or *Ilm el nizan*. There is also *Il el quimija* or the Science of Chemistry. It is an age-old jewel of wisdom. Some time around A.D. 900 we find it in Venice where the foundations of Freemasonry were laid by the adoption of the Syrian legend of Hiram and the linking of the individual grades with the building of Solomon's Temple. In this way, the science became a monopoly of the masonic lodges."[20]

"They (the modern Moslem brethren) studied and researched and discovered in the writings of the *Rosicrucians* and in those of the Alchemists, that these had given an accurate account of the 'Science of the Key' in their books. The exercises of the oriental Freemasons, what is more, are nothing but a work carried out on themselves, for improvement and gaining higher knowledge. It will become clear, as we continue our exposition, that they reveal the secret of the *Rosicrucians* and Alchemists and demonstrate the preparation of the Stone, which was the object of the seeker's desire" (p. 19).

"The exercises have persisted in the usage of the three signs of recognition of the modern masons: Sign, Grip and Word, except that originally, these three were not signs of recognition, not merely symbols, but *magical operations*, intended *for the assimilation of the subtle radiations of the primal force into the body, thus making it more spiritual*, giving the spirit ascendency over matter. The signs are the three different positions of the hand, which are named after the vocables they represent" (pp. 11, 12). These are the vowels, *A*, *I* and *O*.

"The Grips are made with the hand on various parts of the body" (p. 12).

These are, neck, chest and abdominal grips; the signs and grips being made *only with the left hand*! An old set of instructions says: "Take the Steel of the Wise (Chalybs, the index finger), strike the scintilla (the spark). Take the second steel (thumb) and put the magnet in operation (= the *A* sign), which attracts

---

[20]Hence the occult knowledge of the so-called "Venetians" (Walen).

the elements and provides you with the water for which you thirst" (p. 35).[21]

"This is the water of life which so often occurs in our mythological stories, the alchemist's *aqua vitae*" (p. 36).

"The water is 'our Heavenly Water' which does not wet the hands. It is not the ordinary sort although it is nearly always defined as rainwater" (p. 31). That is, when the heavenly effluvia enter the right hand held in a certain position, it feels as if water is trickling through one![22]

Sebottendorf then talks of the Chakras (Sanskrit for *wheels*), the organs of the subtle body. They are so called because of their spinning motion, and are also given the name of "lotuses" as they look something like flowers to the clairvoyant. Now just as the lotus is the fairest flower to the Indian, so is the rose to the Westerner. The Rosicrucian greeting, "May the roses bloom on your cross!" does not refer to the cross over one's grave but to the cross formed by the backbone and shoulders. And then Father Rosencreutz relates in his "Chemical Wedding" how he stuck four red roses in his hat, as much as to say, "I have reconciled four poles of the subtle body, I have developed them in me!" (N.B. the German idiom "to bring under one hat" means to reconcile and the "Chemical Wedding" was, of course, written in German.) The reconciliation of the "roses" is described by the "Wizard abbot," Johannes Tritheim (1462–1516) of Sponheim near Kreuznach.[23] There are seven of them, and they have their correspondences in certain nerve plexuses in the physical body. Anyone who is interested in studying the matter further should read the still obtainable *Theurgischen Heilmethoden* [*Theurgic Methods of Healing*].[24] We shall confine ourselves here to repeating a relevant statement by the Benedictine

---

[21]Jacques Coeur (1400–1456), a French statesman, merchant and financier of Bourges. "The House of the J.C. in B. is decorated with two towers, which represent an index finger and a thumb" (Sebottendorf, *op. cit.*, p. 24).

[22]The *Parabola*, in fact, recognizes the use of all 10 fingers for collecting the heavenly water—"Then I asked the old miller how many water wheels he had and he answered 'ten.' The adventure stuck in my mind and I should have been pleased to know what it all meant."

[23]*Tractatus chemicus* in *Theatrum chemicum* (Vol. IV).

[24]Strauss-Surya (Lorch, 1936).

alchemist, Basil Valentine (ca. 1550): "The king travels through six towns in the heavenly firmament, but in the seventh he holds his court." This is the same as the Indian Tantric rising of the serpent power, or kundalini to the crown chakra or *Sahasrara*!

In this context belong the independent investigations of the college professor, Dr. Ludwig Staudenmaier (1865–1933), who was able to show that different nerve fascicles in the human body can be specially stimulated and can exhibit special effects.[25] These fairly easily stimulated places will give Turkish Freemasonry those fine forces which are said to build (or rather to establish and make independent) the subtle body—the *Puer aeternus*.

These chakras partly coincide with the starting points of the *Rayons Sympathiques* (Sympathetic rays) of the French researcher Voillaume.[26] He gives the following positions: underneath the chin, at the level of the solar plexus (the strongest zone), at the level of the mesenteric plexus, the sacral plexus, above the knee.

MAGNETISM AND HYPNOTISM ARE NOT IDENTICAL

Hypnotism cannot play a part in magnetism—*quite the reverse*. Hypnotism can partly be a matter of "fluids" (Kindberg, Alrutz, and others). Suggestion may be involved in both hypnotism and magnetism—as in all life activities. The question is sometimes raised, did the Rosicrucians know about hypnotism too? No question about it! It has always been one of the secrets of the mysteries and the Rosicrucians certainly investigated the latter. It was especially the healing secret of the Essenes, who are by way of being precursors of the Rosicrucians, if it is conceded that they are a mother society for Freemasonry (Dr. A. Kohn: "Die Essäer als Freimaurer des Altertums," in *Der Zirkel*, Vienna, 1897).

Besides, hypnotism is found in the Yogic texts, which were translated into Arabic over a thousand years ago (Hauer) and

---

[25]*Magie als experimentelle Naturwissenschaft* [Magic as an experimental science] (Leipzig, 1922).
[26]Dr. Albert Leprince. *Le Pouvoir mysterieux des Guérisseurs* [*The Mysterious Powers of the Healers*] (Paris, 1942), p. 125 ff).

the Rosicrucians obtained their knowledge from Arabia. The records show that certain Rosicrucian personalities gave examples of the power of mass suggestion. Albertus Magnus (1207–1280) performed a successful experiment during Epiphany 1249 in the frozen monastery garden in the presence of King Wilhelm of Holland (1247–1256). According to Abbot Trithemus, "the winter was transformed into a summer's day enriched with flowers and fruit." However, when grace was said after meat, the hocus-pocus came to an end and the guests were as hungry as ever! A similar fools' paradise was conjured up by suggestion by the "chief rabbi" Jehuda Löw ben Bezalel (1513–1609) in his ghetto home in Prague in the year 1592 for the royal alchemist Rudolph II (1576–1612) and his retinue, among them the astronomer royal Tycho Brahe (1546–1601). (And now, by way of comparison, let us add that in 1949 a certain Dahege was deported from Lebanon to the Persian border for the persistent practical jokes which he performed by magical arts. He would, among other things, invite his friends to a feast and entertain them for hours with the finest food and drink while they listened to soft music and skilled story-tellers. It was only on their way home that they heard their empty stomachs rumble.)

What is more, the induction of hypnotic sleep was well known to witches, whether the subject was themselves (auto-hypnosis) or others (heterohypnosis). They used it on themselves in order to withstand torture without pain or suffering (*Maleficium taciturnitatis*),[27] and on others to make them come to some sort of harm or to deliver them from harm as the case might be. One need only look at the picture "The Bewitched Groom" by Hans Baldung Grien to see this (1475–1545)! It was made in 1544 and shows a groom stretched out on the floor in a state of catalepsy. He had been "frozen stiff," so to speak by

---

[27]We find a typical example in one of the *Arabian Nights* stories, where a man was "turned half into stone" by a sorceress. Having bent him to her will, she put a spell on his legs so that they were too stiff to move, but she left the skin of his back sensitive. Every day, at the same hour, she came to the room where she was keeping him and dragged him off ferociously for a smacking to remember. Because he was under her mesmeric control, he did not try to escape from her or even to resist her with any great effort.

fright hypnosis with the sudden shrill shriek of a witch.[28] Fright hypnosis was a predilection, much later, of J. Custodi de Faria (1755–1819), who entered the world of fiction in "The Count of Monte Christo."

Now, it is safe to assume that what was familiar to the "sisters of the left-hand path" was also known to the "brethren of the right-hand path"—except that the latter, true to type, did not use terror but induced sleep by look, word and passes made with the hands (á la Dr. Dodds). They may also have used "conductors" (batons), the traveling-staff of Odin with which he could entrance people, the magic wand of fairy tales.

Finally, the "Philosophus teutonicus" Jakob Böhme (1574–1624) who was very close to the Rosicrucians in time and outlook, fell into a trance on gazing at the "jovial" light reflected by a pewter dish.[29] Nowadays this would be called autohypnosis by the method of fixation.

What is more, the Rosicrucian Order probably had a considerable knowledge of the nerve centers (the planets); which leads us to a consideration of the *hypnogenic zones*, i.e., the nerve points that can be manipulated to induce a trance.

The skin on certain parts of the body is especially responsive to stimulation according to Pitres. The *zones hypnosigènes* described by him are sometimes unilateral and sometimes bilateral. Individuals exist, so it is said,

---

[28]Fairy stories and fables frequently stress the high-pitched cackle of the witch and the charmer's falsetto. Perhaps it is not too far-fetched to recognize in the laugh "He! He! He!" words of bewitchment that could produce a trance. Alexandra David-Neel reports that Tibetan monks given to black magic would expel the soul (or subtle body) through the skull by chanting the syllable "Hick!" which is reputed to create a characteristic opening in the head. In Egypt, according to Sebottendorf, some Whirling Dervishes can levitate while uttering the word *"Hai."* Dr. Arnoldo Krumm-Heller ("Meister Huiracocha," 1865–1916) occasionally intoned the sacred "Om" in a curious high-pitched register he had been taught to use by Papus (Dr. Gérard Encausse 1865–1916) for the purpose of "opening the door" (Dr. H. Fritsche). The term "opening the door" was coined by Hieronymus Cardanus (1501–1576) and means the release of the astral body through a self-induced trance.
[29]See Abraham von Frankenberg, also Martensen's *Jacob Boehme*, tr. T. Rhys Evans. London: Rockliff, 1949.

who may be hypnotized when these areas are mas-
saged. The most noteworthy of the areas are the crown
of the head, the root of the nose, the elbows and the
thumbs. Croq, working in Brussels, later confirmed
Pitres' findings regarding these zones. Indeed he discovered other points, some of which varied from individual to individual. Croq believed that he had
excluded the possibility of suggestion here. According
to Chambard and Laborde gentle scratching of the
skin of the neck induces hypnosis. I myself have met
several people who declared that they could only be
hypnotized if I touched their foreheads. It has often
been said that touching their foreheads will make
many persons strangely sleepy (Purkinje, Spitta). An
Englishman named Catlow used to gently stroke the
forehead to magnetize (Bäumler). Equally, there are
people known to me who, in order to go to sleep more
easily, get their partners to stroke them on other parts
of the body, e.g., the head or the soles of the feet.
Eulenburg maintains that pressure on the cervical ver-
tebra is able to bring about hypnosis and Petersen recognizes the ovaries as hypnogenous zones.[30]

The electrobiologist, Dr. J. Bovee Dodds (USA) in 1850–
1860 produced the "psychological condition" by pressure on
the ulnar nerve and the median nerve.[31] He also placed his
thumbs on his (the subject's) forehead, a little above the root
of the nose (!) and kept them there. In this category come the
so-called corresponding poles with which Cora Tappan obtained good results.

For instance, when she wanted to act on the brain, she
worked on the region around the eyes and at the back
of the neck, for the lungs she operated on the cheeks
and on the back between the shoulder-blades, for the
heart she treated the palms of the hands and for the

---

[30]Dr. Albert Moll *Der Hypnotismus* [*Hypnotism*] (Berlin, 1907, p. 42).
[31]Vairagyananda. *Hinduhypnotismus* [*Hindu Hypnotism*] (Berlin, n.d., Talisman-
bücherei, pp. 26–27).

nervous system she generally treated the soles of the feet.[32]

Mention must also be made in this connection of the Chinese healing method known as acupuncture (in Chinese, Chin kieou), in which key points are pricked with needles made of noble metals. However, I can not enter into further particulars here.[33]

It is entirely possible that acupuncture was known to individual Rosicrucians or people who were intimately connected with them. I am thinking here of Paracelsus (1493–1541), who was not unaware of the Chinese *pulse diagnosis*.[34]

Finally, the *erogenous zones* are places where remote control can be exercised. "Sexual stimulation can occur not only in the sex organs. There are places all over the body which are especially liable to sexual stimulation, the so-called erogenous zones." In addition to the genitals, such places are the skin of the back, the skin inside the upper part of the thigh, the nipples (especially in a woman, which become filled with blood and stiffen, like the male penis), the region around the anus, the lips and the ear lobes. There is hardly anywhere on the skin which is not subject to sexual stimulation in a higher or lower degree. Different people display different reactions in this respect.[35]

Another medical writers says: "Other (distinct points) are the palms of the hands, the bend of the elbow, the hip area, the backbone and the inner surface of the upper thigh." And now a historical example of the use of these zones in practice. Not only was the royal mistress a national institution, but the king's infatuation became a public spectacle. How else could we learn from the annals of history how Louis XV of France (1715–1774) used to kiss Madame Du Barry? Certainly, she made no

---

[32]Riko, op. cit. sub. 10; pp. 32, 33.
[33]Willy Schrödter: *Streifzug ins Ungewohnte* [*A Venture into the Unusual*] (Freiburg i. Br., 1949, pp. 77, 78).
[34]G.W. Surya (1873–1949) *Paracelsus—richtig gesehen* [*Paracelsus Rightly Viewed*] (Lorch i.W., 1928, pp. 189, 190).
[35]Dr. Wilhelm Reich *Sexualerregung und Sexualbefriedigung* [*Sexual Stimulation and Sexual Satisfaction*] (Vienna, 2nd. Ed. 1929, p. 11).

secret of it, and others at court did not refrain from recording it.

Observe the anatomical accuracy with which the courtiers have described these kisses. The king kissed the lady in question in "four places." He planted his kisses over the right eyebrow, then under the left eye, and went on to kiss the root of her nose on the right side and over the corner of her mouth on the left. A complicated ritual. What is more, some of these places are mentioned as stimulatory centers in old Indian sources[36, 37]

Apart from the passes over certain sensitive centers in order to induce magnetic or hypnotic sleep, there are manipulations for the relief or removal of suffering in the waking state.

The Swiss physician, Dr. Otto Naegeli (Ermatingen) published his *Therapie von Neuralgien und Neurosen durch Handgriffe* [*The Treatment of Neuralgias and Neuroses by Manipulation*] in 1894, in which he described "his" discovery and the attendant results in considerable detail. Because this excellent work had been written for the medical profession and was difficult for the layman to understand and apply, the well-known lay-hypnotist Reinhold Gerling (1863–1930) brought out his booklet, *Sofortige Schmerzstillung durch Handgriffe* [*Prompt Relief of Pain by Hand Pressure*] and added the method of cardiac manipulation.[38]

There is not a shadow of doubt that the Rosicrucians knew how to relieve pain by manual methods, for these have come down to us from antiquity and the Fratres made a close study of classical literature in search of this type of material, as has been shown by the "demonic knight," Heinrich Cornelius Agrippa von Nettesheim.

I shall now give, for the reader's benefit, a few of these useful methods:

For a Pain in the Neck
Massage the hollow of the knee.

---

[36]In the *Kamasutra*.
[37]Karl N. Nicolaus, *Die Küsse der Mme. Dubarry* [*The Kisses of Madame Du Barry*].
[38]Verlag Wilhelm Möller (The Wilhelm Möller Press), Oranienburg bei Berlin. The 7th unaltered edition with 10 illustrations.

For Muscular Cramp (in the calf)
When the left leg is affected hold the big toe of the left foot tight in the right hand and vice versa. Rub the cramped muscle with an old steel key or a piece of copper!

For a Fainting Fit
Massage the ring finger of the left hand vigorously (and lay three cold keys over the heart).

For Hiccups
Grip the thumb of the left hand with the right (Augustinus, 354–430). Scratch the palms of the hands! (Blinius, 23–79). The ring fingers are driven, without the other fingers, into the hands. The secret here, is the distraction afforded by this somewhat difficult task.

For Choking
Say when a foreign body is stuck in the glottis or trachea (windpipe): strike the back between the shoulders with the flat of the hand.

When a Person has Stopped Breathing
In small children, where they are holding their breath in a fit of rage for instance, strike the back between the shoulders with the flat of the hand as before.

For a Nose Bleed
Bind up the little finger between the nail and the first joint, making sure you do this to the finger on the same side as the nostril from which the blood is flowing. Bend the ring finger of each hand inward and tie them tight. Bend the little finger of one hand and squeeze it tight with the other hand. If the blood issues from the right nostril then bend and squeeze the little finger of the left hand and *vice versa*.

For Epilepsy, Mental Excitement
Press a piece of cold iron into the hand of the epileptic. The agitated person should catch hold of an earth (a gas or water pipe, central heating unit, metal sheet lamp support, etc.) for a few seconds.

•   •   •

In conclusion, the following notes on *epilepsy* may prove interesting:

As is well known, there are certain sensitive spots on the body, the so-called *hysterogenic zones*, which, when touched, can initiate fits of an epileptic or hysterical type. Dr. Cloziers of Beauvais read a paper on this subject to the Académie des Sciences in January 1895, adding that he had also discovered places where a touch would stop the said attacks. According to him, touching them would control fits of various kinds of different persons. These points were the region over the apex of the heart, the highest part of the palate and perhaps others requiring further investigation.

Tests have already shown that, in a large number of women and young girls, fits of hystero-epilepsy, spontaneous somnambulism, hallucinations and nervous coughing can be cut short by firm pressure applied for approximately thirty seconds to the above-mentioned areas.

As a matter of fact, similar information has already appeared in older works on magnetism and in the communications of clairvoyants. Thus, years ago, the *phreno-mesmerists* produced or removed various phenomena by touching certain areas on the skull. Any competent magnetizer of an earlier generation would have known that epileptic fits, for example, can often be inhibited if the fingers are placed *with the tips bunched together* and applied to a nerve plexus, while the place is breathed on magnetically at the same time. Hence, there is nothing really new in all this.[39]

ADDENDA

1) Dr. Georges Dujardin-Beaumetz (1833–1896), in the course of his studies on the vasomotor disturbances in the skin of an hysterical patient, discovered "hypnogenic, hypnolytic, spasmogenic, spasmolytic and idiogenic points."[40]

2) The above "idiogenic points" bring us to the research findings of Prof. Giuseppe Calligaris, M.D., Professor of

---

[39]Riko, pp. 113–114.
[40]Jacques Marcireau, *Une Histoire de l'Occultisme* [*A History of Occultism*] (Poitiers, 1949, p. 133).

Neuropathology at the University of Rome. "On the surface of the body there are lines, points and hypersensitive patches of skin which are in close communication with our organs (by resonance), with the organs of other persons (consonance), with our own thoughts or with those of other people whether present or absent."[41]

3) Calligari's "meridians" and Chinese acupuncture are matched by the Zone Therapy developed by Fitzgerald and Bowers in 1917.[42] They identified points which produce pain, insensibility and death and those which, by conduction, exert a healing action on remote organs.

4) One of the surest and most infallible signs that a person was a witch, was the so-called *stigma diabolica* or Devil's marks. If one or more spots insensitive to pain were found on the witch's body, this was taken as proof of guilt and further inquiry was thought to be completely unnecessary. According to the old records, such "anaesthetic zones" were quite common. They are, in fact, a characteristic symptom of hysteria.[43]

5) Placing one hand on the forehead and the other on the solar plexus produces a loss of motoricity (capacity for locomotion), with full consciousness.[44]

---

[41]Dr. Albert Leprince *Les Ondes de la Pensée* [*Thought Waves*] (Paris, ca. 1940, p. 59). Calligaris managed it by pushing small metal cylinders onto given fingers in such a way as to stimulate the nerve positions. This must surely remind anyone of the magic rings of the old tales. He also made diseases detectable on the surface of the skin by similar means. See, Leprince, *Les Radiations des Maladies et des Microbes* [*The Radiations of Diseases and of Microbes*] (Paris, 1939).

[42]Op. cit., pp. 63, 64. See also, Fitzgerald, *Zone Therapy* (Columbus, OH, I.W. Long).

[43]Prof. Alfred Lehmann (1858–1921) *Aberglaube und Zauberei* [*Superstition and Magic*] (Stuttgart, 1925, p. 622). Albert de Rochas: *Die Ausscheidung des Empfindungsvermögens* [*Transference of Sensitivity*] (Leipzig, 1909, p. 133). Dr. G.H. Berndt *Das Buch der Wunder* [*The Wonder Book*] (Leipzig, n.d. Vol. I, pp. 299–303).

[44]J.B.L(oubert): *Le Magnetisme et le Somnambulisme devant les Corps Savants, la Cour de Rome et les Théologiens* [*Magnetism and Somnambulism and Scientific Bodies, the Court of Rome and the Theologians*] (Paris, 1844, p. 448; fn 1).

6) I myself know two poles with which it is possible to cause serious cardiac disturbance by placing the two hands on them. There is even the possibility of cardiac arrest.

7) In the region of the navel (the solar plexus or abdominal brain) there are pressure points which, when touched, can evoke sensations of discomfort, anxiety and even mortal terror (own observations).

8) If a metallic point is brought close to the root of the nose, a peculiar, unpleasant tingling is felt. The Manas Chakra is affected (*Manas* is Hindustani for human). Goethe (1749–1832) writes, "I feel as if my whole self is compressed between my eyebrows." In folklore, compressed eyebrows are a mark of astral travelers of all kinds (werewolves, witches, etc.).

9) Because of the significance of the crown of the head as a starting point, and because I have accumulated so much material on the subject of this center, I shall have to set about composing a small monograph on it. Here it is possible to summarize only by saying that it can be manipulated with the naked hand, with the wand, with other conductors and with the pendulum. The latter is not used here as a passive, divinatory or diagnostic instrument but as an active, magical therapeutic one.

10) Gustav Meyrink (1868–1932) represented his Dr. Cinderella as performing an *Asana* (Indian body position) on the pattern of "a small dark bronze . . . excavated from the sands of the Theban desert, the imitation of an Egyptian hieroglyph." This *asana* brought about the projection of the *Ka* (Egyptian for the *Doppelgänger*—a soul or astral body) and induced a partial loss of motoricity even after the *Ka* had returned: "since that time I have been paralyzed; the two sides of my face are different and I drag my left leg." The *asana* consisted in lying in bed and, before going to sleep, raising both arms over the head and lowering the fingers until the nails rested on the crown of the head.[45]

---

[45]"Die Pflanzen des Dr. Cinderella" ("The Plants of Dr. Cinderella") in *Des deutschen Spiessers Wunderhorn* [*The German Duffer's Story Book*] (Leipzig, 1948, p. 233 ff).

11) The *asana* used by "Seelchen" to travel in his astral body seems to have been more harmless: "When I lie down, I stretch myself out to my fullest extent, then push my hands under my hair,[46] and then I venture in spirit into the land of my childhood. I must think of nothing else, I must will strongly, it is essential for me to have eaten sparingly[47] and I must keep quite still."[48] "Seelchen" is the main character in Agnes Günther's (1863–1911) novel *Die Heilige und ihr Narr* [*The Saint and her Fool*] (1913). According to Meyer, "her emotionally overcharged novel was one of the biggest best sellers and, in 1929, had run through 112 editions."

12) The Indian Icvaracharya, Bramachari, was aware that, "certain places in the body are very sensitive to given manipulations, especially in the female sex. These places are the navel, the heart, the adam's apple, the root of the nose, the nape of the neck and the temples. Pressure on various parts of the vertebral column is often very effective."[49]

In regard to "pressure at the root of the nose," the Indian magnetizer revealed this: "Press steadily and somewhat vigorously—without however causing any pain—at the root of the nails of the index and middle fingers of the two hands of your subject, who must keep his eyes closed in the meantime. This pressure will in itself be sufficient to induce sleep in the very sensitive."[50]

13) By placing the thumb or index finger of the right hand in the *pit of the throat*,[51] it is possible to remove a persistent mucus

---

[46]The ominous "crown" itself!

[47]If "Eating and drinking keep body and soul together," abstention from food (= fasting) must sever them.

[48]G.W. Surya: *Das Okkulte in Agnes Günther Die Heilige und ihr Narr* [*The Occult Implications in Agnes Günther's* book, *The Saint and the Fool*] (Lorch i. Württ., 1929, p. 96).

[49]*Magnétisme hindou* (Paris, Durville, n.d. p. 17).

[50]Op. cit., No. 48, pp. 17–18.

[51]The term "pit of the throat" is used for want of a more precise designation; what is intended here is the hollow formed at the beginning of the neck where the trachea descends behind the collar bone. In other words it is found by following the contours of the Adam's apple over the thyroid gland until one reaches the breast bone. This is the location of the *Vishuda chakra*, which has its physical counterpart in the pharyngeal plexus. Pantañjali has the following

obstruction caused by excessive smoking on the previous day (author's own observation).

14) As far as I can tell, Cora Tapan's "corresponding poles" are identical with the "Head's Zones" discovered by the English mental specialist, Professor Head, M.D., at the turn of the present century. According to him, the internal organs are linked with various parts of the head by certain nerves. Or, to put it another way, *the Head's Zones are projection areas of the internal organs.*

This is the basis of the use of the *Chiropa Krallenkam*—the equivalent of the scraper used at the baths by the ancient Greeks (the xystra)—to stimulate the capillaries.

More information is obtainable from Wilhelm Wild, Heifelberg. Apart from Head, Morell Mackenzie showed that diseases of the most various sorts act through the nervous system to cause pain in definite skin and muscle zones. Prof. Friedrich Dittmar utilized this fact to create a subtle method of diagnosis: "The investigation of reflector and painful disease signs."

15) In Japan, forceps are no longer used for tooth extraction. The fingers are used instead. This requires considerable strength which has to be developed by special exercises from childhood onward. The father dentist gives his young hopeful a little board to play with in which there are small holes with tooth-sized pegs stuck in them. These wooden pegs are driven in more and more firmly over the years. But this is not the main point, our interest lies in the fact that, although painless dentistry is the rule in Japan, the dentists there (at least those of the older generation) operate without chemical anesthetics; they use a certain grip in which the hand exerts a pressure on one of the cranial nerves and in this way blocks, with complete reliability, any sense of pain.

16) My friend Dr. Busse, who is a qualified dentist, informed me on May 8, 1952 that "an epileptic fit can be immediately arrested by the simple firm grip between the thumbs and index fingers."

---

to say of it in his Yoga sutra (III 37) "By concentrating his mind upon the nerve center in the pit of the throat, the ascetic is able to overcome hunger and thirst."

17) An especially important treatment point is the small bone called luz, which is so often mentioned by Rosicrucians, Hermeticists and Qabalists. However, it needs further investigation.[52]

18) Another, and as yet unsolved, secret is the so-called "*La Main d'Or*" (the Golden Hand). Perhaps what is meant is a hand which has been energized by certain training (*á la* Turkish Masonry). Gold is a synonym for the sun. Ancient Egyptian hypnotists spoke of the "Sun finger." The Romans used to call the index finger *medicus* (i.e. doctor)! The *Main d'Or* was a band of brigands in the South of France during the 17th century who were able to throw their victims into a deep sleep with a touch of their hands as soon as they had surprised them. (*Kiesers Archiv*: Leipzig, 1820, Vol. VI; Part 1, p. 168). Similar secrets were rumored to be in the possession of the *Mersener Bockreiter* of the Lower Rhine.

---

[52]The small bone called luz has not been identified to everyone's satisfaction. It is a Qabalistic grip which was used on it and it is generally assumed to be the coracoid process of the breastbone.

MAKING GOLD

> But now concerning (and chiefly in this our age) the
> ungodly and accursed "gold-making". . . . We there-
> fore do, by these presents, publicly testify that the true
> philosophers are far of another mind, esteeming little
> the making of gold, which is but a parergon; etc.
>
> —*Fama*

Making gold was nothing more than a parergon (incidental
matter) as far as the Rosicrucians were concerned; God was
their ERGON (main consideration), as we see in the sequel to
the above-quoted statement:

> And we say with our loving Father R.C.C. Phy: aurum
> nisi quantum aurum, for unto them the whole nature
> is detected: he doth not rejoice that he can make gold,
> and that, as saith Christ himself, the devils are obedient
> unto him, but is glad that he seeth the heavens open
> and the angels of God ascending and descending, and
> his name written in the book of life.[1]

In 1923, a booklet was published at Hattenheim (Rheingau)
entitled "Gold Making." The author was P.R. Eichelter (Ragnit
bei Graz). The argument of the booklet was this:

> If we accept the "historical" evidence as incontrover-
> tible that a prince of the Cherusci called HERMANN

---

[1] *Fama Fraternitas, etc.* ed. Dr. Ferd. Maack, (1861–1930) in the compilation,
Geheime Wissenschaften, Vol. I (Berlin, 1922, 3rd edition), p. 58.

fought the Varus battle in the Teutoburg Forest; that a certain GUTENBERG invented printing and that a "heretic" Augustinian monk called Martin LUTHER nailed his famous 95 theses to the gate of the castle church in Wittenberg; then it is an unassailable fact, on the basis of information *of equal validity*, that since the beginning of the 17th century there have been *at least seven people who knew how to make a preparation by means of which base metals could be transmuted into the purest gold!*

Eichelter closes with an example which he has taken from the *Geschichte der Alchemie* [*The Story of Alchemy*] by Prof. Karl Christoph Schmieder. However, I shall not hand out stale news here, but shall try to show that in comparatively recent times gold making has been done by genuine alchemists (not swindlers).

1) The butcher, Johann Reichardt, who was born January 4, 1897, went on his travels after serving his apprenticeship and, at age 22, set up on his own account, beginning, at that time, a practice in natural healing, after spending years poring over old herbals and spellbooks. He received a message at a spiritist seance telling him to dig at the old city wall. There, in company with his friend, Gräfe, he discovered a receptacle from the time of the Thirty Years' War and, inside it, a set of handwritten instructions, a phial of oil and a black and a white powder.[2]

Tests were then performed, in the presence of witnesses, at his home dispensary and at civic schools, all of which were eventually successful. Experiments in Nuremberg and Berlin followed. In May 1930, it was reported that half a pound of genuine gold was obtained on one occasion. "Not all tests were *equally* positive, but gold was found eventually *on each occasion.*"[3]

---

[2]Edward Kelly (1555–1597) found a book written in the old Welsh language, when staying at an inn in Wales and, with the book, two ivory spheres, one containing a white and the other a red powder. His find enabled him to carry out the transmutation of metals with Dr. John Dee (1527–1608) on and after the year 1582. Karl Kiesewetter: *John Dee, etc.* (Leipzig, 1893). Gustav Meyrink: *Der Engel vom westlichen Fenster* [*The Angel of the Western Window*] (Bremen, 1927). Schmieder: op. cit., p. 302 ff.

[3]"Der Goldmacher" ("The Gold-maker") in *Astrale Warte* [*The Astral Watchtower*] (Memmingen, August, 1930, p. 168 ff).

It was verified, on further enquiry in G. . . . (southern Germany) and in a statement made to me on July 7, 1950, that:

> Mr. Reichardt was really successful in making gold by alchemical means during the years 1925–1935. In 1929–1930, the press all over Germany reported his sensational experiments, which were corroborated by scientific experts.

Through a chain of circumstances such as often frustrates us when dealing with "occult" matters, I was unable to accept an invitation to visit Mr. Reichardt.

But, anyway, I wonder whether, if I had been able to call on him, I should have been able to do anything more than to confirm the facts of the case. Probably Mr. R. did not know the composition of the materials, in which case he would have been *unable* to tell me anything useful; but, even if he did know what it was, he would not have been *free* to reveal it, if tradition is anything to go by! *Therefore*, I have suppressed his name here.

In any case, in this age of radium (which turns into lead after losing helium, etc.) and atomic fission, the transmutation of metals can no longer be disputed. As my extremely knowledgable hermetic friend, "AME" of Hamburg, wrote to me July 1, 1946, as follows:

> Atomic fission has brought about a revival of the long-dead art of alchemy and it is in splitting the atom that the promising future of alchemy lies in great measure. Atomic analysis and synthesis is the alpha and omega of the whole hermetic art. Official chemistry will resurrect the memory of ancient alchemy and confer upon it an honorary degree! The natural process will be accelerated in the laboratory, in the same way as plant growth and the formation of human bodies at spiritist seances is a speeding up of what happens by slow organic action in nature.

2) The well-known psychic researcher G.W. Surya (Demeter Georgiewitz Weitzer, 1873–1949), a man whose sincerity places him beyond suspicion, made known in a letter dated May 27, 1940, and written to our mutual friend Ernst Alt (1889–1945) what I can now reveal since they are sadly no longer with us:

Before the World War, that is to say before 1914, I
and a chemist in S. . . . who was at that time assistant
at the Chemical Institute of the University, repeatedly
transmuted Hg (mercury) into sol (= the sun in an
alchemical sense, i.e., gold) *in three different ways*. On
one occasion we succeeded in making a transmutation
of 40 grams. It was a really fine gold made out of
mercury! The only trouble was that it was still a little
too expensive to make commercially. I have also known
for some time a man in Germany who has artificially
made much larger amounts of Au (gold), by trans-
muting lead into sol. Only his sol (gold) had the dis-
advantage of being unable to withstand the action of
fire on many occasions, so that on being heated
strongly it changed back into lead again. Unfortunately, I lost my fortune during the war and am no
longer able to perform the fairly costly and, at times,
lengthy experiments. And, besides, anyone who tried
to fit out a laboratory for such a purpose would be
watched so closely nowadays.[4]

Surya further related in a conversation with assistant
schoolmaster Alt, at Salzburg on July 20 and 22, 1940: "I have
prepared Sol (gold) on three occasions. My attempts cost RM
20,000. The third time we obtained the 40 grams with the help
of liquid air and were paid the equivalent in ordinary fine gold!

3) The "Reviver of Occult Medicine"—himself a gold-maker—
informed us that Will-Erich Peuckert[5] had a meeting with an

---

[4]Document from my collection, "Correspondence with Cognoscenti" (Briefwechsel mit Wissenden).
[5]Will-Erich Peuckert (born in 1895), Silesian poet and scholar. He was the
author of, among other works, *Die Rosenkreuzer* [*The Rosicrucians*] (Jena, 1928),
Pansophie [Jena, 1930], *Von schwarzer und weisser Magie* [*Black and White Magic*]
(Berlin, n.d.). Peuckert also spent three summers panning gold in the Iser-
gebirge, nine hundred meters high among the mountain ridges. He soon
learned to trust the information given in the old *Walenbücher*. (*Zauber der
Steine* [*Magic of the Rocks*] (Leipzig, 1936, p. 8 ff).

alchemist. Surya wrote September 19, 1942, to Ernst Alt[6] to the following effect:

> Finally, I have come across the article (pasted into a book unfortunately) by Will-Erich Peuckert: *The Last Alchemist*, a remarkable event which took place in 1923; it was published in the "Münchener Neuesten Nachrichten" (No. 6, Friday, January 7, 1927). According to this article, Peuckert was at the apartment of a certain Dr. Jägerloh, in Breslau, between the hours of eleven and twelve, and witnessed the transmutation of lead into gold with a minute amount of shiny-grey and greasy-looking powder. The quantity of gold obtained was not very great, only about 10 grams. A twentieth of a gram of the "greasy, shiny-grey powder" was employed. Hence the latter had a transmuting power of 1 : 200. In order to be quite sure that he was not the victim of a conjuring trick, Peuckert provided the crucible, lead, coal, and glass vessels and other necessities; items which he had himself purchased for the experiment. All that Jägerloh did was to hand him 1/20 gram of the transmuting powder, which Peuckert himself threw into the molten lead. The lead then gradually congealed and finally turned into gold. Unfortunately, Jägerloh died a few years after this transmutation, so Peuckert informs us. He learned from a woman who occupied the same house as Jägerloh that, before his death, the latter had destroyed all his glassware and other vessels and his furnace, and had burned his books.

4) Around 1890 there was a mystic school, well-known in informed circles, sited in Darmstadt, which was led by an in other respects uneducated and almost illiterate weaver called Mailänder.[7] Those who belonged to it included, among others, Karl

---

[6]From my Collection "Briefwechsel mit Wissenden" ["Correspondence with Cognoscenti"].

[7]Karl Weinfurter: *Der brennende Busch* [*The Burning Bush*] (Lorch, 1930, pp. 206, 207). Franz Dornseiff: *Das Alphabet in Mystik und Magie* [*The Alphabet in Mysticism and Magic*] (Leipzig, 1922, pp. 152, 153).

Weinfurter (died 1942), Gustav Meyrink (1868–1932; a student there from October, 1892); Dr. Franz Hartmann (1838–1912); Helena Petrovna Blavatsky (1831–1891), the Indian Babij and Chief of the Austrian General Staff, Schemua (a friend of G.W. Surya). So Mailänder must have been a rather unusual man.

I shall now recapitulate from letters[8] written by Meyrink, Surya and "Baron Müller," the following details, so that they can be preserved in print and gain wider publicity:

On his return from a prolonged sojourn in India, Dr. Franz Hartmann landed in Naples in 1889. He was able to recognize Christian mystics in quite humble people (Mailänder among them) and practiced with them. Mailänder used the so-called "Kerning exercises" by which he professed to be able to understand the language of the animals.

However, we are interested in someone else who belonged to this group, one P., a Rosicrucian. He was named Prestel and had the ability to convert base metals into noble ones.

Mailänder later came to Germany in an ox-wagon and obtained a position as a weaver near Darmstadt, where he was presented with a small house and grounds by one of his female pupils (a rich aristocrat).

"This man Mailänder," said Meyrink, stressing that the latter had never told a lie, "saw one winter's day in. . . . near the Church of the Holy Cross, the snow stained as red as blood in a certain place, and declared that an adept of the Middle Ages (Paracelsus, 1493–1541) had buried some of the red tincture and that the red coloration in the snow had been caused by emanations from this tincture." The "blood" was impressed at five places around the Church and many others saw it besides Mailänder.

Now Prestel was one of those who came to Germany. He was a nomadic and mysterious old man. He was a master joiner by profession, but could produce magical phantismagoria, etc. In his possession there was a bottle containing a grey salt. According to him, it was the *unfinished* elixir of life. He always kept it near the warm kitchen stove. One day a real blue serpent appeared in the bottle and Prestel said, "I am going to die." He

---

[8]The Collection, "Briefwechsel mit Wissenden" (Correspondence with Cognoscenti).

did die, too. The elixir was never perfected. After his death, it was passed on to a certain Gabele in Darmstadt who became his brother-in-law and, today, this unfinished product is in one of the cities of southern Germany.

Writing of Prestel, Dr. Franz Hartmann[9] said: "Prestel also had the power[10] to transmute base metals into noble ones and I possess some examples of this."

Surya saw one of these examples of alchemy, "an apparently gold-metal cross in the form of the German Cross but a third smaller, but it was at least a finger thick and really solid. "Look," said Hartmann to him, "this cross is made of alchemically manufactured metal, yet it is neither silver or gold but an *intermediate substance*[11] halfway between the two. I have satisfied myself that it is a noble metal. I have carried it about with me for many years on my travels, even in India[12] and Ceylon, and I have noticed that all base metals and even silver itself lose their brilliance, but this cross, which was given to me by a genuine Rosicrucian, has never tarnished."[13]

At this point, Dr. Franz Hartmann undid a small screw at the end of the cross. "Here in this hole," he said, "there is a

---

[9]*Lotusblüten [Lotus Flowers]* (1900, p. 154).

[10]This remark sounds as if transmutations were carried out with mental or spiritual powers alone, not with the "unfinished salt."

[11]One can make only half-finished products with half-finished "fluid stone of the wise" (*Tinctura Physicorum*)! By the way, even August Strindberg (1859–1922) once made a halfway metal—from copper. It was no longer copper but it was still not gold! According to Privy Councillor, Prof. Karl Ludwig Schleich (1859–1922) in *Besonnte Vergangenheit [The Sunny Past]* (Berlin, 1930, p. 267), it was examined by Professor Hans Landolt. He kept this transitional metal to the end, saying, "It is not without emotion that I can look at this piece of gold tinsel of Strindberg's which I have in my possession."

[12]This seems to show that Hartmann must have known Prestel *before* his return to Italy from India if we are to take it that the little cross had been "transmuted" (or perhaps it would be preferable to say "alchemically treated") by the latter.

[13]Sinbad (Korv. Kap. Frdr. Schwickert, 1855–1930): *Das Lebenselixier [The Elixir of Life]* (Leipzig, 1923; pp. 13, 14). However, the foreword, in which this episode is related, relies on Surya, "a man who is completely trustworthy" (Sebottendorf). There were also "certain experiments shown to Sinbad before the World War and *this is where* he got the information for what he has written" (Surya in a letter to assistant schoolmaster Ernst Alt dated May 27, 1940).

drop of the elixir of life. Just smell it!" I did so and a sweet, fine vanilla-like odor floated toward me. I have never been able to forget this smell. This happened and was seen and smelled in Algund near Merano in the year of Our Lord 1910!

Naturally enough, we have made enquiries as to the whereabouts of the cross with the elixir of life and received the following answer from "Solarius" on March 17, 1942:

> I very much regret to say that I do not know what became of *the golden cross* owned by Hartmann in which was contained a drop of the true *elixir of life*, although at the time (1910) when Hartmann showed the cross to me, the liquid had long since dried up. There was just this wonderful aroma as of violets which streamed out of the hollow which had been bored in the cross as soon as Hartman took out the screw which closed it. I suspect that this golden cross was inherited either by Miss Nandine von Rantzau, who remained with Hartmann until his death or by his sister, the Countess Sperdi.[14]

DISCUSSION

> Everything trusts in
> Everything thrusts after
> Gold . . .
>
> —Goethe, *Faust*

"Everything that happens to us is—so to speak—a continuous alchemy" (Schelling, 1775–1854).

"And, anyway, what is so very marvelous about changing lead or mercury into gold with the help of a chemical preparation? Is it not equally wonderful that the juices secreted by our stomachs, livers and intestines convert strong cheese into muscle, bones, nerves and brains, and is not each fruit-grower an "alchemist" when, by grafting, he compels a simple crabapple

---

[14]From my private collection "Briefwechsel mit Wissenden" ("Correspondence with Cognoscenti").

to bear fine dessert fruit?" (Eichelter, *op. cit.* p. 8). To put the record straight, we should remark that it is not the fruit-grower but the tree that is the alchemist; indeed, *every* plant is an alchemist. Photosynthesis will produce materials which were not in the plant, the soil, or the air originally.

"Take a pot of earth and confirm, by prior chemical analysis, that there is no lithium in the earth. Now sow the pot with tobacco seeds and, when the tobacco plants are grown, burn them. Their ashes will be found to contain sufficient lithium. But from where does it come?" (Surya).

As long ago as 1937, uranium was bombarded with neutrons to produce trans-uranium; this then decayed into eka-rhenium then into eka-platinum and, eventually, in 2½ hours, "eka-gold" was brought into being. The Italian scientist, Fermi, initiated the tests, which were continued by Professors Hahn and Meitner.

However, the old alchemists accomplished this transmutation without huge electrical equipment. What we have to do is to discover their secret. The ancients had techniques of metalworking which have been lost to us. For example, in Delhi there stands a 6,000 kg iron pillar dating back to 350 B.C. made of rustless wrought iron. The secret of this rustproof iron has not been solved even today. In 1942 we found blocks 3 meters high in the old Aztec city of Tectohua, and these blocks were hard as iron, yet so light that a 10-year-old child could lift them without difficulty. Experts believe that this "super duraluminium" is an alloy of iron and clay, and they believe that this technique, which was lost when the Spaniards conquered Mexico, has not yet been recovered.

How strange it is that with no knowledge of atomic weights, the alchemists usually started with mercury as their prime matter (projection base), which, especially in its isotopes, has an atomic weight so near to that of gold!

A challenging remark put forward by Therese Schiffner holds good here: "Don't you think it is extremely significant that the old research workers, who called themselves alchemists and 'theosophists' came so close, by the exercise of their intuition and without all the apparatus available to us today, to the substance of current findings and theories?" (*Blutzauber* [*Blood Magic*] Leipzig, 1923, p. 26).

I think that I have been able to show, in the accounts given earlier, that gold has been made by alchemical means (that is to say, chemically, and not physically with very powerful equipment).

Even people who refuse to place any credence in these accounts will no longer be able to deny, in view of the alchemical powers of plants described, the possibility of the transmutation of base metals into noble ones. My readers will hardly be expecting me to present them with a recipe for manufacturing gold. Of course, I have none to offer and, even if I had, I should certainly be careful not to disclose it—for reasons uniformly stated by the adepts in their writings.

Thus the *Uralte Ritterkrieg* [*Ancient Knightly Combat*] says: "The wise man knows well enough the mischief and evil which can arise in human life and society when the knowledge of this great secret is disclosed to the ungodly; therefore he always treats it with much caution and speaks or writes in riddles which are only to be solved by those whose work and industry God pleases to bless."

Also, Lord Lytton (1803–1873) makes the Chaldean adept, Mejnour, say in *Zanoni*: "Dost thou think that I would give to the mere pupil, whose qualities are not yet tried, powers that might change the face of the social world?" (*Book The Fourth*, chapter 5).

Finally, there is a curious phenomenon which, strictly speaking, cannot be explained except on an "occult" basis: World-famous chemists such as Hermann Kopp (1817–1892) and Edmund von Lippmann (1857–??) have spent a large part of their lives writing histories of alchemy in order to disprove the reality of gold-making. And yet, according to their training and knowledge, it is only nonsense anyway! One wonders why all this expenditure of energy?

In my opinion there can be only one explanation lying in the deep psychological layers of the mind. In other words, they are driven by a karmic, subconscious belief in the actuality of the transmutation of metals. It is as if they were alchemists in a previous existence!

THE ELIXIR OF LIFE

Not as people say: let alchemy make gold and silver!
This is the task: let us make the ARCANA and use it
to cure diseases!

—Paracelsus
Paragranum, Tract. III

Nothing is nearer related to the human body than the
UNIVERSAL.

—Brotoffer
Elucidarius Major, 1517

Sensible people will not imagine that they are going to be offered a perfect recipe for the *elixir of life* which can be used
without further ado. We would have to be very foolish to expect
any such thing! Nevertheless, most readers will want to learn
something new, regarding the *effects* of regular use of the elixir
and the *prime material* from which it is made.

In general, the elixir of life is seen only as the *absolute,
radical tonic* which will give freedom from all diseases (also
known by the Greek word, *Panacea*, or "heal all"), the guarantee
against falling ill again, immunity of the body which will persist
into an exceptionally great age.

In individual cases (according to the dosage employed), the
Tinctura Physicorum not only preserves the body, during a very
long life, in the same physical condition as that in which it was
in when the elixir was taken, but will make it younger by a
process of rejuvenation.

All three kingdoms—the mineral, plant, and animal kingdoms—and even the air kingdom, are taken or indicated as the case may be.[1] The animal kingdom includes the human kingdom.

And now, as promised, we will demonstrate something which will come as a revelation to many; namely that the "Universal Tincture" not only made gold and bestowed health but imparted spiritual powers. That is to say, it increased the human senses until they became super-sensitive or clairvoyant, clairaudient, clairminded, and the astral body—the basis of every occult phenomenon—gained ascendancy over the physical body and became competent to act on its own account (astral travel, the Indian, *mayavirupa*).

This was called the *Glorification of the body of salt*. One of the things used for the prime material was the atmospheric air! However the following points were also made to elucidate its nature:

1) *The elixir of life is the precursor of the "Stone of the Wise"* (Latin: *Lapis Philosophorum*). It is, in a fluid (and so less concentrated and less productive) form, what "our Stone" is in a fixed form.

2) *The "Stone" is a maximum of "Life Force" bound to a minimum of matter* (Papus [Dr. Gérard Encausse] 1865–1916).

3) The "Natural Remedy" resembles a sponge to a certain extent, and it absorbs the Life Force from the fourth state of aggregation (the etheric or radiant) through the third (the gaseous) into the second (the liquid, that is to say the elixir) and finally into the first (the solid, or "ER" itself) by a process of transmutation and condensation, and thus stores it up or accumulates it.

---

[1]As a matter of interest: Among the "human" materials taken were blood, as a "special juice" and later "semen virile" as an even more concentrated life essence, for 1 gram of sperm is the equivalent of 70 grams of the "Red Tincture." (See the *Berlinische Monatsschrift* for June 1786!) These facts are taken from Eberhard Buchner's *Medien, Hexen und Geisterseher* [*Mediums, Witches and Spirit-Mongers*] (Albert Langen, Munich, 1926; para. 237 on p. 351).

4) To put it in a nutshell: *The Elixir is the liquidized etheric Life Force and the Stone is the solidified etheric Life Force, stored up in a minimum quantity of fluid or solid as the case may be.*

5) Taking the Elixir in homoeopathic doses in natural wine (once a day for from 3 to 30 days) strengthens the *Archaeus* described by Paracelsus and necessarily imparts the "Force" to the deficient organs, making any diagnosis redundant.

And so the hermeticist James Butler could say to J.B. van Helmont (1577–1644) at Vilvoorden near Brussels in 1617: "My dear Friend, if he had not reached the stage where he could cure any type of disease whatever with a single remedy, he would remain a tyro still however old he might be."

6) The *Archaeus* (i.e., Regulator or Force Distributor) is located in the brain; apparently it is the *pineal gland* (epiphysis), in which Renatus Cartesius (René Descartes, 1596–1650) saw the seat of the soul. In addition to being the mathematician who invented analytical geometry, this French philosopher was also a Rosi-crucian!

The body's power supply, it can be said, is a brain-electrical matter and not a heart-motoric one!

> It would be silly to believe that the universal remedy heals broken bones, destroyed organs or the like. Since it contains that vital power which is the same in all three kingdoms of nature, it needs only a little of this power to impart to those patients who have a defi-ciency; simply introducing into the body's metabolism a solar activity (*activité solaire*) which will restore energy to the brain and the regulatory organs governing phys-ical and chemical life. All it is is a strengthening agent, a mighty tonic. (René Schwaeblé. *Alchimie simplifiée* [*Simplified Alchemy*] Paris, n.d., p. 37.)

7) *In the "Life Force" we have Baron Karl von Reichenbach's (1788–1869) OD, which belongs to the fourth state of matter.*

8) The Indians came to the conclusion, thousands of years ago, that it was not the air as such which supported our life, but the "ethereal or super-air" contained in it, to which they gave the name *Prana*. This acts on the nervous system (and therefore

on the brain!), and when it is absorbed in excess of requirements occult powers are stimulated into activity (the *siddhis*). Thus the yogi attains by physiological exercises (breathing exercises) what the hermeticists sought by chemical means!

9) Dr. Manfred Curry[2] has, in recent years, identified a vital ingredient in the air, which he calls "Aran," an ingredient which is essential for organic life. In my opinion, this is no more than the time-honored *Prana*!

Having now made a preliminary survey, we can investigate the following:

a) What did the ancients understand by Od/Prana/Aran?

b) What *cerebral* effects did they ascribe to its use in liquefied form?

c) What method did they employ in order to extract the "nature of air" or "air mother" from ordinary air and to condense it into "Primeval Force Elixir"?

The Hermetic authors who have dealt with Prana, Od, or Aran are:

1) Michael Sendivogius (Sensophax, 1566–1646) said in *Novum Lumen Chymicum* [*The New Light of Chemistry*] (1624): "Est spiritus in aere qui coagulatus melior est quam universa terra" [There is a spirit in the air which, when coagulated, is better than the whole earth].

2) George von Welling wrote in his *Opus mago-caballisticum* [*Mago-caballistic work*], Homburg v.d.H., 1735, II, para. 42,

---

[2]Dr. Manfred Curry (born December 11, 1899) comes from Boston (USA) and lives in Ammersee. He has written a two-volume work called *Bioklimatik* [*Bioclimatics*] and a single-volume work called *Schlüssel zum Leben* [*The Key to Life*] on his researches (published by the Schweiz. Druck- und Verlagshaus, Zürich). His findings were originally mentioned in the German press at the end of 1949. Aran is a fairly fixed ozone and can be detected in the "Aran apparatus" devised by Curry and built by Siemens. It "determines the oxidation value of the air." Curry has developed a new system of human types out of the response of the individual to Aran!

p. 191: "No one who has seen the true light can gainsay that this angels' food, which strengthens and preserves the inner man, is contained and concealed in all bodies including elementary bodies, and therefore in the air, food and drink we enjoy."

3) Onuphrius de Marsciano commented in *Sendschreiben [Correspondence]* Para. 35 (Vienna, 1744): "Also in the air we inhale, there is this hidden nourishment . . . yet it is diffused in such rarefied amounts and mixed with humors, vapors and water, etc." The old Hermeticists also identified this "super air" with the *solar ether* (Prof. Osk. Korschelt, 1880), "sun *gold*," "astral *gold*," the fire from heaven or gold which flows from heaven (The Golden Fleece).[3]

4) *Uralter Ritterkrieg [Time-Honored Knightly Combat]* (Leipzig, 1604): "We unceasingly take this *astral gold* into us with our breath; its astral particles penetrate our bodies; what is more, they are exhaled from the latter without intermission."[4]

5) Peter Steiner says, in *Von der Universal-Materie [The Universal Matter]*: "The great, transcendentally perfect Stone of the Wise is none other than a pure, concentrated and congealed heavenly fire."

6) Fictuld (Baron von Meinstoof): *Aureum Vellus (The Golden Fleece)* 1747: "If we play with the meaning of the word ("Golden Fleece"), it becomes fluid or liquid gold, which flows down from heaven—a solar, astral, fiery substance which reduces to actual, essential things, giving to them all life and growth because it is their seed and soul."[5]

---

[3]Trans. note: The play on words between the German "Vlies" and "fliesst" meaning "fleece" and "flows" respectively, is peculiar to German.
[4]Very good: "Od vapor."
[5]Hence the "Stone" is the "Golden Fleece" (Latin *Aureum Vellus*) in the Greek story of Jason. It was represented in the highest Spanish Order of the same name, instituted by Duke Philipp III of Burgundy on January 10, 1429. This is the highest and most ancient European order of chivalry. Karl der Kühne [Charles the Bold] (1433–1477), bore this golden fleece, according to his own declaration, as possessor of the "Godly science" (of the stone), an attainment he owed to "true friends." Unfortunately, he died a violent death.

Finally, it should be mentioned that *potable gold* is a misleading name for the elixir of life. It is a translation of the equally erroneous Latin term *Aurum potabile*. The expression is really derived from the Hebrew word[6] *Aor* (= light) and the Latin word "potabile" (= drinkable), and therefore means "drinkable light" or "drink made of light."

Orpheus (1400 B.C.) derived the mysteries which have taken his name from this "congealed sunlight."

> The name Orpheus is the Greek form of the Phoenician Arpha, and is constructed from the words *AOR* = light and *ROPHAE* = healing; hence it signifies one who heals by means of light, through the drinkable light, *Aor*, *Aur* or *Aurum potabile* (potable gold).[7]

What do hermetic authors have to say about the cerebral effects brought about by using the elixir of life? The following list provides a brief explanation.

1) John of Padua, *Witness*: "And the remedy wonderfully improves the mind of man."

2) *Microcosmisches Vorspiel* [*Microcosmic Prelude*] (1720): "When the tincture will no longer work, the end of life is near. But since you know God, in Christ Jesus, as one friend knows another, you will not tremble at the gentle sleep of death free from infirmity, but will be joyous and confident of entering *the distantly viewed land of the living*."[8]

3) Josaphat Friedrich Hautnorton Sneci[9] said in his *Tractat vom philosophischen Salz* (1st edition, 1656), chapter VIII: "Von der Wunderkraft unseres Salzwassersteins" [*Treatise on the Philo-*

---

[6]Trans. note: The German original says, by mistake, that "Aor" is a Greek word.

[7]Max Retsclag: *Die Alchimie und ihr grosses Meisterwerk* [*Alchemy and its Great Masterwork*] (Leipzig, 1934, p. 160).

[8]"I had fainted, unless I had believed to see the goodness of the Lord in the land of the living" (Psalm 27, v. 13).

[9]The son-in-law of Sendivogius, in Livonia. *Hermaphroditisch Sonn- und Mondskind* [*The Hermaphrodite Sun and Moon Child*] (Mainz, 1752). Trans. note: Sendivogius married Seton's widow, according to Mackay, quoting Lenglet du Fresnoy, in *Popular Delusions*. London, G. Routledge & Co., 1841.

sophical Salt: chapter on "The marvelous power of our salt-water stone"]: "Its use is 1) the knowledge. . . . of his own glorious future state."

4) The Cosmopolite, Alexander Setonius Scotus (died January, 1604) said: ". . . and I behold the glory of our future life with my eyes and rejoice over it."

5) Dr. Thomas Vaughan (*Eugenius Philalethes*) wrote in *Lumen de Lumine* (1651): "I have to my reward a light that will not leave me."[10] (A.E. Waite's translation, p. 305 of the collected works.)

6) Dr. Edmund Dickinson wrote a book called *Chrysopoeia, sive quinta essentia Philosophorum* [*Gold-making, or the quintessence of the Philosophers*], which was published at Oxford in 1686, containing an open letter written by a French adept, Theodor Mundanus, with the following remarks on the Rosicrucians among others: "And they treasure the power of the Elixir most of all because— when used with care—it imparts a wonderful sharpness to the spirit." Dickinson was personal physician to King Charles II of England (1660–1685); Mundanus was a gentleman of high rank, wide culture and great wealth; the two were friends from their university days.

7) Edward Bulwer, Lord Lytton (1803–1873) wrote in *Zanoni* (1842, Book The Fourth, chapter 4): "Because the very elixir that pours a more glorious life into the frame, so sharpens the senses that those larvae of the air become to thee audible and apparent. . . ." Lord Lytton was a high grade initiate; a member of the "Hermetic Lodge" at Alexandria, and a practicing magician. His novel, *Zanoni*—"the much-loved work of his maturity"—was, he said, "a novel, yet more than an ordinary romance." In other words, it is partly autobiographical: hence, we cannot ignore his opinion on the elixir.

---

[10]What he means is the compass of the "inner light" (John 14:17). Many perceive this guide as an "inner word." Cf. Johannes Tennhardt (1661–1720), *Das innere Wort* [*The Inner Word*] 1712! We read of King Saul (1030–1010 B.C.) that the Lord no longer answered him by the "Lights" (I Samuel 23:6). The reference is to the High Priest's breastplate with the divinatory stones, the Urim and Thummim, in all probability.

What did the hermetic authors have to say about the extraction of the elixir of life from the air? In 1459, A. Christian Rosencreutz (1378–1484) was nominated "Knight of the Golden Stone" (Latin: *Eques Aurei Lapidis*). This means that he had been initiated, had performed the "Great Work" (Latin: *Magnum Opus*) and had made the "Masterpiece" (Latin: *Magisterium*)—the gold stone, which also promotes health and spiritual powers!

And so we turn to *Chymische Hochzeit Christiani Rosencreutz, Ao. 1459* [*The Chemical Marriage of Christian Rosencreutz*, 1459], which actually went to press at Strasburg in 1616 for the first time. There is certainly no sound reason for the assumption that Johann Valentin Andreae, the "Württemberg clergyman (1586–1654), was simply writing an occult "romance" here.[11]

On the contrary, repeated and thorough study has led to the view that we have here the *Diarium spirituale* [spiritual diary][12] of an astral traveler recording his mystic development[13] right up to "gold ripeness."[14] What is more, it is not an imitation of the year 1616 but the real thing from 1459. To demonstrate this in detail would be valueless for the generality of readers and would entail a good deal of time-consuming philological argument.

---

[11]The *Chymische Hochzeit*, it can be proved, was being passed round in ms as early as 1602. This means that Andreae, if he had written this basic book, would have done so at the age of 16, which is surely out of the question! Trans. note: The counter-argument to this is that Andreae was assisted in his writings by his mentor, Prof. Christoph Besold (1577–1638).

[12]"Spiritual Diary" Emanuel Swedenborg (1688–1772) wrote one! A better name would be "spiritual nightbook" because it records nightly astral journeys. Trans. note: Another play on words. The German word for "diary" is "day-book."

[13]On the "First Day" of the Chemical Marriage the writer tells us, "I stuck in my hat four red roses." This means, "our beloved father" developed four roses on his (back) cross and, in this way, had subjugated the "Lower Quaternary" in order to let the three upper roses of the cross-beam (= the collarbone) burst into bloom.

[14]Gustav Meyrink (1868–1932) says somewhere: "It was the function of alchemy to make men of gold out of mere animal men." Nevertheless, Meyrink took an interest in chemical as well as spiritual alchemy and held the opinion that struvite (magnesium ammonium phosphate hexachloride) was the "prime matter." He discussed it humorously in the *Stachelschwein* (*The Porcupine*) many years ago!

In the "Sixth Day" chapter of this symbolic book is described a furnace for the preparation of the Stone, the heating for which is provided by the rays of the sun concentrated by mirrors:

I saw the globe hanging from a strong chain in the middle of the room. In this room there were nothing but plain windows, with everywhere a door between every two windows. The doors simply covered great polished mirrors and these windows and mirrors were optically adjusted with regard to one another in such a way that although the sun (which now was shining brightly) fell only on one of the doors, its light (after the window facing the sun had been thrown open and the mirrors had been uncovered) flooded the whole room and was concentrated by skillful reflection on the golden globe hanging in the center; and, because the latter was highly polished, the brilliance prevented us from looking on it directly, but we had to avert our eyes to the windows until the globe had been thoroughly heated and brought to the required state. I ought perhaps to say, at this point, that these mirrors presented a most wonderful sight in that as soon as the sun came out there seemed to be suns everywhere and the globe in the middle shone even more brightly so that we could not look at it any more than if it had been the sun itself.

On this it should be remarked that: 1) The Arabs, who were the most skilled enamelists in the Near East, used to employ concave mirrors in ancient times in order to melt their enamel and for carrying out chemical processes in general. 2) The concept of furnaces operated by the reflected rays of the sun, as described above, was a novelty as far as Europe was concerned.

"This idea, which was unusual for Europe at that time, is a further indication of the *Arabic* origin (or, more correctly, the Arabic connections) of the Brotherhood of the Rosy Cross, an origin which had been claimed for it by its pseudonymous adversary, Eusebius Christianus *Crucifer* in his "Brief Description of the New *Arabian* and Moorish Fraternity" [Kurtzen

Beschreibung der Newen *Arabischen* vnd Morischen Fraternitet] (Rostock).[15]

Arndt wrote in 1599: "The 'Philosophers' Stone' can be manufactured without artificial fire, if the sun's rays are concentrated by means of lenses."[16] This was written a century before the mathematician and physicist, Ehrenfried Walter, Count von Tschirnhaus (1651–1708), who invented modern lenses! Arndt was a confidant of Johann Valentin Andreae.

In 1670, Montfaucon[17] gave a recipe for making pulv. sol. (*poudre solaire* or sun powder) with which control could be gained over the elemental fire spirits (the Salamanders). "Gaining control over" implies "making contact with" initially and this can happen only if these spirits are first observed. In other words, we must sharpen our senses until they are supersensitive:

> If we wish to recover empire over the Salamanders, we must purify and exalt the Element of Fire which is in us. . . . We have only to concentrate the Fire of the World (i.e., the sun) in a globe of crystal, by means of concave mirrors; and this is the art which all the ancients religiously concealed, and which the divine

---

[15]Willy Schrödter: *Streifzug ins Ungewohnte* [*A Venture into the Unusual*] (Freiburg/Brsg., 1949, p. 143).

[16]Johann Arnd (Arndt) was a theologian who was born on December 27, 1555, in Edderitz (Anhalt) and died May 11, 1621, as Superintendent-general in Celle. His works *Vier Bücher von wahren Christentum* [*Four Books of True Christianity*] (1609) and *Paradiesgärtlein* [*A Small Garden of Eden*] (1612) plead for a living and wholehearted Christianity (Brockhaus). The work or ms in which Arndt mentions the use of lenses is called: *Zweytes Silentium Dei* [*The Second Silence of God*].

[17]Nicolas Pierre Henri de Montfauçon de Villars (1635–1673) was the author of *Le Comte de Gabalis ou Entretiens sur les Sciences secrètes* [*The Comte de Gabalis or Information on the Occult Sciences*], which was published by Claude Barbin on September 8, 1670. In this book he poked fun at the central secret of the Rosicrucians, which is intercourse with elemental spirits. In 1673, the Abbé was assassinated while not far from Dijon on his way from Paris to Lyons. Stanislaus de Guaïta (1860–1898) wrote in his copy of the above-mentioned book: "The Abbé de Villars, who profaned the arcana of the Rosicrucians, into which he had been initiated, and had turned them into an object of amusement, had sentence passed upon him and was executed on the highway in broad daylight." The recipe given above is taken from the second Discourse of *The Comte de Gabalis*.

Theophrastus discovered. A Solar Powder is formed in this globe, which being purified in itself and freed from any admixture of the other Elements, and being prepared according to the Art, becomes in a very short time supremely fitted to exalt the (life) Fire which is in us, and to make us become, as it were, of an igneous nature . . . and when your eyes have been strengthened by the use of the very holy Medicine. . . .

As regards the elementals belonging to the three other elements:

One has only to seal a goblet full of compressed Air, Water, or Earth and to leave it exposed in the Sun for a month. Then separate the Elements scientifically, which is particularly easy to do with Water and Earth. It is marvelous what a magnet for attracting Nymphs, Sylphs and Gnomes each one of these purified Elements is. After taking the smallest possible quantity every day for some months, one sees in the air the flying Commonwealth of the Sylphs, the Nymphs come in crowds to the shores, the Guardians of the Treasures parade their riches.[18]

In his *Memoirs* for March 1764, Giovanni Jacopo de Seingalt Casanova (4.2, 1725–6.4, 1798) related the following of the celebrated Comte de Saint-Germain.[19] "He showed me a white

---

[18]The author reverts to this "aerial commonwealth of the sylphs" in his Fifth Discourse. It is interesting that the famous Qabalist, Zedekias, prevailed on the army of the sylphs to appear in the air during the reign of Pepin the Short (714–768). The populace called it sorcery and "weather magic" and Charlemagne (768–814) and Louis the Pious (814–840) decreed severe penalties against "air pirates" in their Capitularies. There is evidence that the "kingdom of the fairies drew near at that time" both in the reports of Zedekias and in those of other contemporary authors and by the above-mentioned legal sanctions against air spirits enacted in the edicts of the Carolingian monarchs. Hence we need hardly be surprised to learn that, as late as 1725, the Hohenzollern Hechingen Forestry Commission was still offering rewards for the apprehension of water sprites! This royal statute of the Hohenzollerns was dated February 5th. It is still extant in the Hechingen city archives.

[19]He was born on May 28, 1696, and was the son of Prince Francis II Rakoczy (1676–1735) of Siedenbürgen and Princess Charlotte-Amelie of Hessen-Rheinfels.

liquid in a well-corked phial, which he called *ato éther*; this he claimed was the universal essence of nature, and the proof of this he said was that the spirit escaped if one made the tiniest pin-prick in the wax. He gave me a pin, and I pierced the wax; in a moment the phial was empty."[20]

Perhaps this *ato éther* was the "air elixir" . . . ?

Charles Baudelaire (1821–1867) sings in his poem "Elévation":

> drink, as it were, a pure and holy draught,
> the limpid fire pervading open space!

Madame Blavatsky wrote in 1888.[21] " . . .pure air. Which if separated *alchemically* would yield the Spirit of Life, and its Elixir."[22] "He who would allotropize sluggish oxygen into ozone to a measure of alchemical activity, reducing it to its pure essence . . . would discover thereby a substitute for an 'Elixir of Life' and prepare it for practical use."[23] According to Lützeler,[24] a Nepalese adept[25] recommended ozone[26] to a private German

---

[20]Casanova's *Memoires* (Brussels, 1838, Vol. X, p. 56 ff).

[21]Helena Blavatsky, true name Ielena Petrovna Blavatskaia, née Hahn, the Russian theosophist, born at Ekaterinoslav in 1831. She traveled in North America, India, etc. She died in London on May 8, 1891. Known, for short, as HPB, she had as her successor to the leadership of the Theosophical Society Annie Besant (née Wood, born October 1, 1847). Her opponent on the astral plane was P. Beverly Randolph (1825–1874).

[22]*The Secret Doctrine*, London, 1888 (Part I, p. 686).

[23]Op. cit., p. 168.

[24]Egon Lützeler (Cologne): *Er ruh el mssaferi* (Die wandernde Seele) [*The wandering soul*] (Leipzig).

[25]Sri Mahatma Said Radsch Guru, of the village of Pawalar at the foot of the Dhauwalagiri. He was born in Delhi but his family came from Mesopotamia originally. His father was Said ben Mustapha ibn Soliman and, like his son, a Parsee. After the Indian Mutiny of 1857, the wealthy fled to the valleys of the Himalayas where they could dedicate themselves to the study of nature and of the *Zend Avesta*.

[26]In the *Erläuternden Anhang* [*Illustrative Supplement*], p. 98, illustration 40, Lützler enlarges on the state of the knowledge of ozone at that time:

> Ozone or active oxygen is a modification of ordinary atmospheric oxygen. It was discovered by Schönbein at Bâle in 1859 on the basis of earlier observations. The new chemical entity was given the name

pupil as a means of dissociating[27] the physical and astral bodies. Since the little book is as interesting as it is hard to find, I shall quote the most important places here:
"And can or will you tell me what is in this little bottle, the essence of your supernatural wizardry?"

Ozone (from the Greek, 'Ŏzō to smell) on account of its peculiar odor. It occurs in the atmosphere after thunderstorms but only in very small amounts. It is always obtained mixed with oxygen, from which it can be separated by the cautious application of pressure and by strong cooling into a very explosive blue liquid. When dilute, it is fairly stable at ordinary temperatures and only gradually decomposes at temperatures above 400°C with increase in volume and formation of atmospheric oxygen. Ozone is distinguished from the latter by its smell, its extremely powerful oxidizing and bleaching action and by its bluish color. The ozone molecule consists of three atoms of oxygen, whereas ordinary oxygen molecules have only two atoms. Hence its chemical formula is O_3. Ozone is prepared by electrifying a slow current of pure oxygen with a nonsparking electric discharge. Ozone has been easily confused with hydrogen peroxide in the past and the same mistake is still made today, because H_2O_2, which is a clear, syrupy liquid, has similar properties. Part of the trouble arose from the false assumption, which used to be quite widespread, that ozone is a regular component of healthy air, such as woodland air for example, whereas it is never present here. Ozone fiercely attacks the respiratory mucous membranes and, even in very attenuated form, its prolonged inhalation will bring about catarrh, drowsiness and a deadening of the sensitivity of the skin. *Therefore the use of ozone inhalations and so-called ozone water against various diseases has proved a failure.* On the other hand, ozone has a much more powerful action than ordinary oxygen on the vitality of organs, it kills harmful germs and is highly disinfectant. The unmistakable, characteristic smell of ozone is acid and sulphur-like with a touch of turpentine odor. Hammerschmied: *Das Ozon und seine Wichtigkeit im Haushalte der Natur und des menschlichen Körpers* [*Ozone and its Significance in the Economy of Nature and of the Human Body*] (Vienna 1873); Fox: *Ozone and Antozone* (London, 1873); Engler: *Historisch-kritische Studien über das Ozon* [*Historico-critical Studies on Ozone*] (Leipzig, 1880).

This concludes our extract from Lützeler. As already mentioned, ozone was discovered by Schönbein, who was born in Metzingen (Württemberg) on October 18, 1799; he was appointed professor at Bâle in 1828 and died on August 29, 1868, in Baden-Baden. In addition to ozone, he discovered guncotton, collodion etc.

[27]*Dissociation* (French, *déboublement*), or "spirit travel" is the fairly well-known projection of the astral body or soul. The Tibetans call such astral wandering

"It is called 'ozone.' "

"What, ozone? . . . oxygen?"

"You've said it!. . . . Are you still going to see it as miraculous, as supernatural, this agent, this source of power, which has been known to your learned men for more than fifty years already?. . . . Admittedly, they went only half way. They found the clue in oxygen, in the life essence, to which they gave the chemical formula O, and followed this clue until they had discovered the concentrated form of active oxygen, that is to say ozone. I have no need, Mr. Chemist, to recount any details of this for your benefit. But what I would say is that, this point having been reached, the light provided by your clever formulas failed you. The formula O_3 was proudly written for the newly-won element and it was decreed, in arrogant self-deception that 'ozone does not occur in the pure form!' merely because it would not fit in with your scheme! . . . . Nevertheless, what is beyond you has been accomplished by us, the 'freelance researchers,' as long as 3000 years ago . . ."

"So this deep blue fluid is . . . ?"

"Pure, liquid ozone with all its wonderful life force!"

"And is it possible to use this ozone to . . . ?"

"*In the first place,* when it is administered to the organism, ozone revivifies and promotes the general vitality and the primary matter associated with it. The stimulated force tends to concentrate. The intensified self-consciousness develops its unconscious drives into conscious self-will and the will having been able to concentrate all the cohesive power atoms of the cellular fabric, the remaining cell structure is left behind as dead material; the liberated, newly-formed primary force, or soul, manifests as the independent psychic creation of the 'I will.' "

"But what of the abandoned body?"

"The body is dead without the soul. It is lifeless matter which, as in death, is liable to decomposition. It is true, that by

---

delog and the Indian name for fully conscious projection of the astral body (with freedom of observation and liberty of action) is *mayavi rupa.* The fact of sorties onto the astral plane has been known from the dim past; therefore Lützeler refers to the following classical authors at the beginning of his book: Acosta, Book V, cap. XXVI; Herodotus, Book IV, cap. XIV; Plinius, *Historia natural,* 1, Book VII, cap. LIII.

impregnating the cellular tissues, ozone inhibits the normal course of decay . . . but take care that your soul does not travel too far and does not remain too long outside the body—its substance is inexorably subject to natural laws—if you wish to return to your vacated shell and find it unharmed! *Above all avoid using the agent too often, avoid over-stimulation of your life-force and do not forget that ozone will gradually corrode and weaken the organism.* . . . This agent is intended only for the beginner, for the impatient novice. The Master, who is consecrated to the Deva, will more surely achieve his object by means of unceasing research and study."

Like Lord Lytton's *Zanoni*, this article raises the question, is it fact or fiction? Presumably, it is both. It deserves a place in a study of the elixir of "air" simply as an idea. In 1918 van den Meulen[28] announced that he had succeeded in the alchemical decomposition of a fluid substance present in the air; claiming that it was a remedy for tuberculosis, dropsy and other diseases.

The following statement was issued by a distinguished Dutch Theosophist and alleged Rosicrucian[29] in 1922:

> The vital energy of the physical body is to be found in the etheric body. If that is strengthened, a man will attain health and a long life. The ingestion of condensed ether is the easiest method of succeeding in this enterprise. So far, our experts have *not* succeeded in manufacturing it and therefore they think it impossible to do so. However, the impossibilities of today are the commonplaces of tomorrow. . . .

Accordingly, I shall say something here about the preparation of the elixir of long life, impossible as it may sound. The

---

[28]The chemist, A.A. van den Meulen in *Het vraagstuk van de zuurstof [The Problem of Oxygen]*, which was published by The Rosicrucian Press, Hilversum, in 1921, the founders of which were Anthroposophists. In fact, the above quotations have been taken from the *Histoire des Rose-Croix [The History of the Rosicrucians]* by the Antwerp lawyer Fr. Wittemanns (Paris, 1925, p. 174).

[29]Fr(ater) Syntheticus in "*Meinung und Wirklichkeit*" ["Belief and Reality"], which appeared in the Dutch periodical *Eenheid [Unity]* March 16 and 23, 1922); quoted in Fr. Wittemans' *Histoire des Rose-Croix [History of the Rosicrucians]* (Paris, 1925, pp. 187, 188).

ether is set in motion by the rays of the sun, and anyone who manages to refract and concentrate the sunlight by means of mirrors and lenses can cause certain waves in the ether. And whoever knows how to unite the force of the elemental fire with that of the *ignis essentialis* (the true fire) will see eventually that very slow but regular drops make their appearance, the like of which cannot be found as a curative agent for countless diseases!

He will vindicate the alchemical maxim: *Scias enim summum artis secretum in ignis consistere.*[30]

At this point we might remember those remarkable lenses of the ancient Indians, "lenses of special construction, capable of reflecting (sic) or concentrating certain certain forms of solar energy, etc." ("Rosicrucian optics") and also that the Indians had an optical mirror system with the special property of attracting or repelling, as required, given forces in sunlight, i.e., cosmic rays.

Finally, mention should be made once more of Peter Steiner's definition of the Stone of the Wise in his *Universal-Materie*: "The great, super-perfect Stone of the Wise is none other than pure concentrated and congealed fire."

DISCUSSION

I am firmly convinced that it is possible to keep individual human beings alive forever in natural conditions, because I believe that such test persons can be nourished from the air and by the transmission of force from other suitable subjects.

Carl Buttenstedt
Übertragung der Nervenkraft, p. 48

The *Sophi* sought the "Stone of the Wise" and its modification, the "Elixir of Life," in all the kingdoms of nature—mineral, vegetable and animal (including the human) and also in the atmosphere. The latter species of seekers were called "Air Fishers," about whom we read the following in the *Rechten Wege zur*

---

[30]"But know that the greatest secret of our Art lies in fire!"

hermetischen Kunst [*The Right Way to the Hermetic Art*] (1773): "The *Air Fishers* seek the little bird of Hermes before the rising of the sun, when it enters Aries and is fiery and full of *Astral Salt.* They try to gather a good supply by inhaling the open air and breathing it into suitable glass vessels." Who knows what may come of this?

The Indians have a history of practicing energy recruitment, and so prolonging life, by means of breathing exercises (*pranayama*). An immense amount has been written about these practices and yoga has become popular in Europe, too. One speaks of the "life-breath," but the chemical transformation of air into the elixir of life is no longer seriously discussed. Nevertheless, its special use is part of the process which makes supermen. Professors Leon Binet and Strumza, in 1952, fitted some of their examination candidates with oxygen masks, while the remainder took the tests without extra oxygen. The standard of performance of the students whose brains received additional oxygen was spectacularly higher. So the Hermeticists had the correct general idea when they tried to extract the elixir of life from the air. Their reasoning was, "No air—no life, so special air means a special (inspired) life."

But was an elixir of life ever prepared?

Robert Boyle (1627–1691) learned of the recipe for a medicinal wine from the French chemist Nicholas Le Fèvre, who had been brought to London by Charles II in 1664. A friend of the French savant had administered the potion to a 70-year-old woman. After she had been taking it for ten or twelve days, her periods started again, she became more animated and her face grew more smooth and attractive. She was so upset that the test was discontinued. Unfortunately, Hargrave Jennings, from whose book *The Rosicrucians* this account is taken, does not say where to find the recipe in Boyle's writings.

Johann Wolfgang von Goethe (1749–1832), who on December 7, 1768, was apparently dying from his indeterminate Leipzig illness, was restored to life in Frankfurt am Main by a very secret "universal medicine," a "salt" administered by the alchemist physician Dr. Johann Friedrich Metz (August 1, 1724–July 22, 1782). In *Dichtung und Wahrheit* [*Fiction and Truth*] (II, 8), he himself relates that a friend of his mother's, the pious Miss Susanne Katherina von Klettenberg (1723–1774), had recommended the Hermetic doctor. As a consequence of the mysterious healing, young Goethe, in company with Dr. and Mrs. N. who were kindred spirits, threw himself enthusiastically into those alchemical and Qabalistic studies which are thought to have been of fundamental importance to his whole world view (Maack)!

Nowadays, people are trying to define the "elixir of life" on a *hormonal basis*. However, this is nothing new, at least not as far as fundamental ideas are concerned. Thus we read in *Des Hermes Trismegisti wahrer alter Naturweg* [The Authentic Old Natural Way of Hermes Trismegistus] (1782): "Man, the microcosm, is the sum and extract of the macrocosm. Within the microcosm lies the grand Arcanum of the macrocosm, the great universal secret."

The adept Fictuld (Baron Meinstof) expresses this rather more clearly in his *Goldenen Vliess* [*Golden Fleece*] on March 7, 1747: "Adam knew that he was a concentration of all the powers of the Great World and that within his own being he carried a fire for alimentation and digestion *and the noblest medicine*. Anyone who does not recognize this in himself, will not find it without."

The Qabalist, Dr. Erich Bischoff (1865–1936) came to the conclusion after prolonged alchemical studies that the *elixir of life must be a radioactive preparation* (From *Der Sieg der Alchymie* [*The Victory of Alchemy*] Berlin, 1925, p. 131). When the traveler, Fridericus Gallus visited the adept, Reichsgrafen von Trautmannsdorf (1462–1609)[31] at his Wälsch Michael hermitage in the neighborhood of Trent, he was shown a golden jar in which the Lapis Philosophorum was kept. "When he put out the light and opened the jar, the object inside threw *a distinct gleam on the wall*. When examined in the light, it looked oval, and was about the size of a bean; it was as red as a garnet and exceedingly brilliant and, since it weighed two-and-a-quarter ounces, was more dense than gold" (Schmieder). Apparently the "Stone" shone by its own light: it produced "emanations." A noteworthy observation!

---

[31]Trans. note: von Trautmannsdorf shows from the dates of his birth and death that he did indeed possess an elixir of life. He lived to be 147 years old!

Then again, the "Fortalitium scientiae" of Irenaeus Agnostus dated August 13, 1617, published at Nuremberg, records the following formula, or should we say pipe-dream, of the Rosicrucian Brotherhood: Take pulverized turnips, mix with two ounces and three drachms of rye flour, add three grains of the "Philosophers' Stone," and make up into pills with linseed oil when Jupiter and Mars are in conjunction in 225° (sic) Aquarius. Three pills taken as required will preserve normal health for five months, without recourse to other food or drink.

In the Autumn of 1952, Dr. Walter Strathmeyer (Regensburg) created a considerable sensation with his "Paravita." This researcher, who was born in 1900, demonstrated that it was possible to survive on a daily dose of 20 g. of the sweet brown fluid for weeks or even months! Two coffeespoonsful were taken morning, noon and night, and the calorie intake was only 20! However, the vital force obtained from our daily food does not come from calories but from *radiant energies*. A lettuce leaf, for example, does us no good in itself; the virtue is in its "radiations of life-force" (Harvey T. Rowe).

And so the Rosicrucian dream was fulfilled. If Strathmeyer's test subjects continued to take small quantities of normal food, it was only to prevent their stomachs from shriveling due to months of inactivity. For the same reason, the above-mentioned Rosicrucian preparation was to be used for not more than five months, and the very fact that the precaution was proposed leads us to inquire whether the recipe was not something more than mere wishful thinking. If the elixir keeps the body alive, not to say rejuvenates it, there should be no difficulty in accepting that it will enable it to survive for a long period of time without a substantial meal.

One final point: it may be that some wiseacre will say, "That's all very well, but if there is such a thing as the elixir of life, why haven't the adepts kept themselves perpetually young?" The facts of the case are quite otherwise, however. Each one of us, whether with or without the elixir, has an allotted span of life which may not be exceeded, although *with* it we can live the full term and remain healthy and active to the end. But, quite apart from this, there are higher considerations. When Lord Lytton made the sage of Aleppo, in his novel *A Strange Story*, say that "he had thrice renewed his own life, and had resolved to do so no more. . . . The soul is not meant to inhabit this earth in fleshly tabernacle for more than the period usually assigned to mortals," he knew what he was talking about.

In 1885, Sri Ramakrishna Paramahamsa (1833–1886) contracted the "preacher's disease," and severe laryngitis developed into cancer of the throat in spite of attention. "Why don't you employ your yogic powers to heal yourself?" someone asked. He replied, "These powers of the soul have been consecrated to the Lord; do you expect me to take them back again and use them on the body, which is nothing more than a prison for the soul?" (Dr. Carl Vogl, died 1944).

When Pandit Malvija felt his mental and physical strength slipping away, he entered a yoga trance for 72 days, and, on rising from the place where he had allowed himself to be buried, he exhibited a youthful vigor such as he had not displayed for several decades. Once more the ravages of age began to show themselves after some years and one of his followers pleaded with him to undertake a *processus vitae interruptionis* (a process of suspended animation, in which life force is accumulated) yet again, a process we shall be discussing in detail later. The yogi simply replied, "My time has come," and attired himself in a change of raiment. Now this happened as recently as 1950! His wisdom, like that of the last Indian prophet, Ramakrishna, was even greater than his power.

All three men—the hero of the novel and the two spiritual sages of flesh and blood—knew that they would receive a far more glorious wedding garment in exchange for their tattered earthly mantle!

What purpose would there have been in delay?

We shall read of another type of rejuvenation—without chemicals or even special air—in the chapter on the "Great Work." There we shall find an alchemy which is no longer chemical but physiological, an alchemy which has been and still is treasured by the Rosicrucians and by the adepts of the Far East. Baron von der Goltz writes (in 1893) concerning this Chinese physiological alchemy as follows:

Today's seekers of *chin-tan*, the pills of immortality (named after the secret sect *Chin-tan-tao*) no longer try to obtain endless life by external means; they engage in *Tsa-Kung-yün-ch'i* and other mystical exercises designed to transform the body into an etheric substance.

The theurgist of Graz, Dr. Alfred Strauss, LL.D. (died 1935), has termed this "etherizing."

I have already pointed out that "the chemical transformation of air into the elixir of life is no longer seriously discussed." *Dies diem docet*, however (i.e., day teaches day—something better). Hardly had I penned the above sentence than an apparent chance placed in my hands two relevant reports which served as a sharp reminder that one must never treat anything as final!!

I refer to the remarks of Dr. Fritz Quade (1884–1944), an investigator of Reichenbach's Od, who wrote in his book *Odik* (Pfullingen i. Württ., 1924, p. 10):

> A further source of Od in the atmosphere (possibly of a different polarity) could perhaps be found in evaporation, which according to the results of Reichenbach (1788–1869) and Durville (1849–1923) is accompanied by odic luminosity. Od which is thus due to evaporation must be particularly concentrated over water surfaces and in meadows and woodlands, not to speak of *waterfalls*, the invigorating influence of which can be felt by those with above-average sensitivity. There the Od produced by friction is added to that caused by evaporation.

Folklore has it that "at the fall dwells the fay," meaning by the fay the animating element of water.

Turning now to *Die Magie als Naturwissenschaft* [*Magic as Natural Science*] (Leipzig, Vol. II, pp. 145, 146), by Baron Carl du Prel (1839–1899), we read: "A trance medium prescribed for a sick person baths of cold water pouring off a millwheel, although in his waking state he knew nothing of the electrical excitation present in sprayed liquids" (Cited from the Bibliothèque du magn. an. VIII, 229).

We must all, at one time or another, have remarked the refreshing effect of a tumbling mountain stream; an effect which depends on the momentary production of negatively and positively charged ions in the water droplets. In modern medical "spray treatments" the positive ions are removed electrically so that a stronger stimulus will be created which is beneficial in asthma, eczema, hay fever and general exhaustion. In 1950, the Institute for Meterology and Climatology in Hanover found out by chance that students who were using certain water atomizers for plant treatments regularly experienced a boost when inhaling the air during the atomization. Professor Grundmann of the College for Horticulture and Agriculture in Hanover has been carrying out further investigations on the subject.

The Hamburg biochemist Lipsky was able to supply the human organism with large amounts of stimulating oxygen (without increasing the respiratory action), by using his Lanthasol Method in which the oxygen contained in the air is concentrated by a micromist of cerium. This is not the place to go into the technical details, but we can at least say this that at the Weserland Clinic in Vlotho the process employed proved helpful in many of the symptoms of old age, such as high blood pressure, hardening of the arteries, cardioasthenia, etc. The treatment was introduced in 1949 and, within the period to 1951, thirty thousand patients had regained their health by breathing dry, noble-metal mists!

ELEMENTAL SPIRITS

You must know, my sweet one, that there are beings
in the elements which look almost like you (children
of men) but do not let you glimpse them very often . . .

—Fouqué[1]

Nobody should be surprised at the existence of such
creatures, for these things do not daily meet our gaze
but quite seldom.

—Paracelsus[2]

Among other things, there were in the vault where Father
Christian Rosencreutz (1378–1484) lay buried "wonderful artificial songs."[3] These were used for calling up spirits, as may
be seen from the words: "How pleasant were it that you could
so sing, that instead of stony rocks you could draw to the pearls
and precious stones, instead of wild beasts, *spirits*, and instead
of hellish Pluto, *move the mighty Princes of the world?*"[4] "The
mighty Princes of the world" are the *Spiritus olympici vel gubernatores firmamenti* (The Olympic spirits or governors of the

---

[1]Friedrich de la Motte Fouqué (1777–1843) in *Undine* (1811).
[2]Paracelsus (1493–1541) in *Liber de Nymphis*.
[3]*Chymische Hochzeit Christiani Rosencreutz Ao. 1459* [*The Chemical Wedding of
Christian Rosencreutz*] ed. Ferd. Maack (Berlin, 1913), Includes *Fama* (first
published in 1614), New impression, p. 53.
[4]*Confessio* (first published in 1615), Chap. IV. New impression, p. 67.

firmament), the planetary archons of the *Arbatel*.[5] What then of the other spirits? They can only be good or at least neutral, for they are mentioned in the same breath with the "angels"— "through the service of the angels and spirits."[6]

These are the spirits of the elements:

> Salamander soll glühen,
> Undene sich winden,
> Sylphe verschwinden,
> Kobold sich mühen.[7]
>
> Salamanders burn and glow,
> Undines ever waver so,
> Sylphs into thin air flow
> And Gnomes do toiling go.

The Knights of the Rosy Cross esteem their obedience better than the making of gold.[8]

And we need hardly wonder at the scarcity of genuine Rosicrucian writings on the *transmutatio metallorum* (transmutation of metals) when, generally speaking, no instructions have come down to us for summoning the elemental spirits.[9] What

---

[5]*Arbatel oder über die Magie der Alten* [*Arbatel or the Magic of the Ancients*, known in English as *The Arbatel of Magic*] the main body of a magical primer with a somewhat biblical flavor. It is concerned with ceremonial magic and the evocation of the planetary intelligences. The *Arbatel* was published as an appendix to the *Occult Philosophy* of Henry Cornelius Agrippa von Nettesheim (1486–1535) quite early on. It is apparently of Arab origin, and might even have been brought back to Europe and translated by "Father Rosencreutz" himself. In any case, it seems to be based on the *Sumus al-anwar wa kunuz al-asrar al-kubra* of Ibn al-Hagg al Tilimsani (died 1336). It teaches the ceremonial summoning of the planetary spirits (*ruhanija*) for the procurement of elemental spirits (*Afreets*) for service (serving or familiar spirits). Cf., Dr. A.H. Winkler: *Seals and Characters in Moslem Magic* [*Siegel und Charaktere i.d. Muh. Zauberei*] (1930).

[6]*Confessio* IV (p. 66 in Maack's edition).

[7]Goethe: *Faust* I; Reclam, vv. 1273/76.

[8]*Fama*, Maack's ed., p. 58.

[9]Apart from the brief account transmitted to us from antiquity by the "Demonic Knight" in his *Occult Philosophy*: "Hermes saith that . . . if a fume be made of that (i.e., *spermaceti*) and lignum-aloes, red storax, pepper-wort, musk and saffron, all tempered together, with the blood of a lapwing, it will quickly gather airy spirits together."

we do know of such conjurations, we owe to the indiscretion in the form of a contemporary lampoon!

The Abbé Nicolas Pierre Henri de Montfauçon de Villars was born in 1635 in the vicinity of Toulouse. He came to Paris in 1666, and on September 8, 1670, published his famous *Le Comte de Gabalis*[10] through Claude Barbin, as an attack on the occult sciences. Then, at the end of 1673, he was found dead on the highway from Paris to Lyons near Dijon, with a dagger between his ribs.[11]

This lampoon leads to the following observations on commerce with spirits as practiced by the Rosicrucians:

---

[10]The Paracelsist, Oswald Kroll (Crollius, died 1609), personal physician to the Prince Christian von Anhalt-Bernburg, treats of a sidereal human Gabalis in his Basilica Chymica! It is easy to see that the word *Gabalis* is derived from "Cabbala," or QaBaLa, (Hebrew for "Tradition"). The *Gabal* of Paracelsus = "A telephone connection with the unconscious," to put it in modern terms.

In 1681 Giuseppe Francesco Borri (1616–1695) published in Geneva his *La Chiave del Gabinetto del Cavagliére Giuseppe Francesco Borri, milanese* in ten letters [*The Key to the Cabinet of the Chevalier Giuseppe Francesco Borri of Milan*]. The first two letters were written in Copenhagen in 1666 and deal with a conversation with a Danish nobleman on the subject of elemental spirits.

In his book, Montfauçon de Villars referred to conversations with a German nobleman from near the Polish frontier on the elemental spirits. It would be interesting to know who inspired whom! In all events, Alexander Pope (1688–1744) says in the foreword to his *Rape of the Lock* addressed to Mrs. Arabella Fermor (1712): "The Rosicrucians are a people I must make you acquainted with. *The best account I know of them is in a French book call'd Le Comte de Gabalis.*"

Trans. note: an English edition of *Le Comte de Gabalis* issued by The Brothers in 1913 comments as follows on Borri's book: "To a politico-religious source may therefore be ascribed the ingenious fiction that *Comte de Gabalis* is a direct translation of an Italian book *La Chiave del Gabinetto*, by Giuseppe Borri, published in 1681, eleven years after the appearance of the first edition of these Discourses. Thoughtful comparison of *La Chiave del Gabinetto*, with the contemporary French and English editions of *Comte de Gabalis* reveals the fact that the Italian book is but a faulty translation and expansion of the former, masquerading under the guise of letters dated from Copenhagen in 1666, which imaginary date was employed to lend colour to its pretension to priority, and to cast discredit upon the Abbé's book" (pp. xiii–xiv).

[11]In his *La Rôtisserie de la Reine Pédauque* (1893), Anatole France (1844–1924) brought the Abbé de Villars to life again as the Abbé Jérome Coignard, and the Count of Gabalis as Mr. d'Astarac. His novel is intended to poke fun at the Rosicrucians in general and at their commerce with elemental spirits in particular.

What chiefly drew attention to them (the R+C) was their belief in certain *elemental spirits*, who—although invisible to the eyes of ordinary humans—gave their confidence to the initiates. Before getting to know them it was necessary to have one's eyes cleansed with the universal medicine,[12] and to have special glass flasks chemically prepared with one or other of the four elements and exposed to the sun's rays for a month. After these preliminaries, the initiate would see a host of beings of a *shining substance*,[13] *but loosely textured and diaphanous*.[14] These beings populate the elements all around us.

Those of them which inhabit the air were called *Sylphs*, those who dwell in the earth, *Gnomes*, those belonging to the fire, *Salamanders*, and those who have the water as their home, *Undines*. Each of these entities is said to hold extensive sway in the element inhabited by them. They are supposed to be able to produce winds in the air and to raise storms at sea,[15] they shake the

---

[12]The same thing is said by Lord Lytton in *Zanoni* (1842) in Book 4, chapter IV.

[13]The wizard abbot Johannes Trithemius (1462–1516) answered the Emperor Maximilian I (1493–1519) as follows on question six of the Eight Questions, i.e., on *"the power of sorceresses"* (= witches) in regard to aerial spirits: "The Platonists maintain that the demons which *fly in the air like the thickest fiery snow* have regularly shown themselves to those who wished to see them if the latter gazed fixedly into the sky for some time on a sunny day. Nevertheless, I do not know whether the objects seen are real or are false images induced by stopping the movements of the eyes. *I myself have made this experiment*, though not without some small prejudice to my eyesight!" What we have here is the so-called "seeing stars." The book by Trithemius to which we refer was printed at Oppenheim in 1515 (and many times since) and has the Latin title: *Curiositas regia sive octo quaestiones theologicae a Maximiliano I propositae et per Joannem Trithemium solutae* [*A Royal Inquiry or Eight Theological Questions asked by Maximilian I and Answered by Johannes Trithemius*]. In it he patches together a demonology taken from the Neoplatonist Psollus and from old German mythology (according to Kiesewetter).

[14]Trithemius (true name Johannes Heidenberg) in *loc. cit.* "The *spirits of the air* can descend to the earth and—*by assuming a body of densified air*—can make themselves visible to men on many occasions."

[15]Trithemius, the teacher of Agrippa von Nettesheim, in *loc. cit.*: "By the permission of God, the spirits of the air often raise stormy winds, produce

earth and terrify its denizens with devouring flames.[16] However, they pretend to be more frightening than they really are, for all are subordinate to man and yield ready obedience to the initiates themselves.

The gnomes, who own the mines and occupy the interior of the earth, freely give the hidden treasure they guard to the men who become their associates.[17]

The four species of elemental spirits are partly male and partly female but the feminine sex seems to predominate in all four.

We are given to understand that they live longer than humans do but that, when they die, their existence ceases altogether. And so, in the course of time, they have developed a passionate longing for immortality and have found a way to achieve it. If they are fortunate enough to arouse desire in one of the initiates and lure them into marriage, then the soul of the Sylph

---

thunder and lightning (and conspire to destroy the human race)." Cf., Shakespeare's *The Tempest*! (ca. 1611).

[16]"They (the *Devarajas* which control and reign as kings over the four elements together with the nature spirits and elemental essences dwelling in them) are very important to us as regents of the earth. *Fire is extinguished by their power.* A Moslem offered to exorcise the fire of Hamburg (May 5–8, 1842) for the City Council for the sum of 60,000 Marks" (Ferdinand Schmitt: *Okkulte Magie [Occult Magic]* Leipzig, 1908, p. 26). In his *Autobiography*, the Italian sculptor, founder and goldsmith, Benvenuto Cellini (November 3, 1500–February 13, 1571) records that when he was a boy he saw a *Salamander* in the parental fireplace. To insure that he would remember this rare experience as long as he lived his father boxed his ears severely! Later on, the artist of Francis I (1494/1515/1547) chose the salamander as a heraldic beast with the motto: *J'y vis et je l'étains* (I saw [it] there and extinguished it). He also participated in an evocation of spirits in the Colosseum at Rome, as mentioned by Goethe in his biography of the sculptor.

[17]E.g. to the so-called Walen ("Welsh" or foreigners in the sense of Italians living in Germany) and *Venetians* (from whom we get the expression, *Ars venetiana*) who worked with earth mirrors, divining rods, and evocations. The wizard of the Ore Mountains of Saxony, Pater Johann Adalbert Hahn (February 14, 1750–September 23, 1825) was a master of hocus-pocus (fascination, binding, casting spells on thieves) and gave out that he came from Venice and used the "Venetian art."

bride of a blameless man, by growing into his nature, becomes immortal.[18] On the other hand, should she unite with some immortal being who would thus fall to her estate, the said exalted being would be compelled to conform to the law under which his wife lived and would become completely mortal.[19]

An oath was taken from neophytes on the occasion of their admission to the secrets of the Order that they would preserve perpetual chastity in regard to (mortal earth) women.[20] For this sacrifice they were well repaid by the likelihood that they would make contact with a sylph, a female gnome, a salamander,[21] or a nymph,[22] any of whom would be far more ravishing than the

---

[18]Cf, the same theme in the pathetic story, *The Little Mermaid* by Hans Christian Andersen (1805–1875)!

[19]This can mean only an originally immortal *angel* like those who once found the daughters of men so attractive (Gen. VI:1–4). The Apostle Paul issues some highly significant instructions (regarding the wearing of head coverings) for the protection of women from angelic interference (I Cor. 11:10)! So the possibility of intercourse between angels and humans is an item of dogma!

[20]Alexander Pope (1688–1744) had this to say in the *Rape of the Lock* (1712): ". . . the *Sylphs*, whose habitation is in the Air, are the best-conditioned creatures imaginable. For they say, any mortals may enjoy the most intimate familiarities with these gentle Spirits, upon a condition very easy to all true Adepts, an inviolate preservation of *Chastity*." In *loc. cit.*, Pope refers expressly to the *Rosicrucians*!

[21]The late Professor Strauch of Hanover, a spiritist of many years standing, claimed success in the materialization in Hanover of the spirit of a girl named Vanina, who had been stabbed by a jealous officer at Turin in the 18th century. Strauch remained in contact with Vanina until his death in 1947! He informed his wife Erna that the girl was a so-called "Salamander" with whom he was involved in love-making! (from a newspaper report Sept. 1950).

Dr. Andreas Justinius Kerner (1786–1862) wrote on April 12, 1836, to Sophie Schwab: ". . . Mayerin, a female court usher, had full intercourse with the spirit and thought more of him than she did of her husband. She said that her life had been quite miserable since the spirit had departed. . . ."

[22]Thus the Rosicrucians tried to get in touch with such things for the purpose of forming "ultraviolet misalliances," in order to redeem these transparent entities by "soul impregnation," Hebrew *Ibbur* (the very same thing that the Comte de Gabalis preached as a "mission"!) while at the same time making use of their superhuman wisdom and four-dimensional powers. In contrast to this, the Indian yogis (Latin, *juncti* = joined, i.e., to God) were wary of seduction by feminine entities in fine-material forms, the so-called *Siddha* = Women!

fairest earthly woman and would not lose her beauty by the aging process.[23]

In the works of Paracelsus we read:

> Now they (the elemental spirits) are certainly people but, like the animals, they have no souls. Now if a marriage takes place between a female water-sprite and a son of Adam, so that she takes him as husband, sets up home with him and bears him children, she knows that the children of the union will take after the man. Because the father is a descendant of Adam, a soul will be poured into the child, which will be a proper man with a soul and everlastingness. You should understand further that a wife of this sort, receives a soul on marrying so as to be redeemed by and through God like other women. . . . It follows from this that they go wooing men, seek them out assiduously and work secretly. . . . Yet not all of them are able to marry us. The water folk are those most capable of doing so, since they are closest to us.[24]

The final statement, however, is at variance with what he had said earlier: "*The sylvans*[25] *are closest to us*, for they too are supported by our air."

Trithemius is of the same opinion and he, as the reputed owner of a "serving spirit," is presumably an authority.[26] "The

---

[23]William Godwin: *Lives of the Necromancers, etc.* (London, 1876, p. 22).

[24]Two such contacts of humans with watersprite lovers are mentioned by Paracelsus and Gabalis: Count Raymondin von Lusignan entered into a union with a water fairy, who became the ancestress of his family; hence she obtained the names "Mère des Lusignans," "Mère Lusigne," Merlusine and finally Melusine. (In the Latin prose romance written by Jean d'Arras, the secretary of Duke Jean de Berry in 1478), Sir Peter(mann) Dimringer von Staufenberg (Ortenau) died when he broke his marital vows to a water-wife.

[25]I.e., the air or woodland spirits (in French, *sylvains*).

[26]No less a personage than the *Praeceptor Germaniae* (The Preceptor of Germany) Philipp Melanchthon (1497–1560) reported that Trithemius possessed a serving spirit. When he said the word "Adfer" it would produced cooked pike at his window (*Theatrum diabolorum*, Frankfurt au Main, 1565, fol. 112). In the same way, many years later, the serving spirit of Johann Georg Schröpfer (1730–1774) used to bring letters to the window from far away. See my

air spirits are the second race of daemons. They float around in the air and linger in our neighborhood. *They chiefly assist the sorceresses* (= witches) *in their spells,* as they are much more cunning than the others (i.e., the other elemental spirits) and are characterized by the greatest impudence."[27]

Of the highest significance is the voluntary confession of the convicted magician Beaumont, made in 1597 at the Castle of Chinon (Indre-et-Loire) before the parliamentary speaker, Jacques Auguste de Thou (1553–1617), the Governor of Tours, Gilles de Souvré and the Chancellor of Navarre, Sofroy Calignon. The prisoner stated that his (white) magic consisted in the art of *dealing with the heavenly spirits of the air,* who also revealed to him the secrets of nature.[28]

The Milanese physician and legal expert, Facius Cardanus (1443–1526) had a *spiritus familiaris* (= familiar spirit, genius, spirit guide, control?) of the class of aerial spirits, about which his son, Hieronymus Cardanus (1501–1576) had this to say in *De subtilitate,* Book XIX:

> On August 12, 1492 at two o'clock in the afternoon, there appeared to my father, when he had just said his prayers, seven men in silk garments in the Greek style. They wore purple half-boots and shining carmine red shirts. Their stature was unusually large. The heads of the spirits were uncovered and they looked to be approaching the age of forty although they themselves affirmed that they were over two hundred years old. When asked who they were, they replied that they were air spirits which arose in the air and dissolved into it once again, though they were able to prolong their lives to three hundred years, etc. They remained with my father for more than three hours.

One of these air spirits (according to Cardanus further on) accompanied his father for thirty-three years after this as his

---

The Rosicrucians for further information on these serving spirits (Lorch i. Württ, 1952, p. 74 ff)!

[27]Trithemius in his *Eight Questions.*

[28]*Memoires de la vie de Jacques-Auguste de Thou etc.* (Amsterdam, 1713, Book IV, pp. 329–332). A translation of the full text will be given in my next book, *Rosenkreuzer-Historien [Rosicrucian Histories].*

spiritus familiaris and gave him replies to his questions. These answers were truthful when Facius adjured him, but otherwise they were deceitful.

According to the old records, the aerial spirits are the nearest neighbors to mankind and are also closest to us in nature, and these were the entities with which the Rosicrucians must have made their compacts. I am supported in this conclusion by three more recent authors, authors who were Rosicrucian initiates themselves!

The first of these, and the earliest of the three, is Edward George Earle Lytton, the first Baron Lytton of Knebworth (1803–1873), a magician of knowledge and power.[29] In his *Zanoni* the "well-loved work of my matured manhood" as he called it, he makes the hero begin the initiation of Viola by invoking "the loveliest children of the air to murmur their music to her trance."[30, 31] Bulwer was followed by Marie Corelli (1864–1924), the English novelist of Scottish-Italian extraction, who was initiated (after being trained for a musical career[32] in a French institute run by nuns) by an Armenian "Count"[33] whom she calls "Heliobas," shortly before 1866. She has put her experiences in the form of a novel, *A Romance of Two Worlds*.[34] In keeping with traditional reticence, she has not disclosed the written instructions given to her by her initiator for increasing her bodily electricity preparatory to gaining out-of-the-ordinary accomplishments.

Having been born with musical talent, she was more fortunate than Zanoni's Viola, in so far as a sylph, whom she calls "Aeon," inspired her with lyrical improvisations for the piano. Heliobas taught her the theory of sylphs as "Twin Flames" or "Twin Souls." The twin soul of the celibate Dr. Heliobas was called "Azúl," that of his equally unmarried sister, Zara, is not

---

[29]Sinbad. *Das Lebenselixier* [*The Elixir of Life*] (Leipzig 1923, pp. 18–20, in G.W. Surya's foreword).

[30]Needlessly: Viola paid them no attention, her mind being fully occupied with Zanoni.

[31]Book 4, chapter 9.

[32]Sensitives and those susceptible to spirit intercourse tend to be musical, as further examples will show.

[33]Corelli says "Chaldean."

[34]Published by Tauchnitz, Leipzig, 1888, No. 2549/2550.

named. In the words of an English poet, Zara was a "woman, waiting for her demon lover." This "demon lover" approached her as "a ring of light like a red fire, which seemed to grow larger and redder always."[35]

Surya[36] knew of a 20-year-old musician into whose hands there came a book of Latin conjurations of the elemental spirits. A young theological student who was a friend of his translated his find for him and he then undertook the preliminary abstinence from meat, tobacco, alcohol and women for several months. At the expiry of this period he uttered the prescribed conjurations, upon which "two female sylphs appeared to him." One was slightly built but the other was very big and tall. Like her companion, she had a mass of golden hair. He asked her if she would be his friend and they began to spend much time together. As the days went by she became more and more substantial; she no longer needed to fascinate him with looks and words but had him in her physical possession. Her love-making became so prolonged and vigorous that he was unable to stand the physical and mental strain.[37] Therefore he decided to part

---

[35]Corelli, Vol. I, p. 210.

[36]G.W. Surya, whose real name was Demeter Georgiewietz-Weitzer (1873–1949), informed me on July 26, 1942, that even as a child of 6 or 8, his elder daughter had been able to see nature spirits. She has confirmed in personal interviews that she retains this ability to a great extent provided she leads a quiet life amid natural surroundings.

[37]He was weakened by two distinct emissions of "Od." First of all the air spirit took of his substance to materialize a solid body for herself and second she depleted him sexually. Here are two similar cases: Christian Reimers, a musician living in Manchester although German by birth, died under the non-stop sexual attentions of his mistress, a spirit called "Betty" (Cf., "Erfahrungen eines Deutschen in Spiritualismus in England"—*The Experiences of a German in English Spiritist Circles*—in *Psychische Studien* [*Psychic Studies*] Leipzig, 1874–1879).

Books on Faustian Magic led a man to invoke evil spirits. He called on the name of the great wanton Jezebel, mentioned in the Bible and swore to be hers if only she would grant his wishes. "From that day to this," he complained, "I have had no peace from this creature. She visits my bed twice a week and I am unable to resist her successfully as she wraps herself around me. My whole body has been weakened and damaged by her. As soon as she comes near me I feel myself being imprisoned in an indescribable net-like thing. I have tried to break free by living a chaste life, but it is no use. When I awake I usually have a dim memory of a fierce struggle" (pp. 152 ff). This

from her, but this was easier said than done and it was only with the assistance of a practical Qabalist that he was able to regain his freedom.[38]

I have on file testimonies taken from the most reliable and critical individuals that even in this day and age elemental spirits have been seen, successfully summoned and, what is more, *photographed*. For example, a Hamburg hermeticist and friend of Gustav Meyrink (1868–1933), who has been immortalized by the latter as "Baron Müller" in his *Der Engel vom westlichen Fenster*[39] told me that a late teacher, F.W. Krippner, who used to write extremely interesting articles for *Das Wort* [*The Word*], a magazine for students of the Illuminati, articles on such subjects as "Apollonius of Tyana" and "King Solomon," frequently used to invoke the elemental spirits in his *Idyllum naturae* in what was, at that time, the wildly romantic Gross-Borstel region not far from Hamburg. While they swung on the branches of the hazel bushes, he conversed with them and had collected many fascinating notes. This magus also "healed" by magical means but would let no one look at his cards. Shortly before he died—it was before the First World War—he bequeathed to my informant his magical cloak, pointed hat and sword.[40]

---

account by someone who came to him for help, was published by the well-known hypnotist, Hans Ertl (then in Munich) in the *Zentralblatt für Okkultismus* (Leipzig, 1910). Jezebel (Greek, Iesabel; German, *Schön Ilse*—beautiful Ilsa; Spanish, Isabella) was the daughter of King Ethbaal of the Zidonians (known today as Saida). She was the wife of King Ahab of Israel (877–854) and high priestess of the sexually orientated worship of Astarte. Captain Jehu, in 842, had her thrown out of the window of her ivory palace at Jezreel. She was about 50 at the time. As the "prophetess of the left-hand path" she offered an "occult revelation" (II:20). Astarte impulses are traceable right up to modern times, a fact which I have demonstrated in a monograph on "Jezabel" [Jezebel].

[38]Surya: *Das Okkulte in Agnes Günther Die Heilige und ihr Narr* [*The Occult in Agnes Günther's The Saint and her Fool*] (Lorch i. Württ., 1929, pp. 91, 92).

[39]Published at Leipzig in 1927. The "angel JI" described in the book is no angel, but an amoral intermediate being who enticed the two magical operators John Dee (1527–1608) and Edward Kelly (1555–1597) into wife-swapping!

[40]Reported by "AME" on June 1, 1946, December 1946, and April 10, 1950. The original letters, which I may publish later on using pseudonyms for persons still living, are in my files marked "Correspondence with Cognoscenti."

The American essayist Prentice Mulford (1834–1891) made the following comments on the subject of "twin souls" and the possibility of an alliance with them:

> The priests of many religions[41] take vows of chastity, not because they would renounce wedlock in the highest sense but because the wife of a true priest, that is to say of an almost divine man has, as his spiritual half, nothing to do with the visible side of life but sends inspirations into his soul from above.[42] If this man formed close ties with another woman, she would form a wall, a coarse element, separating him from his priestly companion, his true mate, with whom he must be united again in some form of existence. It is impossible for men or man-made laws to separate those who have truly been destined for one another from eternity. It is quite within the bounds of possibility for one soul mate to be incarnate while the other leads an existence in the invisible realms.[43]

Posterity may recognize the possibility of achieving *a real connection* between such separated souls, by

---

[41]Rosicrucianism is a religion and every *genuine* Rosicrucian is "a priest for ever after the order of Melchizedek" (Hebrews 5:6). What is more there is a theurgic "Offering of praise of Melchizedek" (Karel Huysmans: *Là-bas*, the Potsdam edition, 1921, p. 265 ff).

[42]Cf. Egeria, the "ultraviolet" adviser, said to be a nymph, of the Roman King Numa Pompilius (715–672)! I propose writing a monograph to show that this hero was a Rosicrucian (in the widest sense of the word and hence in character). He knew, among other things, how to invoke "Jupiter Elicius." A clumsy attempt to follow his example cost his successor, Tullus Hostilius (672–640) his life. The Senate treated it as a case of fire.

[43]"Is this what Beethoven (1770–1827) means by his reference to the 'Far Beloved?' Or what Swedenborg (1688–1772) means when he says that he will be married to Countess X beyond the grave? Or is this the 'spiritual marriage' of certain religious Americans which Hepworth Dixon was never able to comprehend?" (August Strindberg: *Ein drittes Blaubuch* [*A Third Blue-Book*] Munich, 1921, p. 1265). Dixon (1821–1879), an English writer, traveled to the USA in 1866 in order to study the ways of the sects; he was the author of *Spiritual Wives* among other books (which appeared in German as *Seelenbräute*, Berlin, 1868). Cf., also what Franz Vencenz Schöffel has to say in his *Irrwege des Sexualtriebes* [*Offbeat sexual appetites*] (Pfullingen, 1922, pp. 13–23) on Les Vince, Kolly Kowac, and Ayscha.

means of the continuous fusion of their thoughts. Were the man to enter into a deep relationship during his lifetime with another woman he would be parted more than ever from his true spouse. A new barrier would be formed between him and her and many incarnations would have to pass no doubt before he regained that clarity of spiritual vision which would enable him to *know*[44] the one who was truly intended for him.[45]

Sédir[46] gives the following instructions for seeing sylphs: "After the usual purifications, go into a wood in the early morning and look for a place where the trees grow sufficiently close together to cover you completely from the sky. Then sit down and half-close your eyes with a fixed gaze and call the "sylphs" *mentally*, by which I mean the spirits of the woods. It does not matter what names you use to call them, they will certainly show themselves to you, especially if you offer them water or cereals and if you persist in your endeavors for several days."[47]

---

[44]Notice the double meaning of the word "know"!

[45]*Unfug des Sterbens* [*The Nonsense of Death*] (Munich, 1919, pp. 118–119). Mulford dared only to introduce as "future possibilities" what he knew as past and (less often) present facts; for he was a member of the theurgic circle known as the "Society of the White Cross" (founded in Nebraska in 1881) an offshoot of a society of the same name formed in Manchester around 1853 by the wholesale merchant William Oxley, who was a follower of Swedenborg. In 1886, the American branch published Mulford's writings under the title of the "White Cross Library." Author Max Dauthendy (1867–1918) found his twin soul through conscious meditation in which he said, "Somewhere in the wide world lives a female soul who is the perfect complement to my soul. May I eventually find her and be happy with her." And that is how it turned out. One day he got to know a Swedish lady who was the fulfillment of his long-felt desire.

[46]Paul Sédir (real name Yvon Leloup, 1871–1926) in *Les Plantes magiques* [*Magical Points*]. Sédir quotes from a certain H.J. Bjerregard.

[47]Cf., *Viertes Buch der Geheimen Philosophie*, ascribed to Cornelius Agrippa [*The Fourth Book of the Occult Philosophy*]: "Provide a table at the place of the invocation covered in a clean linen cloth and with pure water or milk in new earthenware vessels, together with a new knife and fresh bread. Seats for the spirits who have been invited must be set round the table." Cf., Agrippa's *De Occulta Philosophia* [*Occult Philosophy*] Book III, chapter 32, New impression: Vienna, n.d., p. 184 (in German). Cf., further: Carl Kiesewetter: *Faust* (Vol. II, p. 20 ff).

I once passed these instructions on to a "nature lover" and he carried them out with *immediate and complete success*. However, I will not relate his observations as I do not wish to influence anybody by suggestion.[48] Sédir goes on to explain that:

> These beings belong to the class which the xenologists term elementals. They are the inhabitants of the astral plane who are attempting to incarnate. They are endowed with a certain instinctive intelligence and adapt their form to that of the flesh-and-blood being by whom they are enchanted. *It is they who were employed by the old Rosicrucians to perform their miraculous cures*, for they are servants and are naturally inclined to obey men of a high spiritual order. They have fairly considerable influence over the material plane, because they dwell on the borders of this plane with the astral. They can produce healings and astounding visions, in exactly the same way as the elementals of the mineral kingdom bring about all alchemical phenomena when strictly controled, and the elementals of the animal kingdom produce the great majority of spiritist manifestations.

A recent example of the beneficial intervention in healing of these denizens of the astral threshold is to be found in Dr. Hermann Haupt's *Die strahlende Lebenskraft und ihre Gesetze* [*The Radiating Life-Force and its Laws*] (Althofnass bei Breslau, 1922, pp. 91, 92), concerning the ex-journalist who later became a spiritual healer, Gustav Adolf Egmont Roderich Müller-Czerny (1862–1922) who claimed to be assisted by a spirit team consisting of "Roderich of Bern" with his helpers:

> The cures of the recently deceased Hamburg "Miracle Doctor" Müller-Czerny depended mainly on the activities of beings on the other side. Thanks to his special links with a powerful spirit being in the other world, who said he had lived on earth a long time ago, Müller-Czerny had at his beck and call an army of serving

---

[48]Willy Schrödter: *Streifzug ins Ungewohnte* [*An excursion into the Unusual*] (Freiburg i. Brsg., 1949, pp. 270, 271).

spirits who were at his disposal both for individual healings and for mass ministrations. All he had to do was to draw their attention to the health problem in question; he then needed to do no more himself. These spirits belonged to a group which specialized in *unusually profound reactions with the material plane which enabled them quite often to bring about the most amazing organic changes in the shortest time imaginable*—although, admittedly, they could only do so by the permission of a higher Providence. But Müller-Czerny's spirit contacts were themselves highly developed beings and were certainly not the low, seducing kind. So we can see that the achievements of Müller-Czerny, in spite of the roughness of his external bearing which offended many people, gave proof of his spiritual task and presupposed a respectable level of ethical achievement.

Rosencreutz (1378–1484) is known to have brought back to Europe the ceremonial invocations of the planetary spirits and of the star spirits in general which he learned in Arabia and from the natives of Morocco.

Anyway, the knowledge of how to summon the "fairies" (air spirits or sylphs) is also Arabic, and certainly of pre-Rosicrucian origin. In this connection, going backward in time, we have:

1) The Parsifal saga, which has an Arabic source (*Parzival*, ed. Simrod, 416, 17) (453, 11);

2) The delegation sent by Charlemagne (768–814) to Harun-al-Raschid (763–809) in 797 (reciprocated by Harun in 801);

3) The delegation from Pepin the Short (752–768) to Al-Mansur (754–775) in 765; returning in 768.

As far as the third point is concerned, the saga *Flor und Blancheflor* by the Middle High German poet Konrad Fleck (ca. 1220) is the "expression" of a search carried out in the Orient two generations before Charlemagne, which prepared the way for the Rosicrucian Grail-movement in Christendom.[49]

Under the second named Abbasid Caliph, *Abu Giaffar al-Mansur*, the Arabian kingdom reached its greatest extent, but the Persian element was so influential that Frankish documents refer to him as "Rex Persarum" (King of the Persians).[50] *The doctrine of the "Peri" is peculiar to the Persians.* The word *Peri* comes from the Zendish *pairika* = fairy, and denotes a female spirit in Iranian cosmogony. The Peris, who are beneficent but glorious beings, inhabit the empyrean and subsist on the scent of flowers.[51] *They often alight on the earth in order to have intercourse with men. The issue from such unions is of radiant beauty.* When the Persian poets speak of a lovely human child, they frequently call it a *Perizadeh* (= fairy child).

The *Touks* of Central Asia regard spirits of this type as being very powerful. The *Baksas* (= witches) of the Kirghiz-Kazaks (free Kirgheezes between Irtish and the Caspian Sea) often call *on the Peris for help to exorcise Djinns and other evil spirits.*

The Peris have been divided into different groups.[52] In the time of Charlemagne and Pepin, the astral world seems to have drawn especially near. Evidence of this is seen in the Old French poem composed at the end of the 12th century and entitled *Huon of Bordeaux.* Huon went at the Saxon-butcher's command to the Orient and passed through various adventures with the aid of the fairy king, Oberon (French: Auberon; Old German: Alberich).[53]

---

[49]Walter Johannes Stein: *Weltgeschichte im Lichte des Hl. Gral* [*Universal History in the Light of the Holy Grail*] (Vienna, 1928, p. 98).

[50]Stein, op. cit., p. 112.

[51]Cf., the alleged sightings of flower fairies! "The Gipsies say that a sure sign that a fairy is flying past is when a foxglove hangs its head." (Villiers-Pachinger: *Amulette und Talismane* [*Amulets and Talismans*], Munich, 1927, p. 74, under "Foxglove." The Chinese scholar Tschen of Hangchow told Julius Eigner about his relationship with Hsiang Yü (the fairies of a white peony) and their half-sisters the Chiang Hsü (the dryads belonging to a camellia bush) in *Gelbe Mitte-Goldener Kreis* [*Yellow Mid-Gold Circle*] (Hattingen, 1951, p. 230). Cf., *Das Akazienmännlein* [*The Acacia Manikin*] byHofrat Theobald Körner and *A Midsummer Night's Dream* by Shakespeare!

[52]*Larousse du XXe Siècle* (Paris, 1932, Vol. V, p. 480, under "Péri").

[53]Otto Rahn: *Kreuzzug gegen den Gral* [*Crusade against the Grail*] (Freiburg i. Brsg., 1933, p. 138 ff).

During the reign of Pepin the Short (714–768), the famous Qabalist Zedekias wanted to convince the world of the existence of the *elemental spirits*. He invoked the Sylphs, who then appeared in the clouds. The clergy and the populace at large thought they were weather witches and both Charlemagne (768–814) and Louis the Pious (814–840) passed penal laws (Capitularies) against these air spirits.[54]

In the reign of Pepin the Short, Zedekias performed conjurations of the Sylphs and declared that the elements were peopled with spirit beings.[55] *The heroes* ("preux" or champions) *of Charlemagne's century were the issue from intercourse between the sylphs and the daughters of earth.*[56]

In conclusion, we append some comments from several of our own "great spirits" on the spirits of the elements. P. Beverly Randolph (1825–1874), an authority on magic, wrote: "I do not think that elves, fairies, genii and magicians are simply mythical beings. Surely, there must be a grain of truth in the traditional stories which their hearers and readers find so riveting."[57] He is supported to a certain extent by Privy Councillor, Prof. Karl Ludwig Schleich, M.D. (1859–1922):

Schleich was strolling in his garden with a visitor one glorious summer evening when the guest pointed to an old clump of trees and remarked that the garden had such a story-book atmosphere about it that one

---

[54]J.A.S. Collin de Plancy: *Dictionnaire Infernal [An Infernal Dictionary]* (Paris, 1818, Vol. I, pp. 91, 92).

[55]*This belief is, in fact, a dogma of the Roman Catholic Church.* The following formula is used in consecrating holy water: "*Exorcisco te, creatura aquae!*" (I exorcise thee, creature of water = I drive thee out water-creature.)

[56]Jacques Marcireau: *Une Histoire de l'Occultisme [A History of Occultism]* (Poitiers, 1949, pp. 143, 144). Cf., the "giants," "mighty men," and "men of renown" of Genesis 6:4! See also, in the same work by Marcireau (p. 220, para. 25) what he has to say on the love-affairs of Gérard de Caudemberg (1857) with the inhabitants of the spirit world!

[57]Randolph: *Dhoula-Bel*, A Rosicrucian novel (Munich, 1922, p. 133). "It is quite certain that the elemental spirits have taken on life and form—and that not only in the fantasies of trance subjects—and have taken an active part in many a person's fate. Our temporary natural blindness inclines us to treat all such events as amusing stories." From Bruno Noah, *Die Edda*, Berlin-Pankow, 1934, p. 53.

could easily imagine there were elves living in the trees. To this Schleich quietly replied, "Indeed, am I to take it then that you think there are *no* elves living in those trees?" Anyone who looks on this as a jest is the victim of superstitious rationalism.[58]

Nothing irritated Arnold Böcklin (1827–1901) more than when someone called his *Fabelwesen* (fabulous beasts) the products of fantasy. As an art historian who had known him personally often assured me, he would invariably reply that he painted exactly what he *saw* and no more. There is no doubt that the great surgeon, Ernst von Bergmann (1836–1907) was repeatedly struck by the fact of how uncontrived and *organic* his "Fabelwesen" looked, so that he used to say that if it were possible to have creatures of this sort they would have grown *anatomically* to look as Böcklin painted them. An example is the entity in his "Meeresstille" (Calm at Sea) which is pushing off under water from the rocks on which a mermaid and two seagulls are resting.[59]

August Strindberg (1849–1912) talked of astral love-affairs or "mystical impregnations" with special reference to a French "Marquis, who is an occultist." He was referring to Joseph Alexandre, Marquis Saint Yves d'Alveydre (1842–1909). This man, who had been raised to the peerage by the Pope, "formed a connection with the higher forms of existence on what the Theosophists call the astral plane . . . and in those regions he found a wife, etc." Strindberg ends with these highly significant words: "I have absolutely no doubts on the matter, for *I have had a similar experience, and much, much more.*"[60]

Fairies were photographed very early on in England and no less a personage than Sir Arthur Conan Doyle (1859–1930) wrote on the subject.[61] In London, there is even a club devoted to their study!

---

[58]Franz Vincent Schöffel: *Hexen von einst und heute* [*Witches of Yesterday and Today*] (Bamberg, 1931/2, p. 8).
[59]Kurt Aram: *Magie und Mystik* [*Magic and Mysticism*] (Berlin, 1929, p. 572).
[60]Strindberg: *Ein neues Blaubuch* [*A New Blue-Book*] (Munich, 1920; p. 807; *Die mächtige Liebe* [*The Mighty Love*].
[61]Aram: Op. cit., p. 567 ff. (Kurt Aram, Hans Fischer: 1869–1934).

Some time in 1950, one of the most prestigious occultists in the USA, Prof. Fred O. Hamersteen (of Ohio), warned atomic physicists in a confidential circular letter against waging their "war on the elemental spirits." In other words, what our modern physicists, chemists and technologists regard as playing with "lifeless" materials or as a human "victory over the forces of nature," says Hamersteen, is seen on another plane as a struggle against the elemental spirits and these mighty beings feel that their existence is threatened and are likely to take counter-measures. An example of these is atomic poisoning of the human astral body, a plague which cannot be treated by physical means, but only with "evestral" (Paracelsus).

• • •

LITERATURE

Sir Arthur Conan Doyle	*The Coming of the Fairies*, London, 1928
Edward L. Gardner	*Fairies* (with photographs), London, 1945
Geoffroy Hodson	*The Kingdom of Fairies*
Geoffroy Hodson	*Fairies at Work and Play*
Erhard Bazner	*Die Naturgeister*, Leipzig, 1924
Schreiber	*Die Feen in Europa* [*The Fairies in Europe*], 1842
J. Stephens	*Irish Fairy Tales*, 1920
R.L.B. Wolff	*Mythologie der Feen und Elfen* [*Mythology of Fairies and Elves*], Weimar, 1828

SUPPLEMENTARY MATERIAL

Sylph Lovers: An unusual traditional tale comes from Neuwied, which runs like this:

A *sylph*, or female air spirit, used to haunt the place at one time and, as a Neuwied journeyman tiler was lying in bed at night, the sylph pushed open the window and entered his room in the shape of a long, thin ape, which sat on his body and threatened to suffocate him. On his speaking to his master about it the next day, the latter told him to shout for him if the nocturnal spook reappeared. Sure enough, the same thing happened on the following night and the journeyman immediately called his master. The two of them then tried to seize and detain the nocturnal spirit after the master had closed and stopped up every chink and crevice in the room. The night-prowler defended itself, scratching and biting, but was unable to escape because the whole place had been tightly sealed and, eventually, it took refuge beneath the bed.

When the two men got down to take a closer look at this rare apparition under the bed, they did not find a repulsive ape but an extremely pretty young girl, who proceeded to pour out her troubles to them, telling them that she had come from far away after being turned into the ethereal state in which they saw her by a malevolent fiend. She said that she had been looking for nothing more than shelter for the night in question and that that was why she had intruded into the room. Her tears and words affected master and man so much that they decided to keep the young creature with them and things soon reached such a pass that the master married the young woman.

Nevertheless, he could never quite bring himself to trust his young wife, although she seemed so loving and trustworthy. Every evening he stuffed the openings in the windows and doors not wishing to lose his "treasure." His wife used to smile at his odd behavior but did nothing to prevent him.

Little by little the loyalty and love of his wife allayed his fears and, one night, he left the bedroom keyhole unstoppered. When he was ready for bed, he heard a hissing and fizzing sound somewhere near him but of his wife he saw nothing more. The open keyhole had given her the opportunity to return to the unsettled existence of a sylph.[62]

---

[62]W.K. "Sagengestalten unserer Heimat" ["The Folklore of our Homeland"] in the *Westerwälder Zeitung*, Hachenburg, No. 266 dated November 14, 1951, p. 6.

A number of comments can be made on this story: It is certainly "an unusual traditional tale" which contains sylphs. As a matter of fact, I have yet to come across a traditional tale about "regular" sylphs. Melusine, although able to float on wings round Lusignan castle in a farewell lament, was a water sprite. Stories about the misalliances of humans and water spirits are legion, and it was this which persuaded Paracelsus (1493–1541) that the water spirits are our nearest relations. He found confirmation for his thesis in the teachings of the Chinese,[63] whose pulse diagnosis and belief in dragons he knew! (One would like to know his sources!) The air spirits, on the contrary, have an aversion for us base-born sons of clay. They are "proud" as the Celestials say.

"The sylph . . . entered his room in the shape of a long, thin ape." Air spirits are invariably represented as being of more than human size—which explains why this one was "long" or "tall." The sylph was "thin" at first, since she had not fully materialized. However, she moved in quickly to take what she needed from the tiler's assistant, for she "sat on his body and threatened to suffocate him." She vampirized him and might even have been a human "Alpenganger" rather than a sylph. Initially, she looked like an ape because her contours had not yet been filled out. Nevertheless she did have something of a human look and was not completely animal in appearance. The "ape" was a caricature. Afterwards, she took the form of "an extremely pretty young girl," not surprisingly, as it was (and still is) generally accepted that the (usually female) air spirits possess superhuman beauty.

"She had come from far away." The Alpengangers often said that they came from *Engelland* (i.e., Angel Land or the astral plane, not England!).[64] She had been "turned into the

---

[63]"I have to beat the drum which summons the guardian spirits. *One* stroke calls the water spirits. They come gladly . . . , etc. The *air spirits* are proud and wait for *six strokes*" (Nora Waln: *Süße Frucht, bittre Frucht China* [*The Sweet Fruit and Bitter Fruit of China*]; Berlin, 1935, p. 60).

[64]One *Alpengängerin* (female Alpenganger, Waldriderske, Ridimär or Nightmare) said: *"Wat klingen de Klocken/war stuvt de Sand/In Engelland"* [What the bell tolls/Where the sand runs/In Angel Land] (Herm. Lübbing: *Friesische Sagen* [*Frisian Legends*] Jena, 1928, p. 170).

ethereal state in which they saw her by a malevolent fiend."
Alpengangers frequently complained that they were forced to
roam abroad against their will and suffered from a "moral
hangover" next day.[65]

Sexual intercourse with spirits during meditation: Prof. Eduard Erkes
(Leipzig) has this to say in "Die taoistische Meditation und ihre
Bedeutung im chinesischen Geistesleben" ["Taoist Meditation
and its Significance in Chinese Intellectual Life"] (*Psyche*, Stuttgart, 1949, Vol. 3):

> The original significance of meditation . . . consists in
> creating a state of mind in which direct intercourse
> with spirits is possible. It is sexual in kind. Thus, judg-
> ing by its origins, meditation is an erotic affair (p. 372).

> The avoidance of intercourse with women had, to
> begin with, a quite different meaning, generally speak-
> ing. The heavenly sweetheart of the individual prac-
> ticing meditation, the spirit who inspires him, is
> jealous, and if he makes love to earthly women she
> deserts and punishes him. This realization is the real
> reason behind priestly celibacy (p. 376, 377).

The Ancient Egyptians and Serving Spirits: The Imperial Count
Palatine, poet and philosopher, Adam von Lebenwald (died
1690) wrote at Leoben in 1680: "It is a justifiable opinion that
the *Egyptians* put up their pyramids, colossi, obelisks and statues
with the assistance of genii and serving spirits, since they were beyond the constructional capabilities of men at the time they
were erected."

The publisher of this old note, Dr. M. M., a lawyer from
Graz, commented: "The same idea is encountered in
[palæontologist and natural philosopher, Edgar] Dacqué (born
in 1878), who was disposed to think that telekinesis was used
to activate some sort of robot machinery. Genii were, according
to Lebenwald, intermediate entities between gods and men."

---

[65]"It is a national belief that the Waldriderske are girls born in Galli week
(before and after October 16th), who are fated to harm people without being
able to help themselves" (Lübbing, op. cit., pp. 169, 170).

(*Das Neue Licht* [*The New Light*] Purkersdorf b. Wien, 1951, Vol. 11, p. 198 ff. "Ein okkulter Kritikus anno 1680" ["An Occult Critic 1680"]. What is more: "the occult reviewer, Lebenwald . . . ascribes the use of the Qabala to the Rosicrucians" (p. 200).

Jesus Christ and the Elemental Spirits: My honored friend of longstanding, "AME," the Hamburg esoterist and hermeticist, who immortalized no less a person than Gustav Meyrink (1868–1932), his great friend, as "Baron Müller" in his *Der Engle vom westlichen Fenster* [*The Angel of the Western Window*] (Leipzig, 1927), drew my attention (on November 10, 1952) to the passage in Luke 8:23–24, which reads:

> And as they sailed along he fell asleep. Then a heavy squall struck the lake; they began to ship water and were in grave danger. They went to him, and roused him, crying, "Master, Master, we are sinking!" He awoke and rebuked the wind and the turbulent waters. The storm subsided and all was calm.

Only living creatures can be rebuked! The presumption that there was some form of demonic activity behind the storm of wind (devil, witch, undine) can be read in Prof. Adolf Wuttke's book, *Der deutsche Volksaberglaube der Gegenwart* [*Present-day German Folk Superstitions*] (Leipzig, 1925, pp. 37, 159, 294, 302, 303). The Arabs hold the same belief, as can be seen in Hans Alexander Winkler's (died 1945) *Die reitenden Geister der Toten* [*The Riding Ghosts of the Dead*] (Stuttgart, 1936, p. 16) in which he talks about the "Zâr", which is often seen in the nearby desert and many times too on the roads between fields. The *Zóba'ah*, which is a whirlwind, is said to be caused by an evil Jinnee who travels inside it.

Serving Spirits: It is to the Arab world that we owe the teaching on serving spirits. They are known there as Jinns and their section-leader is called *Cutdam*. Belief in them is an Islamic dogma. Their specialities are apports (*Khat*), telekinetic phenomena and, more occasionally, divination (Acts of the Apostles 16:16). In addition, they also behave as demon lovers (incubi and succubi), for they have two genders, like human beings.

Abraham of Worms is credited with a Hebrew manuscript written in 1387, which was translated into German in 1725 by Peter Hammer and published under the title of *Das Buch der wahren Praktik*, known in English as *The Book of the Sacred Magic of Abra-Melin the Mage*, translated by S. L. MacGregor-Mathers. It records how the author traveled through Europe in search of the true magic and finally found it not far from a little town called Arachi, situated on the banks of the Nile, when he met one of the *Chakîmîm* of Bît-Nur, called Abramelin in the book but whose proper name was Ibrahim el-Mu'allim (1281–1412).

He had been resident in Egypt since 1350, looking for documents and, in 1400, spent a whole year initiating the young man into how to control the *Jinn*! On the assumption that the given date of 1387 is accurate, this is the earliest account of the importation of "spirit forces" into Europe I have been able to find.

The abbot Trithemius, to whom we have so frequently referred, is alleged to have possessed a serving spirit. When he uttered the word *Adfer* (Latin for "bring near"), his four-dimensional *factotum* brought boiled pike to the window. At least, this is what Philipp Melanchthon (1497–1560) says in the *Theatrum diabolorum* (Frankfurt-on-the-Main, 1546, p. 112).

More recently, Johann Georg Schröpfer (1730–1774) employed ultraviolet (i.e., invisible to ordinary sight) domestic servants as lightning messengers between Dresden and Mitau in the presence of the Duke Christian Joseph Karl von Kurland (1733–1796). The idea was to avoid having to leave Germany!

The method of procuring a *Jinn* is as simple as it is dangerous and consists of praying, fasting, and keeping vigil. Carl Vett asked three sheikhs about this when he was in Istanbul. The first, Abdul Vehab, instructed that the person making the attempt should "remain standing for forty days and that during this period he must subsist on a daily ration of 200 grams of bread and a few figs. Sleep is restricted to one hour, and there must be no contact with any living thing—human or animal. The time is to be occupied in meditation and spiritual exercises. Occult mantras must also be employed in Aramaic or Syriac, and they must be chanted in a room which has been specially prepared for the purpose. No one must overhear or disturb the magician."[66]

Moses, Elijah and Jesus all went into the desert to be alone, and each spent forty days there, too, in fact. The "specially prepared room" meets us again as a bed chamber both in the Jew of Worms and in his compatriot of a more recent date, Jesse of Hamburg.

The Dane was given identical information by the second Sheikh, Mehmet Aly.[67] His third authority—Ali Hodja—recommended ritual washings in addition, such as the Qabalists also consider to be indispensable in their theurgic procedures, besides *Zihkr* during the night. The latter is a form of swaying motion while sitting, which may or may not be accompanied by incantations in sing-song. "If you persist for several weeks, you will start to see visions, in which your guide will reveal himself and give you further instructions in regard to fasting, praying, forms of magical invocation and so on."[68]

Further to the main psychological conditioning, chemical means were used in support, such as the fumigations described by Cornelius Agrippa, Eckartshausen, and others. They serve to make the operator more sensitive, to disguise the characteristic human smell which spirits find so unpleasant, and to provide a vehicle for any materializations when substances releasing Od are burned.

The exercises for gaining a Cutdam are extremely dangerous. Most of those who performed them either went mad or became physically ill, because it requires almost superhuman strength to be able to bring about substantial materializations strong enough to do human work and actions.[69]

Further information on the subject of the Jinn can be found in the following books: Hans Alexander Winkler: *Die reitende Geister der Toten* [*When Spirits of the Dead Ride Out*] (Stuttgart, 1936); Enno Littman: *Arabische Geisterbeschwörungen in Ägypten* [*Arabic Invocations of Spirits in Egypt*] (Leipzig, 1950); Paul

---

[66]Carl Vett: *Seltsame Erlebnisse in einem Derwischkloster* [*Strange Experiences in a Community of Dervishes*] (Strasburg, 1931, p. 1011).
[67]Op. cit., p. 293.
[68]Op. cit., p. 321.
[69]Op. cit., p. 11.

Brunton: *L'Egypte secrète* [*A Search in Secret Egypt*] (London, 1938) and his *Als Einsiedler im Himalaya*, published in English as *A Hermit in the Himalayas*, p. 165; Willy Schrödter: *Die Rosenkreuzer* [*The Rosicrucians*] (Lorch i. Württ., 1952), which contains a considerable section "On the Jinn" with full details.

Once more, it should be emphasized that only very few are able to stand the nervous strain involved in such dealings and that the risk of possession is correspondingly great: "The spirits that I summoned refuse to go away!" In German folklore, the Devil wrung the neck of Doctor Georg Faust (1480–1540) in the "Lion" at Staufen (Breisgau). In other words, his nervous system "short-circuited" and his body was distorted through the effects of supernormal terror.

DISCUSSION

> Let us invoke the spirits fervently! Otherwise there is no sense in it.
>
> —*The Sixth and Seventh Books of Moses*

As far as I am concerned, the existence of elemental spirits is an established fact, and my conviction is based on the weighty testimony of creditworthy people who are in full possession of their critical faculties. It is no argument to the contrary that these spirit beings cannot be seen by everyone. Mathias Claudius (1740–1815) hits the nail on the head in his folk-song "Der Mond ist aufgegangen" (The Moon Has Risen):

> So sind wohl manche Sachen,
> die wir getrost belachen,
> weil unsere Augen sie nicht sehn.

> And there are many things beside,
> Which confidently we deride
> For that we see them not.

The eminent Qabalist, Eliphas Lévi (1810–1875) expressed the same sentiments when he said that there was no invisible world—merely degrees of perfection of our sense organs. Many of the lower animals have senses very much keener than our own. Thus, an osprey is able to spot choice fish, no longer than the palm of your hand, at more than forty meters, under a choppy sea (!) and will measure with its eye the exact depth below the surface at which its prey is swimming. A barn-owl will chase and catch bats at night, whereas human vision can hardly follow their zig-zag flight at dusk. The bat, in turn, picks up the echo of (what is to us) its supersonic squeak by means of its radar-like ears and is thus enabled to avoid obstacles in its flight path even in pitch-black conditions. And as for the hound, which is able to locate one chicken out of hundreds with its sensitive nose, and the ant, which perceives ultraviolet light and will carry its "eggs" out of a beam of this light which is being played on them experimentally, how far, far superior they are to us in some aspects of their sensory equipment!

But even among human beings there is a considerable difference in sensitivity to external stimuli.

I have already shown what has to be done in order to see spirits of this type. All that is needed is a certain natural aptitude and a fair amount of patience. One of these days, in the words of Lord Lytton, a mechanical tube will be invented through which one may see the "things that hover in the illimitable air." A step has already been taken in this direction, a good many years ago now, with the Kilner screens for viewing the human aura. An account of them can be found in G.W. Surya's, *Okkulte Diagnostik und Prognostik* [*Occult Diagnosis and Prognosis*] (Lorch i. Würrt., 1950, p. 201 ff).[70]

---

[70]Trans. note: also Kilner's own book, *The Human Aura*, written in English and published by Kegan Paul, London, 1920, and reprinted several times since.

PLANETARY SPIRITS

The Olympic spirits are those which inhabit the firmament and the stars of the firmament, deciding and dispensing fate as far as it pleases God and as far as He permits.

—*The Arbatel of Magic*, III/15

The Rosicrucians used to have dealings with beings from higher worlds. Their basic book, the *Confessio* refers to "the service of the angels and spirits" and says invitingly, "How pleasant were it that you could so sing, that instead of stony rocks you could draw to the pearls and precious stones, instead of wild beasts, spirits, and instead of hellish Pluto, move the mighty Princes of the world?"[1]

The summoning of angels is explained in *Das Buch der wahren Praktik in der göttlichen Magie und in erstaunlichen Dingen, wie sie durch die heilige Kabbala und durch Elohim mitgeteilt worden* by Abraham of Worms (known in English as *The Book of the Sacred Magic of Abra-Melin the Mage*). It was published in 1725 by Peter Hammer (Cologne) and was said to have been translated from a parchment manuscript written in Hebrew dated 1387. The first and third white magic parts go back to the same Arabian (Abramelin) sources as those on which the Rosicrucians drew for inspiration. At all events, the Hamburg Qabalist Benjamin Jesse two hundred years ago[2] and one of my own acquain-

---

[1]The *Confessio*, chapter 4, Cassel, 1615.
[2]See the letter of January 30, 1731 in Siegm. Hch. Güldenfalk: *Sammlung von*

tances twenty years ago both operated successfully with this really practical book, the second and fourth parts of which are interpolations containing instructions for black magic ceremonies.[3]

The "mighty Princes of the world" are the seven Planetary Archons (*Gubernatores Olympici*), on which the *Arbatel de Magia Veterum* [*The Arbatel of Magic*][4] provides the best information. The Arbatel is a theoretical torso built on a New Testament basis, while the practice on the Old Testament basis of Leviticus is found in the so-called *Fourth Book* of Cornelius Agrippa's *Occult Philosophy or Magic*, thought to be spurious although written in the same style as the other three books, and also in the *Heptameron, or Elements of Magic* by Peter of Abano (1253–1305; or 1250–1316).

Other books dealing with the Planetary Archons are the *Salamankische Pneumatologia Occulta et Vera* (ca. 1660), the *Erdspiegel* [*Earth Mirror*] of the Capuchin friar, Franciscus Seraphinus Heider, Immenstadt (1658) and the *Heiliggeistkunst* from the library of Prince Rupert II (1785–1793), abbot of Kempten, of the baronial House of Neuenstein, and edited by Andreas Luppius.

In the *Arbatel* I see a de-Mahometanized and Christianized *Sumus al'-anwarwa-kunuz al'asrar a-kubra* of Ibn al-Hagg al Tilimansi (died 1336). The *Gubernatores olympici quibus Deus voluit*

---

mehr als hundert wahrhafter Transmutationsgeschichten, etc. [Collection of more than one hundrd reliable reports of transmutation, etc.] Frankfurt/Main and Leipzig, 1784, p. 120, 122 (Report No. 68).

[3]Trans. note: the English version of MacGregor Mathers, which he translated from a rendering in French at the Bibliothèque de l'Arsenal in Paris, is in three parts or books not four.

[4]In Latin and added to the Collected Works of Cornelius Agrippa in the second volume published at Lyons ca. 1550. The German edition of Andreas Luppius, appeared at Wesel in 1686. The *Arbatel* can have been written no earlier than 1536! Paul Chacornac writes in his *Eliphas Lévi* (Paris, 1926, p. 152) that on May 24 and 25, 1854 (even twice on the latter day) "the great Qabalist" undertook to call up the spirit of Apollonius of Tyana (10–99) by the method laid down in the *Magia Philosophia* (Hamburg, 1573) of Francis Patricius. This book was said to contain the "dogmas of Zoroaster and the works of Hermes Trismegistus." I understand that the book was translated into French in 1926. Regretably, I have been unable to examine a copy but I surmise that it is a precursor of the *Arbatel*.

universam hanc mundi administrari [The Olympian Administrators to whom God has entrusted the whole machinery of this world] are called *ruhanija* in the Arabic texts.

Concerning the two-year stay of Christian Rosencreutz in Fez, between 1398 and 1400) we read in the *Fama*:

> After three years . . . he sailed over the whole Mediterranean Sea to come to Fez, where the Arabians had directed him . . . magic (for in those are they of Fez most skillful). . . . At Fez he did get acquaintance with those which are commonly called the *elementary inhabitants* who revealed unto him many of their secrets. . . . Of these of Fez he often did confess that their magia was not altogether pure, and also that their cabala was defiled with their religion; but notwithstanding he knew how to make good use of the same. . . . After *two* years Brother C.R. departed the city Fez, and sailed *with many costly things* into Spain.

The "magia" which was "not altogether pure" which Christian Rosencreutz found among the "elementary inhabitants" or aboriginal population in the interior of Morocco was the invoking of the stars and of the planets in particular! The Arab historian Ibn Chaldûn (1332–1406) has this to say in fact:

> The Riffs are also given to . . . magic. I have been informed by a sheikh of Morocco that the young women are especially addicted to this art. They are said to possess the power of drawing down the spirit of any star on which they have set their minds and, when they have bound it, of identifying themselves with it. In this way they gain an influence over living creatures entirely in accordance with their imagination.

The reference in the *Confessio* to "hellish Pluto" is worthy of note. He was moved by Orpheus (born 1399 B.C.) to surrender the latter's wife Eurydice. At the end of chapter 59 of the Second Book of Agrippa's *Occult Philosophy*, the reader is referred to the "hymns of Orpheus"—the founder of the mysteries and master of incantations—for details of this type of invocation of the stars. And, in the *Fama*, emphasis is laid on the fact that in the mausoleum of Father Christian Rosencreutz

were found "wonderful artificial songs!" To quote this illuminating passage in full:

> In another chest were looking-glasses of divers virtues,
> as also in other places were little bells, burning lamps
> and chiefly wonderful artificial songs.

The "looking-glasses of divers virtues" were "magic mirrors" for assisting clairvoyance in time and space and for telepathic communication, as well as "earth mirrors" for finding
buried treasure,[5] as employed by the *Walen*. The "little bells"
were cast in "electrum magicum" and were used to summon
spirits.[6] The use of "electrum magicum" or "seven metals" comes
from the Orient and is already mentioned in the Qabala.[7] However, it is known even to the Toba-Bataks of Sumatra (Winkler).
"Burning lamps" could be the "everlasting lamps" of the Rosicrucians, ritual lamps such as are mentioned by Lord Lytton
in his Rosicrucian novel *Zanoni* (in Book 4; chapter 7), or "magic
lamps." A great deal of information is given about the latter in
Agrippa's *Occult Philosophy* and in the magical handbook *The
Great Albert* ascribed to Albertus Magnus (1193–1280). The phe-
monema produced by the *magia naturalis* (natural magic) depend on the wick, the vessel and the composition of the fuel.

The *Fama* does not mention the indispensable fumigations.[8] Hofrat Karl von Eckartshausen (1752–1803) obtained
from a Scot (could he have meant the Welshman, Thomas
Vaughan = Philalethes?) an incense formula for summoning
the living and the dead, which he tried with success. In 1913,
a Swedish lady called Erna Hellberg, a native of Stockholm,
made the acquaintance in England of an Egyptian sage who,
using the same formula, repeated the experiment of the Witch
of Endor (I Sam. 28:7 ff.).[9]

The innocuous recipe used by Eckartshausen and the
Egyptian consisted of white frankincense pounded to a fine

---

[5]Karl Kiesewetter: *Faust*, Vienna, n.d., Vol. II, p. 203 ff.
[6]Ibid, Vol. II, p. 24 ff.
[7]Moses Maimonides: *Moreh Nebukim*, Part III, Sect. 29.
[8]Kiesewetter, op. cit., Vol. II, p. 195 ff.
[9]E. Hellberg: *Telepathie, Okkulte Kräfte* [*Telepathy, Occult Powers*] Prien (Obb.),
1922, pp. 195, 199.

powder then mixed with fine flour and kneaded to a dough after the addition of a blend of egg, milk, and rose-honey plus a little oil. The preparation had to be burned on a coal fire.[10] The reader may recall that the "meat offering" in the Bible was composed of fine flour, oil and frankincense (Leviticus 2:1) seasoned with salt (Leviticus 2:13); on the other hand, the use of honey (or yeast) was forbidden (Leviticus 2:11). In certain instances a "drink offering" of wine was added (Numbers 15:7).

The smoke gives the invisible entities the necessary chemical ingredients for the densification of their ordinarily tenuous materials into something which can be seen by the human eye. The belief in "planetary spirits" or in the teaching that there are living beings in the stars has persisted right down the ages and into modern times.

The scholastic philosopher Thomas Aquinas (1225–1274) said, in his *Opusc* (II, art. II)

> I do not remember seeing it denied, in the works of the saints or philosophers, that the planets are guided by spirit beings. . . . It seems to me that it is demonstrable that the heavenly bodies are supervised by some intelligence, whether it is that of God Himself directly or that of angelic intermediaries. The latter opinion is in agreement with that of Louis the Pious, that God governs all earthly things by regents.

The great Johannes Kepler (1571–1630) endorsed this view in his *Apologia Harmonices mundi* (1622).

In his novel, *Wilhelm Meisters Wanderjahre* (1821), Johann Wolfgang von Goethe told of an earth-bound star in human form called "Makaria," who was responsive to the motions of her cousins in the sky. Theodor Fechner (1801–1887), philosopher, pantheist and founder of experimental psychology, while not going so far as to say that individual heavenly bodies had souls, claimed that higher spirits indwell the planetary systems.

In our own days, the modern Rosicrucian, G.W. Surya (real name Demeter Georgiewitz-Weitzer, 1873–1949), has ex-

---

[10]Eckartshausen: *Aufschlüsse zur Magie [Magic Elucidated]* Munich, 1791, Vol. II, p. 361.

pressed this view in his *Okkulten Astrophysik*, a view which was shared by his collaborator, the astronomer and rocket researcher, Max Valier (1895–1930). The same is true of the Austrian "peasant student" and poet, Hans Sterneder (born February 7, 1889), who said:

> In the Western World, hardly anyone knows that Sir Isaac Newton (1642–1727) had come to this conclusion, that Sir Frederick William Herschel (1738–1822) had maintained the same opinion or that Johannes Kepler (1571–1630) freely acknowledged that there are spirits which control the movements of the stars. And yet these three men were the greatest astronomers in the West! Surely, this is sufficient to indicate that Goethe, in his *Faust*, which is so full of profound occult knowledge, did not intend his *Spirit of the Earth* as a poetical fiction and nothing more. (*Der Wunderpostel* [The Wonder Apostle], Leipzig, 1930, p. 382.)

And just as, right down to the present time, a belief has persisted in the personality of the stars, so *it is only to be expected* that many exceptional people still speak with the star spirits and move them to action.

Thus, *Cheiro* (real name Count Louis Hamon), the most famous palmist in England, commented on May 10, 1912, at the close of his address at the Brahmins at the International Society for Psychical Research in London:

> . . . that they do not so much summon the souls of the dead as the rulers of higher worlds: the powerful beings who permeate the four elements of fire, air, water and earth and the regents of the nine planets. He considered that they were able, by means of mystic invocations, to call these entities into their midst when, although they never assumed human form, they displayed a marvellous intelligence in what they had to say and performed wonders.[11]

---

[11]Ludwig Deinhard: *Wie der bekannte Handleser Cheiro Okkultist wurde* [*How the Renowned Palmist Cheiro became an Occultist*] in the *Zentralblatt für Okkultismus*, Leipzig, July 1913, p. 28).

Cheiro said that he knew people in London, who practiced the same arts but he would not wish to encourage anyone to follow their example as the inherent dangers were very great."

The planetary archons are subordinate to the "Genii of the Zodiac." Preliminary material relating to their evocation can be found in the works of Papus[12] and Buchmann.[13]

However, experiments in evocation are hazardous and, according to a private communication made to me by a Hamburg hermeticist who was a good friend of Buchmann, the latter owed his death to them!

In many of the mediæval German books of black magic[14] the Arabian *Ruhanijas* with their Arabic names are represented by the seven archangels equally recognized by Arab, Jew, and Christian.

It should certainly prove interesting to discover how a notable initiate,[15] Lord Lytton, described the external appearance of such exalted beings, and so, by way of a supplement, I am publishing here for the first time an article of mine entitled "A High Spirit Appears." It immediately follows the discussion.

---

[12]Papus: *Die Kabbala* (translated into German by Julius Nestler) [*The Qabalah*] Leipzig, 1910. Papus' real name was Dr. Gérard Anatole Vincent Encausse. He was born on July 13, 1865, and, after practicing as a gynecologist in Paris, he was killed in battle while serving as a surgeon-major on October 25, 1916. As a leading Martinist, he was in communication with the last Czar over the "Montenegrines," and introduced his spiritual master, Maître Philippe, to him. The thaumaturgist of Lyons, with acknowledged miracle cures to his credit, was known in everyday life as Nizier-Anthèlme Vachod (April 25, 1849–August 2, 1905). This "friend of God" corresponded for a short time with Kaiser Wilhelm II (1859–1941).

[13]Franz Buehmann: *Schlüssel zu den 72 Gottesnamen der Kabbala* [*A Key to the 72 God Names of the Qabala*] (Leipzig, 1919). His pen-name was Naga. He was employed as Head Accountant for the Charlottenburg waterworks. He developed a green and yellow elixir called "Pranoidin."

[14]Cf., the special study which I wrote for the December number of *Das Neue Licht* in 1939 (Purkersdorf b. Wien, p. 260 ff) entitled "Von den deutschen mittelalterlichen Büchern der Magie" ["German Mediæval Books on Magic"].

[15]On Lord Lytton as an intiate, see G.W. Surya: *Das Lebenselixier, etc.* [*The Elixir of Life, etc.*] (Leipzig, 1923, p. 18 ff). The neophyte who had been admitted by Bulwer—Lytton to the "Hermetische Loge von Alexandria" [The Hermetic Lodge of Alexandria], later wrote his memoirs under the pen-name Tautriadelta in "Borderland" (1896), which had been founded by the famous English spiritist and publicist W.T. Stead (1849–1912) in August 1893.

DISCUSSION

> Strongly you have drawn me here
> And put long pressure on my Sphere.
> What now?
>
> —The Spirit of the Earth
> to Faust

It is stated in the *Pneumatologia occulta et vera* (ca. 1660) that the Carmelite, Albert Bajer, of the convent of Maria Magdalena de stella nova in Italy, invoked the Spirit of Mercury on February 18, 1568, and received instruction in alchemy from the latter.

The first to write about this adept Bajer, who is said to have been murdered at Augsburg for the sake of his tincture some time after 1570, was Matthias Erbe von Brandau, personal physician to the Emperor Rudolph II (1552–1612). He left behind a discourse of the alchemist with the Spirit of Mercury on the stone of the wise, which was published at Paris in 1608 by Sendivogius (1566–1646) under the title of *Colloquium spiritus mercuri cum fratre Alberto Bayero sive Bauaro, monacho carmelitano* [*A Conversation of the Spirit of Mercury with Brother Alberto Bayero or Bauaro, a Carmelite friar*]. This title indicates that the friar was as much addicted to alchemy as he was to performing invocations, which would have been familiar to our Bayer (or Bauer) from the exorcisms he had witnessed in Italy and Spain!

Why should there be no Planetary Spirits? We might well join the Emperor Franz Josef I of Austria (1830–1916) in asking the above question, which he had propounded in reply to the query of whether ghosts could really exist. In any event, there is more to be said in favor of the existence of Planetary Princes than there is against it, since the "machinery of the universe" cannot be explained on purely mechanical lines. Nevertheless, if there are Rulers of the Planets, they would not be at the beck and call of a monk called Bayer or of a Count called Hamon (Cheiro). And if they did come . . . who could survive in their presence?

So, let us ask ourselves, *"Have higher spirit beings of a non-human character ever been successfully invoked by man and, if so, which ones?"* The answer is that we can indeed name such beings. First, we might mention the "Zodiacal Genii" with whom Franz

Buchmann and the magnetic healer, Heinrich Hoffmann used to operate. Buchmann is said to have come to a bad end from the contact. Let the curious be warned! Then there are the so-called "Egregors" (Greek: "Watcher" or "Guardian"). They watch over those who have some common purpose, and guard them. The largest body of this sort having a common purpose is the nation (Cf., Daniel 10:13, 20, 21). Such a unit can become a "person" so to speak, as Paul Distelbarth (born 1879) has shown in his *Lebendiges Frankreich* [*Living France*] (Stuttgart, 1948). When a nation is a person, this does not mean that the nature of the egregor assumes a human form. The Egyptian gods looked like animals to the human eye, for example, and, today we speak of the French cock, the Russian bear and the British lion.

These Egregors have been evoked by humans during theurgic sessions. Thus, we hear of this being done in old St. Petersburg from an exceptional source of information!

Count C. . . , whose true name was only known to iso-lated highgrade initiates, was in fact a very unusual person. An experienced magician and an influential member of several esoteric societies, he maintained a permanent relationship for many years with certain Powers of the invisible world. His vocation was so suc-cessful it took him to the imperial court, the way being prepared for him by the Grand-Duke who was a mem-ber of the occult and secret royal lodge which had been founded by "Master Philipp." The Czar wished to meet and question the magician who had become such a topic of general conversation and granted him an au-dience for the first time one day in October, 1910. The mage soon organized spiritist and magical seances within the royal lodge. The spirit of Czar Alexander III (Alexandrovich; 1881–1894) was repeatedly raised and, on each occasion, made the Czar promise to up-hold the Franco-Russian Alliance! But the most bizarre seances were those in which the magician, dressed in his ceremonial robes and with his sword of power in his hand with which to ward off evil influences, retired together with the Czar and the ritual assistants within a magic circle in the center of the lodge, in order to call up *the occult Power which directs the destiny of Russia*.

This mysterious Power appraised the Czar of the tragic events which were to plunge Europe into a bloodbath a few years later. Whenever the Czar inquired the exact date of these happenings, the Power merely replied, "They are now close at hand!" On one occasion the Czar asked after his own fate, but the entity which had been invoked refused to answer. When the magician insisted, there was a horrible noise, the lights went out and the magical altar was overturned! The Czar and the assistants were seized with fear and the magician thought it expedient to resume his conjurations. It was in this way that Nikolaus II (Alexandrovich, 1868–1913) was informed by magical means as early as 1910 of the coming tragedies. I also know, from an unimpeachable source that the magician's suggestions were not entirely ignored in high places . . .

Then Rasputin (1872–1916) appeared in St. Petersburg, more powerful than ever. The party which favored friendship with Germany triumphed and Count C realized that his time was up at the Russian Court so he withdrew into obscurity. (Joanny Bricaud: *Les Mysticisme à la Cour de Russie* [*Mysticism at the Russian Court*] (Paris, 1921, p. 40 ff).

Gustav Meyrink claimed to have had it from an infallible source that it was the Czar's favorite and Martinist Grand Master Papus who invoked the Egregors with the assistance of the Buriatic (i.e., Mongolian) herbalist Pjotr Badmajeff (1821–1923) and so unleashed the forces which produced World War I. The story also goes that, shortly before his death in 1916, Papus openly boasted that he had caused the Russian Revolution.

Egregors which are smaller than those of whole nations are those belonging to provinces. Chinese governors used to pray to them. Still smaller "organizations" are the urban egregors. The ancient Romans included them in their battle plans, as described in Agrippa's *Occult Philosophy* (Book III, chapter

14 gives the names of the entities involved, and Book I, chapter 70 supplies the "modus operandi"). He says:

> It was an observation amongst the *Romanes* in their holy rites, that when they did besiege any City, they did diligently inquire into the proper and true name of it, and the name of that God under whose protection it was, which being known, they did then with some verse call forth the Gods that were the protectors of that City, and did curse the inhabitants of that City, so at length their Gods being absent, did overcome them. The formula they recited can be found in Macrobius (ca. 500) in his *Saturnalia* (III, 9).

How successful the Romans really were in bringing the enemy's guardian divinities over to their own side is hard to decide at this distance in time. However, the successful theurgic invocation of a Greek goddess was undoubtedly carried out in the recent past. It took place on the island of Aìgina during a new moon and followed an ancient ritual in honor of the goddess Aphaia. Prof. Franz Spunda (born 1889) was assisted in the archaic ceremony by his wife Désirée and by the poet Theodor Däubler (1877–1934). The experiment and its results are described in *Griechische Reise* [*Grecian Journey*] (Berlin, 1926, p. 262 ff) in the chapter on "Aìgina." A ball of bright yellow light drifted slowly down over the pine-clad slope of hill near the ruined temple of Aphaia until it was within less than 300 meters (about 330 yards) of the theurgists, who, sensing the immediate threat of danger, fled from the spot in a headlong rush.

It may be worth mentioning at this point that many spirit beings (especially those of the non-human variety) will assume the ideal shape of a shining sphere ("magnetic volt"). Meyrink seems to hint in the final chapter of his *Der weiße Dominikaner* [*The White Dominican*] (Vienna, 1921), that he takes ball-lightning to be the fiery bodies of evil demons. Both popular belief and the uncanny behavior of this rare phenomenon support his opinion. Confirmation that the old Greek gods were still receiving offerings in the first half of the last century will be found in Kiesewetter's *Faust* (Vienna, n.d. Book II, p. 23, fn.).

In addition to the egregors, and tutelary gods or goddesses (e.g., Aphaia), other exalted non-human spirit entities have been invoked, or have manifested themselves through trance mediums. These are *the representatives of ideas* (such as love, truth, etc.), including ideas in the sense of independent beings like the Sephiroth of the Qabala. Rare manifestations of such "abstractions" took place in 1858 in Mödling bei Wien. The experimenter in charge was Johann Heinrich Stratil, one of the most industrious and painstaking investigators of spiritist phenomena in Germany at that time. The medium was his daughter Sofie and the apparatus employed was a much-used psychograph belonging to the family. The material is set out in *Neueste spiritualistische Mittheilungen* [*The Latest Spiritist News*] of 1862, printed and published by the treasurer D. Hornung.

A HIGH SPIRIT APPEARS

Like a rainbow in the clouds on a rainy day was the sight of that encircling radiance; it was like the appearance of the glory of the Lord.

—Ezekiel 1:28

Elohim is the name given by the Qabala to the highest spiritual beings (Hebrew, "Almightinesses"). The Christian mystics call such beings "Archangels" or "throne prince angels." The abbot Johannes Trithemius termed them "Secundi," i.e., those who come second after God Himself, and Jakob Boehme (1575–1624), the *philosophus teutonicus* (German Philosopher) called them "high spirits." Here is how an exalted spiritual being of this kind, addressed as Adonai (Hebrew for Lord), is described by Sir Edward George Earle Lytton, First Baron Lytton of Knebworth (1803–1873), Secretary of State for the Colonies, novelist, and practicing magician of high grade, in *Zanoni* (1842), which he called the "well-loved work of my matured manhood."

And in the lonely cave, whence once had gone forth the oracles of a heathen god [on the Ionian island] there emerged from the shadows of fantastic rocks, a luminous and gigantic column, glittering and shifting. It resembled the shining but misty spray, which, seen afar off, a fountain seems to send up on a starry night. . . . From the column there emerged a shape of unimaginable glory. Its face was that of a man in its first youth; but solemn, as with the consciousness of eternity and the tranquility of wisdom; light, like star-beams, flowed through its transparent veins; light made its limbs themselves, and undulated, in restless sparkles, through the waves of its dazzling hair. (Berlin, 1919, pp. 254–255; Book Four, chapter 9.)

... and through the room [in Paris] rushed, luminous and sudden, the Presence of silvery light. As the Heavenly visitor stood in the atmosphere of his own lustre, and looked upon the face of the Theurgist[1] with an aspect of ineffable tenderness and love, all space seemed lighted from his smile. Along the blue air without, from that chamber in which his wings had halted, to the farthest star in the azure distance, it seemed as if the track of his flight were visible, by a lenthened splendour in the air, like the column of moonlight on the sea. Like the flower that diffuses perfume as the very breath of its life, so the emanation of that presence was joy.[2] Over the world, as a million times swifter than light, than electricity, the Son of Glory had sped his way to the side of love, his wings had scattered delight as the morning scatters dew. For that brief moment, Poverty had ceased to mourn, Disease fled from its prey, and Hope breathed a dream of Heaven into the darkness of Despair. ...

The visitor was gone; but still the glory of his presence seemed to shine upon the spot; still the solitary air seemed to murmur with tremulous delight. And thus ever shall it be with those who have once, detaching themselves utterly from life, received the visit of the Angel FAITH. Solitude and space retain the splendour, and it settles like a halo round their graves (p. 393–394; Book Seven, chapter 13).

---

[1] The word "theurgy" comes from the Greek *theos* = God + *ergon* = work, and therefore means the production of effects with the assistance of God (or of the higher spirits). The theurgist or "God-empowered man" is called "Baalschem" by the Qabalists. The best known of these is Rabbi Israel of Miedziboz (Podolien), the "Bescht" (1700–1760), who founded the sect of the "Chasidim" (= pious) around 1750.

[2] Cf., the Indian perception of Brahma as bliss (Sanskrit: *ananda*)!

The preparations for the theurgic procedure have been depicted in the following manner by the Qabalist[3] Abraham Abulafia (1240–1285) in his *Sépher chaijê olâm ha-bâ* [*Book of Life of the World to Come*]:

> Prepare thyself to direct thy heart to God alone! Purify thy body and retire to a lonely place. . . . Thou canst carry out thy purpose in thy chamber during the day, *but it is better to do so at night*. Withold all thy thoughts from the vanities of the world, for thou art to speak with thy Maker and crave, verily, that He will reveal to thee His power. Wrap thy prayer-shawl (tallith) around thee! Bind thy phylacteries (tephillin) to head and hand, that thou mayest approach with reverence the Shekinah (visible glory of Jehovah), with which thou must converse! Clean thy clothing, *attiring thyself if possible only in white garments*. If it is night, do thou kindle many lights. . . . Unite thy thoughts with the Divine Names and with *the Angels of God, whom thou mayest think of as surrounding thee in human form*. (P. Levertoff: *Die religiöse Denkweise der Chassidim, nach den Quellen dargestellt* [*The Religious Thought of the Chasidim, Illustrated from Original Sources*] Leipzig, 1918, p. 70).

Lord Lytton's description provides the most beautiful model of all for this use of the creative imagination during deep meditation! Abulafia continues:

> Thereupon will the limbs of thy body begin to tremble and *thou wilt think that thy soul is separating from thy body*. But then wilt thou feel a heavenly joy; for, in that moment, thou wilt mark that thou art in a fit state to receive the Spirit of God. Then hide thy face and take off thy shoes . . . rejoice in the lot that has fallen to thee and know thou that it is God's love which bestows on thee this knowledge. If thou wilt but steadfastly

---

[3]The forerunner of the Rosicrucians, Johann Reuchlin (Capnio, 1455–1522), says with good reason of this sort of Qabala: "The Qabala does not leave us creeping about on the floor of the physical world, it draws us upward into communion with God and the angels."

continue in these holy *meditations, so shalt thou go on, little by little, to yet more glorious things.*

Therefore, "Arise, shine; for thy *light* is come" (Isaiah 60:1), for He covers Himself "with *light* as with a garment" (Psalm 104:2) and only in His "*light* shall we see *light*" (Psalm 36:10). The "Cherubinic Wayfarer" Angelus Silesius (Johann Scheffler) sings:

> To God in Light a road must be;
> Would'st see HIM, it must run in thee.

THE MYSTERIOUS
ROTAE MUNDI

Were it not a precious thing that you could so read in
one only book, and withal by reading understand and
remember all that which in all other books (which here-
tofore have been, and are now, and hereafter shall
come out) hath been, is, and shall be learned and found
out of them?

—*Confessio Fraternitatis RC* c. IV

One of the basic Rosicrucian documents, the *Fama*[1] mentions
the *Rotae Mundi* four times:

1) ". . . our Rota takes her beginning from that day when
God spoke Fiat, and shall end when he shall speak Pereat"
(p. 62).

2) ". . . in our philosophical 'bibliotheca' . . . was . . . Rota
Mundi . . . the most artificial (book)" (p. 66).

3) ". . . because first we would overlook our Rotam" (p. 68).

4) ". . . by instruction and command of our Rota . . ." (p.
73).[2]

---

[1]Dr. Ferdinand Maack: *Vier Rosenkreuzerschriften* [*Four Rosicrucian Excerpts*]
(Berlin, 1913). The references are to the page numbers in the *Fama*. *"Fiat"*
= "let it be!" and *"Pereat"* = "let it perish!"
[2]Trans. note: the page numbers given here are taken from the limited Helios
Book Service Ltd. edition of the 1652 English translation by "Eugenius
Philalethes."

To judge from these four excerpts taken together, the *Rotae* are perpetually valid laws, laid down in a very ingenious "book," which were consulted before anything of importance was undertaken. The words *Rota(e) Mundi* come from the Latin and mean "World Wheel" or "World Wheels." The abbreviation "FRC" of the words *Fratres Roseae Crucis* (i.e., Brothers of the Rosy Cross), which also come from the Latin, was once interpreted to mean "Fratres Roris Coctis" (= Brothers of the Boiled Dew). It would have been more reasonable and would have involved less distortion of the original to have read "FRC" as *Fratres Rotae Crusis* (= Wheel Cross Brothers), because:

1) The Brothers accorded such importance to their Rotis;

2) The circle of the wheel, as an archaic representation of the *Rose*, associated with the four-spoke *Cross* of the original wheel, is a complete and perfect emblem of the Fraternity.

3) A "brotherhood of the wheel" did in fact grow out of the Rosicrucian movement.[3]

Is the "Rotae Mundi" an instrument of divination made in the form of a wheel? To revert to out original quotations from the *Fama*, what—we may ask ourselves—is meant by a "book" that will answer all questions? Why was it called a "Wheel?" Perhaps it was not a book in the accepted sense of the word, but an

---

[3]James Harrington (1611–1677), the English historian, was a Rosicrucian. In this capacity, he gathered the "Rotary Club" around him. Rotary Clubs were revived in 1905 by the American attorney, Paul Harris, of Chicago. Its badge is a golden *wheel* worn in the button-hole. Rotary has as its ideal service to the community by business, industry, and the liberal professions. Harrington wrote the "Commonwealth of Oceana" (1656), under the inspiration of the "Atlantis" of Plato (427–347 B.C.) and the *Utopia* of Sir Thomas More (1478–1535), in which he offered a solution for setting up the ideal republican state.

The Rosicrucian, Francis Bacon, Baron Verulam (1561–1626), wrote about a technosophic, ideal republic in his *Nova Atlantis* (1624). About the same time, the Hessian-Cassels university professor, Heinrich Nollius tried to found a "Fraternitas Rotae coelestis" (Latin for *Brüderschaft des himmlischen Rades* or "Brotherhood of the Heavenly Wheel"). Its aim was *"ad restitutionem Hermeticae medicinae ac philosophiae"* (Latin for "to bring about the restoration of Hermetic medicine and philosophy.") He was the author of *Via sapientiae triunae* (1620); *Parergi philosophi speculum.*

actual wheel; a wheel-shaped instrument from which one might read the causal connections between the "train of wheels" by which the world is moved, just as one might read a book?

As a matter of fact, wheel-shaped divinatory instruments have been in use from hoary antiquity right down to the present day.

1) "To the *Druids, who employed wheels in making their most impressive prophecies,* the hub was the symbol of the sun, the spokes represented the heavenly bodies turning round the sun and the rim of the wheel was eternity."[4]

Yes indeed, the *"divinatio per rota"* (divination by means of a wheel) was their most impressive form of divination; unfortunately the *modus operandi* has not been disclosed.

2) Mediæval books of magic reproduce the letters of the alphabet (an *alphabetarium*) in the form of a wheel or dial, with a pointer as the "psychograph" or a pendulum to turn it into the "Great Speaking Wheel of Raphael." This wheel is shown below.

An unusual feature of its use[5] is that the pendulum is not held in the hand but suspended independently. Therefore,

---

[4]C.G. Jung: *Psychologie und Religion [Psychology and Religion]* (Zürich and Leipzig, 1940, p. 200, 201).

[5]The great talking wheel for invocations to Raphael: "This operation must be performed on a bright day when the Moon is waxing. As dawn appears, take the skin of a virgin lamb ('virgin parchment') and write on it with a new

it can not be set in motion by involuntary and unobserved hand and finger movements!

3) Prof. Karl Gustav Carus (1789–1869), doctor of medicine, privy counselor and personal physician to the King of Saxony from 1827, knew of the psychograph (planchette) in its board and in its wheel form.[6]

4) Dutch spiritists are still using the planchette in wheel-form today.[7]

---

goose-quill and with new ink (in which quill has never before been dipped) the design of this talking wheel with the six-pointed star inside it and containing the names of angels and the sign of the spirit with his seal, and put the letters of the alphabet round the rim. After this has been done, consecrate the parchment by sprinkling it with holy water and fumigating it with incense. The next step is to prepare a pendulum made of heavy metal shaped like an inverted triangle. This is suspended from a gold-colored silk thread and is consecrated in exactly the same way as the wheel, with holy water and with incense. The talking wheel is used by spreading the parchment on a table and hanging the pendulum over it. After Raphael has been invoked, the questions are asked and the pendulum supplies the answers by pausing over one letter after another in such a way as to spell out words (H.M. de Campigny).

[6]Carus in his *Über Lebensmagnetismus etc.* [*Animal Magnetism, etc.*] (New impression: Bâle, 1925; pp. 176–177; the section on table-turning and spirit-rapping) had this to say: "Dr. Wenni of Zürich ('Allg. ZTG.' dated April 23, 1854) and my second son, a Dresden chemist (ditto p. 1803) made *round* wooden plates which rotated freely on a vertical axis. The two experimenters claimed that as soon as several persons formed a chain on one of these movable plates, by linking their hands with external fingers touching, the plate started to rotate (note the use of word derived from 'Rota'!, W. Schrödter). I myself have observed this rotation many times and, struck by the high success rate of the attempts, I have attempted to arrive at a scientific explanation for the phenomenon in terms of the nerve currents of the individuals involved, which might be presumed to act in much the same way as magnetism and galvanic electricity combined produce rotation in the copper wheel designed and constructed by Pfaff" (*Allgemeine Zeitung* in a postscript to the article by W. Carus).

[7]Dr. Friedrich Markus Huebner in his *Satan im Tulpenfeld [Satan in the Tulip Field]* (Berlin, 1935, p. 189 ff): "On the plate (the table) lay a chart with letters of the alphabet, figures, and signs. It had been unrolled under *a thin wheel cross of light wood made with four spokes.*" This wooden wheel cross had to be touched by the three sitters "very lightly and with the fingertips only.

"They stretched out their hands to it from three sides and, lo and behold! The piece of wood, which was being held by their six hands rose up above

Is *the "Rotae Mundi" a rotatable disc which points out analogies?* A "spoked-wheel cross" (or planchette), however, is neither a "book" nor "most artificial" in the old sense of being highly ingenious. Therefore we shall have to pursue our investigations beyond the foundational Rosicrucian documents. A true Rosicrucian, Florentinus de Valentia (= Daniel Mögling) says in *Rosa Florescens* (Frankfurt am Main, 1617), that the Rosicrucians possessed Rhythomancy; the use and construction of the "Wheel of Pythagoras," by which that philosopher sought to fathom all things in terms of numbers, even those matters which appertain to God Himself. This is said to have been described by a certain Christopher of Catanea at the end of his *Geomantie [Geomancy]*, a book which I have been unable to obtain.[8]

I have, however, inspected the description given by Dr. Georg Pictorius of Villingen, in his book on *Varieties of Ceremonial Magic known as Goetia*, under the heading, "Onomantia," p. 184 [*Von den Gattungen der ceremoniellen Magie, welche man Goetie nennt*].[9]

---

their hands, apparently of its own accord. Then the questions were put. The cross-frame, dragging the hands of the seance members after it, made wavering curves. Finally, as if tired of hesitation, it started pecking like a bird *with the arrow fastened to its underside* at the letters of the alphabet on the planchette."

It should be remarked that the word "planchette" is used in error here for the alphabet set out on the table. Properly speaking, it is a small board running on castors and a pencil point as used by spiritists for automatic writing. A planchette plus an alphabetic lay-out make the "Ouija" (Larousse). (Ouija is made up of the French and German words for yes, *"oui"* and *"ja"* respectively.)

[8]Gottfried Wilhelm, Baron von Leibnitz (1646–1716) is thought to have taken a cue from the *Rotae Mundi* in writing his treatise *De Arte Combinatoria* (see the preface to *Die Prinzipen der Infinitesimalrechnung* [*The Principles of Infinitesimal Calculus*). It will be ascertained that this figure is an eight-spoked wheel like the so-called Dharma = chakra ("wheel of the law") of Buddhism, in which the eight spokes correspond to the Eightfold Path. As a young man, Leibnitz was secretary to a Rosicrucian society at Nuremberg.

[9]*The Wheel of Pythagoras*: Those who practice onomancy believe that they can predict from this figure the death or recovery of the sick, the falling ill or continuance in good health of the well, besides good luck and bad. The procedure is as follows. The age of the Moon in days is first determined and the number is written down. Then the initial letter of the proper name of

His book is published in the fourth volume which was added to the three books of Agrippa's *Occult Philosophy* at a fairly early date (Agrippa lived from 1486 to 1535).

Now, I do not think, any more than does the Ensisheim medical officer Pictorius, that Pythagoras (580–493 B.C.) was the inventor of this primitive instrument for divination. Nevertheless, the figure of Pythagoras does seem to hover in the background and the unsophisticated character of the device seems to indicate that it has been handed down to us from high antiquity.[10] My own opinion, for what it is worth, is that this "primitive scheme" is not so primitive as it looks, however, but is the simplified corruption, which found its way into popular use, of what was originally an "extremely ingenious" arrangement of concentric rotatable discs full of "correspondences" laid one on top of another. An apparatus such as that (made of copper perhaps) would have been worthy of the Rosicrucians.

Before the time of Rosencreutz (1378–1484) an attempt

---

the individual for whom the inquiry is being made is matched with the number which accompanies it in the outer circle of the diagram and the latter is set down under the number already found. Next, one works out the number of the day on which the person fell ill, whether it was Sunday, Monday or some other day. These three numbers are then added together, their sum is divided by 30 and the remainder taken for reading the oracle. The meaning of this remainder is given in the inner part of the diagram as follows:

Vita	=	Life	Mors	=	Death
Sanitas	=	Health	Morbus	=	Illness
Bona fortuna	=	Good fortune	Mala fortuna	=	Misfortune

The Latin names of the days have the following English equivalents: Sol = Sunday; Luna = Monday; Mars = Tuesday; Mercurius = Wednesday; Jupiter = Thursday; Venus = Friday; Saturnus = Saturday. Some people ascribe the above diagram to Pythagoras, but one may safely assume that the great man would not have wasted his time on anything so trifling. This type of prediction is also known as arithmancy, because it is performed with numbers. Pictorius also wrote *Tractatus de rebus non naturalibus* [*A Treatise on Things Not Natural*].

[10]"These things are generally attributed to *Pythagoras*. Various fortune-telling tables go under the name of Pythagoras. They are listed in Diel's *Handschriften der antiken Ärzte* [*Manuscripts of Ancient Physicians*] (Abhandlungen der Kgl. preuss. Akad. d. Wiss. [Transactions of the Royal Prussian Academy of Science] I. 1907, p. 64) and in Boll's *Catal. codd. astrol. gr.* [*Codified Catalogue of Greek Astrologers*] (VII, p. 21)" (Hentges).

of this sort was made by Raimundus Lullus (Ramon Lull or Raymond Lully, 1235–1315), the "doctor illuminatus." *The Ars magna Lulli* [*Art of Raymond Lully*] aimed at clear comprehension and safe reasoning by using a schematic arrangement of concepts (Brockhaus—publishers of a leading German encyclopaedia).

He replaced the ten categories of Aristotle (384–322) by others of a higher order, and made the extravagant attempt to classify the sum total of human knowledge under a system of key letters. He flattered himself that he could, in the same way, draw inferences about unknown matters, much as algebraists obtain general solutions of mathematical problems by substituting letters for numbers which are not available to them.[11] His scheme of ten is reminiscent of the *ten Sephiroth of the Qabala*! Lully spoke Arabic and spent a long time in the Orient as a missionary to the Mohammedans. It may be that he brought back the idea of his "art" with him from there.[12]

What tends to convince me of this is the title of a book I once saw, which read: *"Vaticinia s. prophetiae abbatis Joachim, et Anselmi episc. Marsirani . . . Quibus Rota et Oraculum Turcicum maxime considerationis adjecta sunt. Una cum praef . . . Paschalini Regiselmi"* (Venetiis, Joa. B. Bertonum, 1600). The book was published in Latin and German with an engraved title page and 20 copper plates in the text. The title of this quarto volume may be rendered in English as *The Predictions of the Holy Prophets Abbot Joachim and Bishop Anselm of Marsiranus . . . To which have been added for Special Consideration the Rota and Oracle of the Turks*, etc . . . Cornelius Agrippa (1486–1535), who comes *after* Rosencreutz (1378–1484) gives a "scheme of correspondences" under the heading, "The Scale of the Number Four, Answering the Four Elements," in his *Occult Philosophy*.[13]

---

[11]Grillot de Givry: *Anthologie de l'Occultisme* (Paris, 1922, p. 233).

[12]"This type of mantic still persists in the East, taking a very complex form at times. It was frequently described by mediaeval and renaissance authors too" (Ernest Hentges).

[13]Trans. note: it is true that details of the Scale of the Number four are to be found in Agrippa's *Occult Philosophy*, but he says nothing about the ALL or the two original opposing forces when discussing the Scale.

It is constructed on the basis of two original opposing forces—expansion and contraction—and displays its effects on the ALL in its maximum and minimum states. The details can be found in Agrippa!

This scheme is very useful and, for that reason, it was seized on by the Hofrat of the Electorate of Bavaria, Karl von Eckartshausen (1752–1803). He mentioned it in his *Aufschlüssen zur Magie aus geprüften Erfahrungen* [*Elucidations of Magic from Trustworthy Observations*] (Vol. II), without stating his sources; possibly he rediscovered it independently.

I found out later that a similar scheme of correspondences had already been known to the Chinese from time immemorial, although admittedly it is based on the number five rather than the number four. Jean Marqués-Rivière gives it in his *Amulettes, Talismans et Pantacles* [*Amulets, Talismans and Pentacles*] (Paris, 1938, p. 205), and so does Henseling (p. 152).

Robert Henseling presents us in his *Umstrittenes Weltbild* [*Disputed Cosmology*] (Leipzig, 1939, p. 124) with a table of correspondences based on the number four (as does Eckartshausen). This "synopsis of relationships" can be traced back to the astrologer, Antiochos of Athens (2nd cent. A.D.) (Franz Boll). Hoené Wronski (1778–1853) designed a "Prognometer" consisting of rotatable copper discs. It was a prognostic instrument based on Zodiacal symbolism. Charcornac has illustrated it and described it in detail (pp. 136 ff). The "Archaeometer" of Joseph-Alexandre, Marquis de Saint-Yves d'Alveydre (1842–1909) was constructed on the same principle, although made of a different material (cardboard).[14]

Hence, to sum up, the inference can be drawn that: ROTAE MUNDI were wheel-shaped representations of the universe in the form of rotatable discs marked with correspondences and looking rather like the old photographic exposure calculators. For the sake of durability, they must have been

---

[14]The Anhalt-Dessau councilor, Julius Sperber (died 1616) invented a *speculum archetypum* or "mirror of archetypes" even before this to supply the meaning of every word and serve as a key to all systems of music. A second device, the "mirror of prototypes" was said to elucidate racial differences. (*Echo der von Gott erleuchteten Fraternitas RC* [*Echoes of the Divinely Illuminated Fraternity of the Rosicrucians*] Danzig, 1616.)

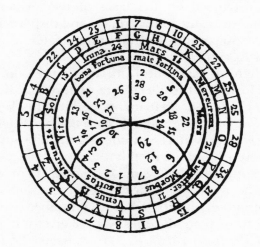

made of metal (copper say, or silver or gold). Presumably, they would have consisted of at least three but more probably of seven, concentric discs or "wheels." After the discs had been correctly adjusted, the correlations and influences ruling the case were read off (as if from a book) in the three worlds and four elements, with the two polarities in their two currently-operating phases, the seven planets and the four kingdoms (mineral, vegetable, animal, and human).

Is the Tarot the same as the "Rotae Mundi"? In 1604, during repairs to the "College of the Holy Ghost" somewhere in Southern Germany or the Tyrol, after a seven-sided sacramental vault had been accidentally discovered and the altar inside, together with the strong brass plate on which it rested, had been moved, the Rosicrucian Brethren found "a fair and worthy body, whole and unconsumed, as the same is here lively counterfeited, with all the ornaments and attires." This was the body of their founder, Christian Rosencreutz. "In his hand he held a parchment book called T., which next unto the Bible is our greatest treasure, which ought not to be delivered to the censure of the world."[15]

The book which, next to the Bible, was their greatest treasure and beyond the understanding of the world must have been the *Rotae Mundi*! But why was it called T.? What was its "official"

---

[15]*Fama*, ed. Maack, pp. 53, 54.

title and how was it named in the world? The answer is this. The word "rota" can be set out on the arms of a cross or "wheel-and-cross" as shown (below) and can then be read in a number of different ways.

Commencing at the top and reading clockwise, we get "rota" but, starting at the bottom and reading counterclockwise, we get its anagram "Tora(h)," a Hebrew word meaning "instruction." If we begin once more with the letter T at the bottom but read in a clockwise direction, we obtain the word "Taro(t)." Possible derivations of "Tarot" are from the ancient Egyptian word *tarut* meaning "that which is consulted" or the Zend word *tarisk* meaning "I seek an answer."

But why refer to a pack of picture cards as a book? A very good answer is that the Tarot has been known as *The Book of Thoth* for longer than anyone knows. The name comes from the ancient Egyptian ibis-headed moon-god, Thouth—the revealer of all primeval wisdom. The Greeks named him *Hermes Trismegistos* (Thrice-Great Hermes) and from this name is derived the word "Hermetic" and such terms as "Hermetic books," "Hermetic chain," "Hermetic philosophy," etc.

The reader may be disposed to wonder whether there is any other link, besides an anagrammatic one, between the word "Taro(t)" and "rota" = a wheel. There certainly is, for the twenty-two Major Arcana can be set out in wheel-formation. As the Parisian magnetic healer and esotericist Oswald Wirth[16] explains:

The real Tarot is limited to the twenty-two philosophical keys and has no connection with the well-known

---

[16]*Das Studium des Tarot, Einführung in die Entzifferung der 22 Arkana* ["The Study of the Tarot: An Introduction to the Decipherment of the 22 Arcana" in *The Grove of Isis*] (Brandenburg/Havel, 1930, No. 11; p. 297 ff).

game of cards with which it is associated. There are twenty-two pictures. This number is that of the letters of the primitive alphabet. The pictures are numbered, with a single exception, which can therefore be regarded as representing zero. The numbered cards total twenty-one, a number having as factors three and seven, which are traditionally the holiest of all numbers.

Before considering each picture individually, it will be as well to try and discover the laws governing the construction of the Tarot as a whole. How is the Tarot made up, looked at logically? The twenty-two major aracana follow one another in numerical order from 1 to 21 and the zero card comes either before the one or behind the twenty-one. This question of the position of the zero is resolved *when the cards are laid out in the form of a wheel as seems to be suggested by the possible derivation of the word rota (a wheel)* from the word Taro.

The cirular arrangement produces, as it does in the terrestrial globe, two opposed hemispheres or, to put it more simply, a northern and a southern series. For easier comparison, the semicircular halves can be stretched in a straight line along their common equator. It then appears that they possess opposite polarizations, for many of the pictures in the northern half can be seen, at first glance, to be opposite in meaning to the corresponding pictures in the southern half.

Thus the Tarot is dipolar; being masculine from cards 1 to 11 and feminine from cards 12 to 0.

And that is not all. A set of four is formed by the arcana 2, 3, 4 and 5, i.e., the Empress and Emperor flanked by the Popess and the Pope. These four make up a sub-group with a meaning of its own which requires investigation. Then, as might be expected, there is a contrasting sub-group in the other half of the Tarot arcana spread: cards 18, 19, 20 and 21 (Moon, Sun, Judgement and World). Anticipations of symmetry lead us to think that there must be another pair of sets of four consisting of arcana 7, 8, 9 and 10 (The Char-

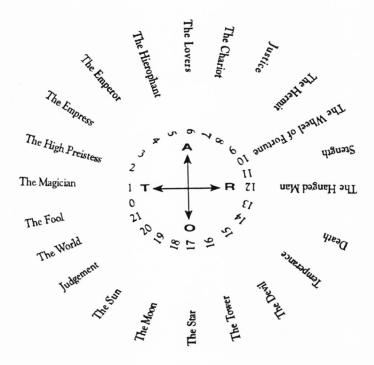

iot, Justice, The Hermit and The Wheel of Fortune) and 13, 14, 15 and 16 (Death, Temperance, The Devil, The Tower). And so there are now four sets of four pivoted, as it were, on arcana 0, 1, 11, and 12 (The Fool, The Juggler, Strength and The Hanged Man) which in themselves make a fifth set of four. Two arcana (The Lovers and The Star) are left over. They occupy an intermediate or "neutral" position, like links between the cards which precede and follow them.

The above structural layout of the Tarot should be borne in mind by those studying the twenty-two major arcana, because it provides an extremely important key to its interpretation. In fact, the major arcana fall into four contrasting sets which, for the sake of reference, can be assigned to the following points of the compass: northwest and northeast in the northern half and southeast and southwest in the southern half.

Since the Tarot is used worldwide as an instrument of divination, it is justly called *Rotae Mundi*, especially when dealt in the wheel-shaped spread. People speak of the "*Wheel* of Fate" and that is exactly what it is!

Papus, too, gives a wheel-shaped arrangement of the major arcana of the Tarot as a "General Key and Analogy" in *Le Tarot Divinatoire* [*The Divinatory Tarot*] (Paris, 1919, p. 169). The question is, who inspired whom?

Eliphas Lévi (the Abbé A.L. Constant, 1810–1875) wrote as follows in a letter sent to the spiritist magnetizer L. Goupy in 1854:

> You have asked me what key I employ in order to decipher and interpret all occult and magical texts; of this key there are three kinds . . .

> The "Proteus" (Fr. *Protée*) or *Wheel of the Rosicrucians*,[17] a hieroglyphic synthesis of the universal language; as once found expression in the Qabalistic alphabet. I will give you a concise account of each key, making sure to supply enough information to facilitate your researches and to enable you to pursue them all in accordance with the high sciences.

Unfortunately, Eliphas Lévi did not redeem this promise completely but discussed the first two keys only, and these do not concern us here.

DISCUSSION

"*Rotae Mundi* as a wheel-shaped psychograph [Greek for 'Soul Writer'] is, to begin with, nothing more than a sensitive detector of the nerve impulses of the body" (Professor of Geology, Albert Heim, Zürich). It is an "ascending pipe to enable material to come up from the depths of the collective subconscious."

Prof. M. Benedikt of Vienna has discovered that the divining rod is considerably more sensitive when placed in the

---

[17]Paul Chacornac, the author of the book *Eliphas Levy* [Eliphas Lévi] (Paris, 1926), from which the above has been taken, adds the explanation: "The game of Tarot" as a footnote to Number 3 (on page 156).

vicinity of an inductive machine, in other words if electrically "influenced." Now, as the pendulum which is suspended over the wheel-shaped pendulum is in effect a "rotating divining rod" (in the words of Julie Kniese), perhaps that, too, would give a better reaction when used near an electric machine of this sort. Here is a hint researchers might like to follow up!

It is only in the rarest cases that spirits manifest through either apparatus (pendulum or divining rod). If they do make themselves known, however, they should be tested by the method laid down in the Bible in I John; chapter 4; verses 1–3 (". . . Every spirit that confesseth that Jesus Christ is come in the flesh is of God: And every spirit that confesseth not that Jesus Christ is come in the flesh is not of God . . . .") Tried and tested! On the "Rotae Mundi" as the Tarot, reference should be made to Joachim Winckelmann's pithy textbook, *Tarot: der uralte Schlüssel Salomonis* [*The Tarot: the Ancient Key of Solomon*] (*Das Buch Thot*), Berlin, 1952.

ROSICRUCIAN TELEPATHY

Thus it is possible, by MAGIC, to hear a voice beyond
the sea and someone in the East may converse with
someone in the West. But you must all understand
this, that the cause resides in the imagination. The
imagination can cross thousands of miles and can make
an impression thousands of miles away too.

—Paracelsus
Phil. sagax, L.I., c. 4

When A. Christian Rosenkreutz (1378–1484) arrived in Dhamar
(Yemen),[1] he was sixteen years old and he stayed there for three
years (1394–1397). "There the wise men received him (as he
himself witnesseth)[2] not as a stranger, *but as one whom they had
long expected.* They called him by his name and showed him other

---

[1] Trans. note: the English edition of *Eugenius Philalethes*, 1652, has Damascus,
not "Dhamar" (or "Damear") in Arabia as the place where Christian Rosencreutz stayed with his teachers for three years, but presumably the German
text is more accurate, seeing it quotes from the original. Internal evidence
alone should, perhaps, alert English readers to the possibility of error in the
Philalethes rendering, because we are given to understand that Christian
Rosencreutz was already in Damascus when he was overcome with a desire
to leave for "Damascus" (or rather "Damear") with his new Arab friends.
Also, when he eventually left this town it was to go from there to Egypt across
the "Sinus Arabicus," not the Mediterranean. It is worth noting, too, that
reference is made to "Damear" in the *Confessio*, which suggests that it could
also have been mentioned in the *Fama*.

[2] Presumably in his "Itinerarium" (Latin for Travel Journal).

secrets out of his cloister,[3] whereat he could not but mightily wonder."[4] *The wise men would seem, therefore, to have had telepathic powers, and to have attracted him to them.* They were also clairvoyant. Having been instructed by them in this art, he taught it in turn to his Rosicrucian brethren, who speak of it alluringly in the following terms: "Were it not excellent you dwell in one place, that neither the people which dwell beyond the River Ganges in the Indies could hide anything, nor those which live in Peru might be able to keep secret their counsels from thee?"[5]

We will put it on record: Rosencreutz brought the art of telepathy with him from Arabia.

Henry Cornelius Agrippa von Nettesheim, M.D. et jur.utr. (1486–1535), who founded the Rosicrucian Fraternity *Sodalitium* at Paris in 1507, a Fraternity which later spread throughout France and to Germany, Italy, Spain, and England, made the acquaintance, during a visit to Würzburg, of the abbot, Johannes Trithemius (or rather Heidenberg, 1462–1516), one of the greatest adepts in magic and the Qabala. He stayed with him at the monastery of St. Jacob and must have learned a great deal from him. The "demonic knight" writes: "And hence it is possible naturally, and far from all manner of superstition, no other spirit coming between them, that a man should be able to signifie his mind unto another man, abiding at a very long and unknown distance from him; although he cannot precisely give an estimate of the time when it is, yet of necessity it must be within 24 hours; and I myself know how to do it, and have often done it. The same also in time past did the Abbot Tritenius[6] both know and do."[7]

The chapter from which this excerpt has been taken is entitled, "Of the wonderfull Natures of Water, Aire, and

---

[3]"Secrets out of his cloister" would be the alchemical experiments carried out with Bishop Florentius Radewijns (died 1393) and Gerardus Magnus (1340–1384).
[4]*Fama Fraternitatis*, Cassel, 1614.
[5]*Confessio Fraternitatis*, Cassel, 1615.
[6]Trans. note: this is how the English version of 1651 spells the name of the "Abt Tritheim" or Abbot Trithemius as we know him.
[7]*De Occulta Philosophia*, 1st ed. (Lat.) Cologne, 1510, 1st. English edition, 1651, Book I, chapter 6.

Winds." Now the Tibetans, interestingly enough, describe telepathy as sending messages "on the winds."[8] Nowadays, instead
of talking about "air" and "winds" we refer to the "ether" and
use radio transmissions as an analogy!

We have testimony to the telepthic powers of Trithemius,
other than that of Agrippa, in the letter written March 8, 1506,
to Privy Councilor Germanus (Germain) de Ganay, subsequently Bishop of Orleans, from Saint-Quentin by Karl Bovillius (Boville) of Picardy, who had been entertained for a
fortnight in 1504 by Trithemius in Sponheim bei Kreuznach.
He related, among other things, how when, on the very first
day of their visit they were talking about someone who had
stolen from them on the way, the Abbot said that he could
compel the thief to come where they were, bringing the stolen
goods with him.[9] Bovillius considered that such a feat would be
impossible without the assistance of *spirits*.[10]

This ability claimed by the learned wizard-abbot,[11] has contemporary parallels:

1) The professional clairvoyant, Max Moecke[12] had his
new hat stolen while he was at a dance in Oberrosen near
Breslau. He announced to the scoffing youths who had
gathered round him that the culprit would restore the hat
before midnight, as he would be too scared to hold on to
it. Sure enough, shortly before twelve, the hat-thief arrived
from Breslau perspiring with fear, and confessed in a
trembling voice, but loud enough for everyone to hear,

---

[8]Alexandra David-Neel: *Mystics and Magicians in Tibet* (Leipzig, 1932, pp. 224 ff).

[9]This letter is to be found in the book by Johann Wier, a student of Agrippa's who lived from 1515 to 1588: *De praestigiis Daemonum [Deceiving Demons]* (Book II, chapter 6). Dr. Wier(us), the Belgian opponent of witch-hunts, had pre-viously studied the "wonders" of the sorcerers in Tunis!

[10]"As soon as people see anything out of the ordinary, they seek in their ignorance to attribute its authorship to demons, and treat as a wonder that which is the work of natural or mathematical sciences" (*Occult Philosophy*, Book I, chapter 1). Trans. note: I have not found this in the English edition of 1651.

[11]"I came to Trithemius and found in him a wizard and anything but a philosopher" (Boville to Ganay).

[12]Max Moecke: *Magie im Alltag [Magic in the Everyday]* Stuttgart, 1932, pp. 15, 16.

that he had been unable to "endure it" any longer. What exerted an influence here was the very concentration on working at a distance, without ceremonies or vehicles for increasing confidence, emotional excitement or degree of visualization.

2) In Westerwald there was a miller who knew how to enchant thieves in the following way: In the evening when all was still—even the millwheel—the miller walked up and down in his room and bowed toward three of its corners in the name of the Father, Son, and Holy Ghost, and asked for the stolen goods "as surely as They were present there" and kept repeating this request for a whole hour while standing in the fourth corner. He continued with the conjuration on the second evening, and once again on a third. It is said that the thief of the moment gradually fell prey to an increasing anxiety which robbed him of sleep and compelled him to restore the stolen goods, however far he might have removed them from the scene of the crime. (Dr. Paul Zaunert: *Hess.-Nass. Sagen* [*Legends of Hesse and Nassau*] Jena, 1929, p. 272.) This is working at a distance with the help of ceremony!

3) In Baden (Wuttke) and in the Kaufunger Forest near Cassel, there are "cunning men" who can trouble thieves and bring about the restitution of goods by constantly turning the wheel of a hand-cart round and round while muttering certain spells. (Zaunert, op. cit., pp. 272–273.) This is working at a distance with the help of vehicles ("crutches" or helps for the imagination).

These methods of charming thieves are very finely divided from black magic ("nocturnal boiling," the sending of nightmarish dreams night after night, death prayers, etc.).[13]
Rosencreutz imported telepathy from *Arabia*.

Since the beginning of the nineteenth century, it has been recognized that the Orientals possess secret

---

[13]Heine, J.F.: *Abusum Psalmi CIX imprecatori oder das Todbeten* [*The Misuse of the Imprecatory Psalm, 109, or Death Prayers*] (Helmst, 1708).

methods of communicating with one another over great distances. Information travels with the speed of lightning. It has become common knowledge that the bazaars possess their telepaths, who transmit and receive messages with their brains direct by their own variety of "wireless telegraphy." They have left it to us Europeans to find ways of doing the same thing by mechanical means! News conveyed like this is called "Khabar"—Arabian news. It is received in the "magic mirror."

The procedure used by the Arabs of the interior of Africa is the one with which I, personally, am most familiar. There they pour a drop of black ink, about the size of a 10 Pfennig piece [a dime] into the palm of the left hand, cover the patch with two or three drops of oil, magnetize the hand by means of passes, settled down comfortably on the soles of their feet and rest the hand on a firm support. The telepath now gazes fixedly into the black spot and awaits, with true Oriental patience, for the news it will bring him.

We may conclude that the radiations sent out into the atmosphere by thoughts and events form themselves into impressions and images when they are picked up by the receiving station of the brain. A transmission of thought takes place.[14]

The Arabs are a conservative people. For this reason, I have never had any doubt that their *present* telepathic methods are exactly the same as they were in our beloved Father's youth. I have found additional evidence for this in the contemporary *Höllenzwang* [Infernal Ceremonial]. In the 72nd chapter of this book there are instructions for "Making Visions appear in the Hand." "Take fine pure oil and chimney-soot and smear them on the palm of the hand. Take a wax candle in the other hand, else you will see nothing. The darker the room is the better: the candle-light will enable you to see the images."

---

[14]Eira Hellberg: *Telepathie, Okkulte Kräfte* [*Telepathy and Occult Powers*] Prien, 1922, pp. 155–157.

In the last analysis, Trithemius' knowledge of telepathy stemmed from Arabia:

Now, even if Trithemius had read the entire contents of his celebrated library[15] on the secret sciences, he would still have lacked the essential key to occult knowledge. He obtained the latter from a certain Libanius Gallus, a learned Frenchman, whom Trithemius had consulted when he was staying in 1495 with the Emperor Maximilian I (1459–1519) at the Diet of Worms. Libanius had spent a considerable time in the company of the famous hermit, Pelagius, on the Island of Majorca and had learned a great deal of hidden wisdom and many occult arts from him, inheriting, after his death, all his books and manuscripts. He had also carried out a lengthy correspondence with the noted philosopher, the Conte Giovanni Pico della Mirandola (1463–1494), and he now saw in Trithemius the worthiest man to whom he could bequeath the store of knowledge he had been accumulating for thirty years. We have it on Trithemius' own confession that Libanius exhibited Nature to him in her majesty, showed him her hidden wisdom and gave him information about things which were previously entirely unknown to him. Pelagius (died 1480) had acquired important occult lore during extensive travels in Africa. He also wrote two books: *De principiis magiae naturalis* [*The Principles of Natural Magic*] and *De magia omnimodo* [*Magic by all Means*].[16]

However, in the time of Pelagius, all that "travels in Africa" amounted to was an itinerary through the Arab-occupied lands of North Africa and Arabia itself!

Turning now to the subject of "telepathic intelligence work," here are two fairly recent examples:

---

[15]Trithemius entered the Benedictine Order at Sponheim in 1482 and prosecuted his studies so assiduously that, by 1483, he was chosen as Abbot, a position which he held for more than twenty-two years, during which time he built up the monastery library to more than 2,000 volumes (Kiesewetter).

[16]Karl Kiesewetter (1854–1895): *Faust* (Vienna, n.d., Vol. II, p. 95).

In 1950, the former Australian accountant, 31-year-old Sidney Piddington, acted as "sender" eight times every half-hour at the London studios of the BBC, surrounded by detectives from Scotland Yard, scientists, doctors, lawyers and journalists as controls. The "receiver" was his 23-year-old wife, a former actress, at the Tower, also under the close observation of prominent witnesses. The sender asked for a volume to be extracted from a pile of books and then for a line from it to be given him for transmission. After a brief period of silent concentration, the receiver slowly repeated the chosen sentence. It goes without saying that both members of the team were searched right down to the skin for micro-transmitters. Piddington claimed that his strange ability was discovered and developed by him during three years in Japanese prison camps. He had achieved similar results on Australian radio programs!

Also in 1950, Dr. Gert Michael, resident psychologist of the weekly magazine *Heim und Welt* [*Home and Abroad*] (Hanover), fell into conversation with a stranger on the subject of "Yogi miracles," while traveling on the famous British express train, the Flying Scotsman, between London and Edinburgh. "Will you be staying for some days in Europe?" I asked my solitary traveling companion. "I shall remain until a message reaches me that I must return," he replied. "I see, you are expecting a telegram," ventured my friend. "No, I do not need a telegram for this," he said, "I am constantly united with the Masters in spirit. My Master is present with me here and now, even when I am separated from India by the oceans and by the continents. His thoughts rush through space and reach me here." "Telepathy?" I inquired inquisitively. "If you will," he replied.[17] The traveling companion was Londoner and ex-journalist, Paul Brunton, better known as a "white yogi." He wrote books on yoga after sitting at the feet of the Maharishi Sri Ramana (died April 14, 1950) of Tirruvanamalai in India, about

---

[17]"Seltsame Begegnung mit Paul Brunton" ["*A Strange Encounter with Paul Brunton*"] in *Das Neue Licht* [*The New Light*] (Purkersdorf bei Wien, Vol. XII, December 1951, p. 227). It is also worth noting that the Dervish sheikhs keep in contact with their pupils by telepathy (Carl Vett: *Seltsame Erlebnisse in einem Derwischkloster* [*Strange Experiences in a Dervish Retreat*] Strassburg, 1931).

whom Scratcherd, Dr. Herbert Fritsche, and Baron Hans-Hasso of Veltheim-Ostrau have also written!

An Indian doctor once informed Surya that, for a period of a month, one should think of the Maharishi (Great Guide) each evening and then, for a further month keep on asking him a question (in spirit). The answer would thereupon be given in a dream or in some other way (from a private communication of July 20, 1940). This tallies with what Gustav Meyrink once told our mutual friend "AME."

> Communion with adepts takes place "on the other side." One must command one's soul, evening after evening before going to sleep, to visit the adept one longs to see and to inform the body so that it will remember the experience on waking. (From a private communication April 14, 1952.)

For many years, this friend of mine "AME" repeatedly made the following "knocking experiment." "My aunt lived in Wernigerode at a time when I was living in Hanover. At night I turned to face Wernigerode with the intention of knocking on the door of her room. A few days later, I received a letter from my aunt in which she wrote, 'My Dear Nephew, what has possessed you to disturb me again, by knocking on my bedroom door so many times and so violently last Sunday night? The time was going on for eleven o'clock. Please stop this nonsense!' " (The hour and day agreed; from a private communication June 23, 1949.)

Tests suggest that it would be possible to transmit telepathic messages quite efficiently by means of knocks and using some such system as the Morse code. However, the same thing can be done without knocks or apparatus, as may be seen from the following:

William Thomas Stead (1849–1912) granted the London paper *Christian Commonwealth* an interview which was published on February 2, 1893, in which he claimed to have telepathized so-called "automatic writing" over a distance of more than 500 miles! He said that he had verified time and again that certain of his friends were able to use his hand as if it were their own, even when removed from him by a considerable distance. It was in this way that, in the summer of 1892, Stead repeatedly received messages from his son, who was staying at Boppard (on the Rhine), writing them out perfectly accurately with his own hand.

"He wrote two or three times perfectly correctly through my hand, but on one occasion the message was completely jumbled. I do not know how this happened, although I conjecture that the causes may have been similar to those which create disruptions in telephonic or telegraphic communication. Perhaps there was a kind of short-circuit or defective insulation permitting other currents to interfere."[18]

Stead went on to achieve one hundred percent success in front of the reporter in a test involving his absent lady clerk.

Even magic is becoming mechanized in this increasingly technological age; so it is not surprising to find "protheses" being employed in telepathy. But, more than two centuries ago, the Hamburg Qabalist, Benjamin Jesse (1642–1730) was using a "Telepathor," i.e., a pointer apparatus with an alphabet that could be operated by the subtle body of the individual sending the "telegram." The message was spelled out on it.

"What is natural to permanently discarnate entities, should come easy to those who leave the body temporarily!"—that is to say, working the planchette or, as in this case, the pointer. Subsequently, the "letter clock" was replaced by the "rotating divining rod" or pendulum and the "Oui-Ja" alphabet.

According to what I have been informed by my friend, the Hamburg Hermeticist "AME," the symbolic magician and spagyric healer, Franz Buchmann[19] often sent "very accurate mes-

---

[18]"Psychische Telegraphie" ["Psychic Telegraphy"] by Werner Friedrichsort in *Sphinx* (Gera, No. 87, May, 1893, pp. 217–223).

[19]On the *Symbolic Magician, Buchmann-Naga,* see his *Schlüssel zu den 72 Gottesnamen der Kabbala* [*The Key to the 72 Divine Names of the Qabala*] (Leipzig, 1925). His partner in the tests was the magnetopath, Henrich Hoffmann in Auerbach. In everyday life, Buchmann was Head Accountant at the Charlottenburg waterworks in his home town. The distance between Charlottenburg and Auerbach is 450 kilometers as the crow flies. Buchmann died shortly after his symbol experiments with my friend, so they do not appear in his *Pendulographie (Pendulography)*! An account of the spagyric healer is to be found in G.W. Surya: *Hermetische Medizin, Stein der Weisen, Lebenselixiere* [*Hermetic Medicine, the Philosophers' Stone and Elixirs of Life*] (Berlin-Pankow, 1923,

sages" by this means between Berlin and Southern Germany and published his researches either in *Prana* or in the *Metaphysischen Rundschau* [*Metaphysical Review*] some time before the First World War.

Dr. Jules Regnault has reported on the publications of the Cavalliere Luigi Zanella, who was similarly successful in sending telepathic messages, this time between Verona and Florence.[20]

Finally, we have the statement of another prominent French researcher into the use of the pendulum, René Lacroix-à-l'Henri, that at Marsan in the summer of 1935, the Radiesthesia Association was able to carry on a regular conversation between two stations more than one hundred kilometers apart by the same method.[21]

DISCUSSION

This magnetic force is especially strong between friends and even acts at a distance.

—Goethe to Eckermann
October 7, 1827

Do you feel how I love you? I am driven to think that you must feel it, even over so great a distance; that you feel it as a faint quivering inside you, just as if you were the receiver in a wireless telegraphy apparatus.

—Rud. Diesel (1858–1913)
to his son in September 1913

Today, the existence of telepathy has been put on a scientific

---

pp. 313 ff). What is more, Buchmann-Naga decided on the 123 (!) ingredients of his arcanum, "Pranodin" or "Shaddai" by using a pendulum!

[20]*Biodynamique et Radiations* [*Biodynamics and Radiations*] (Toulon, published by the author, 1936, pp. 267–268). Trans. note: according to the report in Regnault's book, the sender imparts a given number of oscillations to his pendulum and these are duplicated on the receiver's pendulum.

[21]*Théories et Procédés Radiesthésiques* [*Radiesthesic Theories and Processes*] (Paris, 1942, p. 127).

basis. To the unprejudiced, it has *always* been an established fact. Here is a single everyday observation as a representative of hundreds more which might have been chosen: "I could feel him coming along skulking after me his eyes on my neck," Molly Bloom said of Boylan in *Ulysses* by James Joyce (1882–1941).

One thing is fairly certain: There are straight radiations and counter-radiations passing between individuals, and these account for otherwise inexplicable aversions and likings. So says the Hermeticist, Eris Busse (1891–1947) in *Der Erdgeist* [*The Earth Spirit*] (Leipzig, 1939, p. 322).

Thoughts are buzzing all round us all the time like swarms of hornets: "One never knows whose thoughts one is chewing" (Joyce, *Ulysses*).

The man in the street is unable to resist the influence: "Yes, yes, but how do we come to say the things we do? How easily our thoughts run on! Earthbound man can not prevent any imagination entering his mind, whether it is good or whether it is bad!" says Wilhelm Raabe (1831–1910) in *Das Odfeld* [*The Odic Field*] (chapter 25).

This is why the Yogi strives to become master of his thoughts, realizing that they are not even his own! The notion that thoughts are things with some sort of material reality or that they are forces capable of acting on material objects is not new. Jussuf Abu Al-Kindi (890) proposed in his book, *De imaginibus* [*On Imagination*], that an *actio in distans* (action at a distance) might be possible *per certos radios* (by specific rays)!

The French researchers, Pierre Marie Augustin Charpentier (1852–1916), Paul Broca (1824–1880) and Antoine Becquerel (1852–1908) have demonstrated that, when it is thinking, the human brain emits radiations which are capable of making a phosphorescent screen glow. Tests extending over a number of years conducted by Dr. F. Cazzamali (Milan) exhibit the radioactivity of the human brain. The experimentally established radiations have been named by him "cerebral radio waves." The tones of which the medium being used as a sender was thinking could be distinctly transmitted to a specially constructed wireless apparatus with a wavelength of 4.10 meters.

Thoughts have also been photographed by such men as Dr. Baraduc and Major Darget in France, and by Professor

Tomokichi Fukarai (Tokyo).[22] And so has been fulfilled the prophecy of Christian Morgenstern (1871–1915): "Who knows whether thoughts may not make a very faint sound which could be detected by exceptionally sensitive instruments and could be deciphered empirically?" (in *Stufen* [*Steps Forward*]).

But, anyway, what is so strange about the transmission of thoughts through space? It should no longer cause surprise since the invention of wireless telegraphy.

> To me, as a physicist, the existence of electromagnetic "thought waves" consequent on atomic reactions in the brain, and their reception, due to resonance, by another brain which is tuned into them (and hence the existence of mental suggestion) is as patently obvious as the fact that twice two is four. *If there were no instances of thought transference on record, one would be compelled to look for them* . . . for they simply must exist by the laws of physics where the conditions are right: that is to say, when the sender uses sufficient force and the receiver keeps his mind free from extraneous thoughts.

This is the view of the physical chemist, Dr. Vageler!

A rather unusual case, which also comes under the heading of "Sympathetic Action" was witnessed by the Swiss psychotherapist Dr. Gustav Adolf Farner. After a long wedded life, a husband had to enter a private mental home to undergo the so-called malaria cure for dementia paralytica. "And now, it was interesting to observe that on every day on which the husband, who was separated from his wife and home by many miles, suffered from the artificially induced malarial fever, his wife began to experience a (purely psychogenic) fever too, even though she was unaware of the state of her husband at the time" (*Psych. Schulungsschriften*; Leipzig, 1942, pp. 42, 43).

Arthur Schopenhauer (1788–1860) in his essay on "Animalischer Magnetismus and Magie" ["Animal Magnetism and Magic"] still has something worthwhile to offer to the student of telepathy, even today. It will be found in the volume, *Parerga*

---

[22]Trans. note: Ted Serios in the USA is a more recent example.

und Paralipomena [Secondary and Neglected Items] on the shelves of any University library.

The highest attainment of telepathy is that silent conversation such as was held by Jeanne Marie Bouvier de la Motte Guyon with her father confessor, Lacombe: "Matters gradually reached the stage where I could converse with Father Lacombe in complete silence, with a continuous exchange of thoughts" (Eira Hellberg: *Telepathie, Okk. Kräfte [Telepathy, Occult Powers]* Prien, 1922, pp. 56, 57).

Paul Brunton says much the same thing: "I hoped . . . to sit in the Buddhist monasteries of Burma and Ceylon and to engage in telepathic conversation with the centuries-old yellow sages inhabiting the interior of China and the Gobi desert." (*The Secret Path*, 1937.)

When Count Juan Oaravicino y Arteaga died at a very advanced age at Toledo in 1952, his posthumous records and letters which arrived after his death from India, China, Mongolia, Persia, Peru, Brazil and the USA, revealed that he had been in telepathic communication with numerous spiritual friends and had spent whole weeks in deep meditation.

Finally and very briefly, we ought to mention that *animals are telepathic too*. Karl Rudolf (of Teneriffe) observed hundreds of times how an ant would find a fly sleeping on the ground and then lift and dangle its front legs, making peculiar movements with them. After a few minutes, along came five more ants. Why five? Because flies have six legs. At a given signal—what this was was not entirely clear to me—each ant seized one of the fly's legs as quick as lightning and it was all over! *There can be no other solution*: the finder-ant used wireless telegraphy or telepathy!

The gnat sings, which is a big mistake in one way because it attracts the attention of its chosen victim. Nevertheless, the sound has the important function of attracting the male of the species from far away. The latter's receptors are its antennae, which are tuned to the frequency of the female's call-sign. When the male gnat encounters the "F" waves (female waves), it turns until both antennae are picking up the note equally loudly (consonance). In this way it takes a bearing on the shortest route to its potential mate!

ASTRAL PROJECTION

Odin could change his appearance to the extent that
his body would lie there as if he were dead or in the
deepest sleep. For as long as this lasted he was able to
travel around other lands and bring back tidings from
them.

—Ynglinge Saga (Cap. VII)
Stockholm, 1697

One of the basic Rosicrucian documents, the *Fama Fraternitatis*
states "that every year upon the day C. they should meet together at the house Sancti Spiritus, or write the cause of his
absence."[1] The following opinion was expressed by the late
Hamburg gnostic Ernst (Tristan) Kurtzahn on the place-name
"Sancti Spiritus."

The so-called "house" Sancti Spiritus is a deliberate
blind, as anyone who understands the name in a Ros-
icrucian sense will admit. It is precisely the "Sanctus
Spiritus" who is said to bring the brethren together!
"In Spirit and in Truth shall you gather (according to
Christ's command)."[2]

At first glance, this interpretation looks very attractive, but
it is rather far-fetched and is strongly reminiscent of much

---

[1] The anthology: *Geheime Wissenschaften* [*Occult Sciences*] Vol. 1: "Four basic
documents of the old Rosicrucians," including *Fama Fraternitatis* (Berlin, 1922,
pp. 48, 49).
[2] *Die Rosenkreuzer* [*The Rosicrucians*] (Lorch i.Württ., 1926, p. 21).

trivial Biblical exegesis, in which an allegorical sense is extracted from what should be taken literally (and is an "octave higher" up the scale of truth)!

Genuine Rosicrucians possessed—on their own admission and according to reports by outside observers—the gift of *completely controlled* astral projection. And so, in contrast to the witches, who relied on narcotics, they were able to act positively during the statuvolence[3] associated with exteriorization and, what is more, they were able to recall their experiences.

This seems to show that when they talked of "meeting together at the house Sancti Spiritus" they meant entering the spiritual plane in the spiritual body, the "glorified rose", the "crystallized salt."

The annual assembly on the spiritual plane of existence (called *Devachan* by the Indians) is designated by the true Rosicrucian, Theophilus Schweighard(t) the "peremptory summons of all Rosicrucians to their invisible citadel."[4]

Another aphorism from the pen of the same writer helps to confirm that what we have here is no exercise in Kurtzahnian symbolism but a higher (i.e., spiritual, or at least astral) plane of being: "The College of the Holy Ghost is *suspended in the air* where God works, for it is HE who presides over it."[5] The release of the subtle body—the *Homunculus* in the "Philosophical Egg" (the gross body, or *sthula sharira* as the Indians call

---

[3]*Status* = state, and *volo* = I will; hence the willed state or condition. Both words come from Latin. This is the designation of a new type of induced trance. Cf., *Statuvolence oder der gewollte Zustand* [*Statuvolence or the Willed State*] by Dr. William Baker Fahnestock (Leipzig, 1884)!

[4]*Maenapius Roseae Crucis*, that is the deliberation of the whole Society concerning the hidden and anonymous writer, F. C. Menapio, whether to regard him as a brother. Citation of the same at our duly-installed Supreme Council in libel suit against Florentium de Valentia. Peremptory summons of all Rosicrucians to their invisible citadel. Published by Theophilus Schweighardt by gracious command of the Honorable Society, Ord. bened. Grafiren (April) 1619. Theophilus Schweighardt and Florentius de Valentia are one and the same and—Daniel Mögling of Constance, personal physician and private tutor to the landgrave, Philipp von Hessen-Butzbach. As regards the "invisible citadel" compare the closing section of the *Fama*: "Also our building . . . shall forever remain untouched, undestroyed, and hidden to the wicked world . . ."

[5]Schweighardt: *Speculum Sphincum Rhodostauroticum* (Frankfurt am Main, 1618).

it)—is shown in the table of "ergon and parergon" in the treatise to which reference has been made. It is fully in line with the Chinese description of the "formation of the new birth on the plane of forces."

I have managed to track down the following contemporary references to "astral projection" or soul travel (the soul being equivalent to the astral body in this context):

1) *The Chymical Wedding*, Day Two, Anno 1459. *Quatuor viarum optionem per nos tibi sponsus offert, per quas omnes ad Regium ejus aulum parbenire possis. Per quartam nomini hominum licebat ad Regium parvenire . . . nisi corporibus incorruptibilibus conveniens est.*[6] In English: By us the *Bridegroom* offers you a choice between *four* ways, all of which can bring you to his royal court. By the fourth no man will reach the royal presence . . . except when clothed in an incorruptible body.

2) Prof. Andreas Libau, M.D. (Libavius, 1560–1616) in *DOMA: Wolmeinendes Bedencken von der FAMA vnd Confession der Brüderschafft dehs Rosen Creutzes* [*DOMA: Benevolent Advice Regarding the Fama and Confessio of the Brotherhood of the Rosy Cross*] (Frankfurt am Main, 1616, chapter III, pp. 24–26).

> It is possible for one individual to be living in one part of the world and for a second individual to be living in another and for these individuals to meet at a certain time in one of their countries of residence. The meeting place itself could, *by magic*, take the form of a College, one which is imperceptible to the senses but present in the intellect and the imagination. Anyone who is a Paracelsian Magus and can keep his thoughts and opinions to himself, will be deemed to be in the College, just like Tannhäuser and the faithful Eckhardt, the former in the *Venusberg* and the latter in

---

[6]Op. cit., sub. No. 1, p. 11. The entire *Chymical Wedding* is a reproduction of Eastern astral experiences of Rosencreutz (1378–1484) in 1459. His words, "I stuck four red roses in my hat," inform the initiated that "our father" had "unfolded" four roses on his "back-cross" into consciousness and had become lord of the "lower quaternary." Cf., Matt. 22: 12.

front of it or like old Hildebrand with his comrades in Laurinsberg.[7]

3) Dr. Nicolaes Wassenaer: *Historisch verhael aller gedenkwaer-digheden* [*A Historical Narrative of all Memorable Events*] (Amsterdam, 1624): "They are transported from one place to another in the twinkling of an eye. They make themselves invisible, gather herbs and know how to read the secret thoughts of men." (The Old Dutch reads: *"Dat sij van d'eene plats tot d'andere in een oogenblik vervoert worden; haar onsienlije maken, planten lezen en de secreten det menschengedachten te weten kennen."*)

4) John Heydon (born September 10, 1629) in *The Holy Guide*, Book VI, "Apology":

But there is yet arguments to procure. Mr. Walfoord and T. Williams, Rosie Crucians by election, and that is the miracles that were done by them, *in my sight*, for it should seem Rosie Crucians were not only initiated into Mosaical Theory, but have arrived also at the power of working Miracles, as Moses, Elias, Ezekiel, and the succeeding Prophets did, as being transported where they please, as Habakkuk was from Jewry to Babylon, or as Philip, after he had baptized the Eunuch, to Azot, and *one of these went from me to a friend of mine in Devonshire, and came and brought me an answer to London the same day, which is four dayes jouurney;* they brought me excellent predictions of Astrology, and Earthquakes; they slake the Plague in Cities: they silence the violent Winde and Tempests: they calm the rage of the Sea and Rivers; *they walk in the Air*; they frustrate the malicious aspects of witches; they cure all Diseases.

Libau connects the "College suspended in the air" with the Venusberg. Now, according to the *Halberstädter Sachsenchronik*

---

[7]The clause "who . . . can keep his thoughts and opinions to himself" recalls the basis of yoga, that emptying of thoughts which brings on astral projection among other things. Cf., A. Oppermann: *The Yoga Aphorisms of Pantañjali* [*Die Yoga-Aphorismen des Patanjali (sic)*] (Leipzig, 1925, p. 11)!

[Halberstadt Saxon Chronicle] (15th century): "Chroniclers believe that this youth (Lohengrin), the Knight of the Swan, came out of the mountain, *where Venus is in the Holy Grail.*" Obviously, Venus does not stand for the "demon lover" here but is synonymous with "pure idyllic love." Libau's mountain was thus a *transcendent* reality like Mount ZION, as it is so profoundly described in the Epistle to the Hebrews (12: 22–24), a book which is almost Qabalistic in many places:

> You stand before Mount Zion, and the city of the living God, *heavenly* Jerusalem . . . the *assembly* of the firstborn citizens of heaven, and God the judge of all, and the spirits of good men made perfect . . .

The German theosophical leader, Dr. Franz Hartmann (1838–1912), who wrote *An Adventure among the Rosicrucians* and *With the Gnomes in Untersberg* among other books, had a last meeting with his friend Surya (1873–1949) in 1910 in Algund bei Meran. The latter is the author of *Moderne Rosenkreuzer* [*Modern Rosicrucians*] among other works. Almost as if it were his swan-song, the discoverer of lignosulphite as a curative agent confided to the popularizer of occult medicine: "Yes, it is a fact that the true Rosicrucians assemble *on a certain day every year* in the interior of an *earthly* mountain,[8] although not in their

---

[8]Surya named the "legendary mountain" to me in a letter dated July 3, 1940. Adding, "but please never reveal it anywhere. Hartmann was certainly present at some such gathering in his astral body, as emerges from his story 'An Adventure Among the Rosicrucians' quite clearly." Dr. A. Krumm-Heller (Meister Huiracocha, April 15, 1876–April 19, 1949) had this to say in his *Der Rosenkreuzer aus Mexiko* [*The Mexican Rosicrucians*] (Halle a.d.S., 1919): "We Rosicrucians form an outer and an inner circle . . . only astral bodies enter the inner fellowship . . . (p. 26), and, "We gather annually, first in Bohemia, then in the Hartz Mountains, in the Tatras, in Tiflis, or here in the Yucatan, in Peru or in India, in our astral consciousness" (p. 38). Max Heindel (1865–1919), who successfully made his first "soul flight" from California to Potsdam to the Rosicrucian Temple on the night of April 9, 1910, writes in his *The Rosicrucian Cosmo-Conception or Mystic Christianity* (Third edition, Ocean Park, CA 1911; p. 523): "Gathered like disciples around the Rosicrucian Brotherhood is a number of lay brethren living in various parts of the Western World, but able to leave their bodies consciously . . . these are all, without exception, initiated into the method by one of the 'elder brethren.'" (This has been retranslated from the German. Tr.)

physical bodies, which would hardly be suitable, but in the astral body. *I know this for certain.*"[9]

Jakob (1785–1863) and Wilhelm (1786–1859) Grimm, in their *Deutsche Sagen [German Legends]* (1816–1818), relate how the soul of the sleeping king of the Franks, Guntram (525–593) crossed a streamlet in the form of a mouse over the sword of his bodyguard in order to disappear inside the mountain on the other side. On waking, Guntram related how he had traveled "in a dream" over a great expanse of water by means of an iron bridge until he had reached the opposite mountain and found a treasure buried inside it. Subsequent excavations proved the accuracy of this information. This is an example of *involuntary* astral projection where an actual journey is made to a real place (a mountain in this instance) by a noninitiate.

Here now are two examples of *willed* "journeys" *into* (not on top of) a mount of meeting. The first was one undertaken by a brother of the "left-hand path"—"Jakob Pagel, age 40, told the court on May 17, 1674, that Jakob Kropf, who had already been examined, had entered his house just as he was returning home from the Weinberge and added, 'I smeared him (with witch ointment) and we immediately went together to the *Compagnie* (!) and all went into the Schiesselberg with the parson.' "[10]

The second example is the classic contrast to the procedures of the witch cults with their drugged salves, drinks and fumigations; it is that of the white magician, as told by Abraham von Franckenberg (1593–1652), the author of *Raphael oder Arzt-Engel [Raphael or the Healing Angel]* who, in the Spring of 1624 in the presence of Jakob Boehme (1575–1624), heard at Schweinhaus in Silesia from the lips of the, at that time, almost 60-year-old Bolkenhain physician and philosopher, Johannes Springer, the extremely strange account regarding the latter's spiritual leader and mentor. Seventeen years went by before this man came out with his written report in Tarnowitz about "Joh. Beer's journey from Schweidnitz to Schönberg to the spirits in the Zobtenberg as related by J. Springer in 1624 at the ancestral mansion of a nobleman."

---

[9]Sinbad (Surya): *Das Lebenselixier [The Elixir of Life]* (Leipzig, 1923, p. 14).
[10]Dr. F. Unger: *Die Pflanze als Zaubermittel [Plants as used in Magic]* (Leipzig, n.d., p. 43).

The facts of the matter are these: Meister Beer, who was born in Schweidnitz and held the post of schoolmaster at Reichenau around 1570, had studied the "black arts" in Cracow, much as people used to do in Salamanca or Venice. Then he "saw the light" and burned his magic books, just as the congregation at Ephesis had done in the days of St. Paul, and gave himself up to reading the Holy Bible and the writings of Johannes Tauler (1300–1361), who is held in high repute by the Rosicrucians. By the grace of God and through "praying without ceasing" he was gifted with the natural and supernatural understanding of (herbal) healing and with the power of entering the "doors" of the mountains and visiting the lower parts of the earth. There he preached to the "spirits in prison," it is said, in line with Christ (I Peter 3:18–19), Mohammed (570–632; Sura 72), the Comte de Gabalis (1670) and Oetinger (1702–1782).[11] It was during Easter 1570 that Beer entered the Zobten (718 m) with this purpose in mind. His wife informed Springer that Johann Beer (like the Qabalists) used to talk with the angels at night. He published a little book called *Gewinn und Verlust* [*Profit and Loss*] in 1639; a manuscript entitled *Was Gott der Vater, Sohn und Geist im Menschen wirkelt* [*The Work of God the Father, Son and Holy Ghost in Man*], which must have been a theurgic breviary, has unfortunately been lost. In 1600, Beer finally entered "thy holy hill and . . . thy tabernacles," and "the land of the living" (Psalms 43: 3 and 27: 13).

Beer supplies the answer to why the annual assembly of the Rosicrucians was said to be held on "the day C." What, then, is this "day C"? It is Crucifixion Day or Good-Friday, because on this day Jesus Christ "descended into Hell" in his spiritual body and "preached unto the spirits in prison" (I Peter 3: 19). But to return to the use of a mountain as a meeting place, what is more suitable as an assembly point than a mountain, the most prominent landmark in any district and easy for astral travelers to "home in" on? A big part is played by the "holy mount" in both the Old and the New Testaments, whether it is under the form of Ararat, Nebo, Sinai, Carmel, Zion, the "exceeding high

---

[11] Will-Erich Peuckert: *Die Rosenkreuzer* [*The Rosicrucians*] (Jena, 1928, p. 309; also 24; 337; 425). Also, his *Von schwarzer und weißer Magie* [*White and Black Magic*] (Berlin, n.d., p. 137 ff).

mountain" where Christ was taken during His temptation, the hillside where He preached the "Sermon on the Mount," the Mount of Transfiguration (thought by some to be Mount Tabor), the Mount of Olives, Golgotha—the place of a skull, the mountain in Galilee where His disciples met Jesus after His resurrection or, at the end of the Bible, the "great and high mountains" from which the angel showed John the heavenly Jerusalem decending from God. Other, non-Biblical, moutains which might be mentioned are Olympus, Meru and Athos (Hagion Oros) with its practicers of omphaloskepsis or contemplation of the navel; the mystic monks known as Hesychasts. Mountains are antennae, from which the *genius loci* (spirit of the place) emanates!

To revert to *point b* at the beginning of the chapter, where it is said that any Rosicrucian brother unable to attend the annual gathering should *"write the cause of this absence,"* the apology is understood as being sent *telepathically!* Aegidius Gutmann (1490–1584) of Augsburg[12] and Counselor Julius Sperber (died 1616),[13] both of whom were obviously Rosicrucians to those who know what to look for, are agreed in their writings that *the first initiation takes place in dreams*, the metaphorical language of which is not confined to one human tongue (i.e., it is polyglot).

Hence the Rosicrucians were perfectly justified in announcing, in their Paris poster of March 3, 1623, that, among other things: *"Nous enseignons sans livres ni marques et parlons les langues du pais où nous voulons être."* (We teach without books or written signs and speak the language of any country in which we wish to be.)

The same may be said of a second notice, which appeared a few days later, which contained a statement to the effect that:

If anyone wishes to see us out of pure curiosity, he will never get in touch with us, but if he is really moved by the desire to be enrolled in our Brotherhood, we, who judge men's thoughts, will make him see the truth

---

[12]*Offenbarung Göttlicher Majestät, etc. [Revelation of Divine Majesty, etc.]* (1575, Vol. VIII).

[13]*Echo der von Gott erleuchteten Fraternität, etc. [Echo from the God-enlightened Fraternity, etc.]* (1616).

of our promises, without however disclosing the place where we dwell; because the thoughts which are joined to the earnest intention of the reader will be capable of making him known to us and us to him.

The above is enough to demonstrate that real Rosicrucians make the acquaintance of earnest seekers in the "astral light" and instruct them inwardly by its means. They are also past masters of telepathy, as indicated by their apologist, Dr. Robert Fludd (1574–1637) in his writings.[14]

The Rosicrucians termed the (projected) astral body the "glorified rose." The alchemists called it the "body of salt," while Jakob Boehme (1575–1624) referred to it as the "body which arises in the tincture." The "transmission coils of the electromagnetic substrate" are called "roses" by the Rosicrucians, "planets" by the Hermeticists (who also called them "cities") and "little flames" by Jung-Stilling.

Today, we have a very familiar technical term taken from Sanskrit, "linga sharira," for the subtle (quintessential) body, and the word *chakras* for the "nerve plexuses" or "connections" (for the links with the physical body). The name "lotus" is also employed. The lotus is the fairest flower of the Orient and is the equivalent of the Occidental rose (of the Rosicrucians).

One of Boehme's pupils, the lawyer and mystic Johann Georg Gichtel (1638–1710), reproduced these "planets" in color in his *Theosophia practica* (1696).[15] The abbot, Trithemius (1462–1516) describes their mutual arrangement.[16]

---

[14]Cf., Max Heindel (op. cit., p. 525): "Each good and unselfish deed increases the luminosity and vibrant power of the candidate's aura enormously, and as surely as the magnet attracts the needle, so will the brilliancy of that auric light bring the teacher."

[15]New impression: 1897 the Bibliothèque Chacornac, Paris: "with the original old colored illustrations, in which the human body is depicted with the chakras, each one of which is marked with the name of a planet, as astrologically appropriate" (Ferger). The book's significant subtitle is: "A Short Explanation of the Principles of the World in Man set out in Easily Understood Pictures, indicating where and how each of these has its center in the inner man, in accordance with what the author has discovered within himself by the power of Divine revelation and what he has sensed, proved and observed."

[16] "Tractatus chemicus" [*A Chemical Treatise*] in Vol. IV of the *Theatrum chemicum* [*The Chemical Theater*].

Basilius Valentinus[17] speaks of them as follows: "The King travels through six regions in the heavenly firmament, and in the seventh he fixes his abode."[18]

This journey through seven regions is reminiscent of one which was undertaken through seven islands with the crystal-built (!) town of Thebes, as related in the Arabian tale of the knight Habid and Dorathelguse. I have already discussed the arcane meaning of "glass" or "crystal" in another place. Because the city was of crystal, it was transparent or, in other words, "transcendent, and not touchable with human hands" (Kyber, List). The seven islands must signify the seven planetary spheres through which the soul of man has to pass before it can return to the etheric light of the "cosmic abode" (Thebes).

This parallelism indicates yet again the Arabian origin of the Rosicrucian system of philosophy, a fact which was recognized a long time ago.[19] Hartlaub[20] has drawn attention to the similarity between the meditation of Indian yoga and the Rosicrucian exercises of Prof. Heinrich Nollius for example; and

---

[17]The pseudonym of Johann Thölde of Frankenhausen (Thür.), a court official who was active around 1600 and was Secretary to the RC.

[18]Rudolf Klodwig: *Mythologie und Symbolik* [*Mythology and Symbolism*] (Lorch i. Württ., 1933, p. 138). Baron Rudolf von Sebottendorf (= Rudolf Glandeck, born September 9, 1875) has given a graphic representation of this progress through the 7 planets (or the 12 signs of the zodiac associated with them) in his *Die Praxis der alten türkischen Freimaurerei* [*The Practice of Old Turkish Freemasonry*] (Leipzig, 1924, p. 23). The masonic physician Ibn Tofail (died 1186) showed in his story "Hai eben Yokdhan," "the release of man from matter, his resurrection and his ascent into the higher realms of spirit." Pococke translated this work into Latin under the title, *"Philosophus autodidactus"* (1671); and a French version was brought out in 1900 by Léon Gautier. However, there was really no need to go as far as Arabia—Snow White, in the old German fairy story, lived with the seven dwarves behind the seven mountains; she was laid in a glass coffin and brought back to life by the king's son (= the spirit).

[19]There was published at Rostock in 1618, under the penname Eusebius Christian Cruciger, *Eine kurtze Beschreibung der Newen Arabischen und morischen Fraternitet* [*A Brief Account of the New Arabian and Moorish Fraternity*], where *morisch* (Moorish) = *maurisch* (masonic)!

[20]C.F. Hartlaub: *"Rosenkreuz oder der Mythos des Barock"* ["Rosencreutz or the Myth of the Baroque"]. Recension of the book by Will-Erich Peuckert, *Die Rosenkreuzer (The Rosicrucians)*, in the "Literacy Supplement" of the *Frankfurter Zeitung*, October 27, 1929, No. 803, p. 4.

Marqués-Rivière[21] compared the practices of the Cathars with yoga and the Cathars were a sect that seems to have been greatly influenced by the Rosicrucian movement. "Cathar initiation consisted in the knowledge of the *trance techniques which bring about the separation of the soul from the body*; in many respects these practices were very close to the yogic methods of India."[22] We shall merely add that the Arabian polyhistor Al-Biruni (973– 1048) translated the Yoga Aphorisms of Pantañjali into Arabic.[23]

Finally, we can say with *Ferger:*[24]

Generally speaking, these metaphysical centers are still quite strange and usually unbelievable as well to the European who is not an orientalist, occultist or mystic, even though, in the meantime, biology has found something rather similar in the nerve plexuses,[25] the most important of which is the solar plexus. These occupy *approximately* the same positions in the body where the ancient Indians located the chakras.

They are not observable under the ultra-microscope, it is true, but how long is it since anyone knew much about the nerves and the solar plexus for example, and is it not scarcely a century since the human ovum was discovered? Surely, it is likely that the next hundred years will lead to new findings and perhaps the subtle organs of the body will be identified,[26]

---

[21]Jean Matqué-Rivière: *Histoire des doctrines esotériques* [*A History of Esoteric Doctrines*] (Paris 1940, p. 232).

[22]Déodat Roché: *Le Catharisme* [*The Cathar Movment*] (Carcassonne, 1937, p. 38).

[23]Wilhelm Hauer: *Yoga als Heilsweg* [*Yoga as a Method of Healing*] (Stuttgart, 1932, p. 159 Note 2).

[24]N. Ferger: *Magie und Mystik* [*Magic and Mysticism*] (Zurich and Leipzig, 1935, pp. 216, 217).

[25]The chakras and the plexuses have been compared in detail in: Sebottendorf: *Türkenmaurerei* [*Turkish Freemasonry*] (p. 43); Strauss-Surya: *Theurgische Heilmethoden* [*Theurgic Healing Methods*] (Lorch i.W., 1930, p. 127); Yeats-Brown: *Ist Yoga für dich?* [*Is Yoga for You?*] (Berlin, n.d., pp. 58, 59).

[26]Fritz Grunewald, a professional engineer, has taken the first steps in this direction in his *Physikalisch-mediumistischen Untersuchungen* (Pfullingen i.W., 1920, pp. 53, 54). "For those occultists who have a theosophical background

including some that are designed to absorb part of the cosmic rays[27] which, so we are given to understand, are a hundred times more penetrating than the hardest X-rays?

DISCUSSION

At last, here is another who rises from the physical body unlike so many who only travel out of it.

—Wilhelm Raabe (1831–1910)
(*Aus den Akten des Vogelsanges*)

Instructions in astral projection (exteriorization) are found in Joachim Winckelmann's, *Magisches Training* [*Magical Training*] (Freiburg/Brsg., 1952, pp. 55–57). Gustav Meyrink, who also practiced astral projection, took a traveling-staff to bed with him as an aid to the imagination and then slowed down his heartbeats by emotionally-toned pictures.

I have recorded the interesting case of Franz Richtmann (died 1919) of Baden near Vienna, who could appear in two places at once, in my book *Die Rosenkreuzer* [*The Rosicrucians*] (Lorch i.Württ., 1951). Another, and even more fascinating case, is that of the very high-ranking Austrian official who

---

and are well-versed in the secret sciences of India, the question arises as to whether the magnetic pole-formations discovered by me could be identical with the various centers which are part of what is still regarded as a hypothetical ether by modern science. Further investigations may supply material for deciding this question." Grunewald himself did not go on to supply this material by his own researches because he entered the "bright world of spirits" in his Charlottenburg laboratory in the most mysterious circumstances on July 19, 1925.

[27]Perhaps the spleen. Cf., the curious picture by the initiate, Albrecht Dürer (1471–1528) of a man pointing at his spleen! The mental specialist, Dr. Nic. Müller (Munich) declared as long ago as 1921 that the sympathetic nervous system acts as an accumulator for the crebro-spinal system. The sympathetic system—which collects "electrical forces" in the spleen—charges the cerebrospinal ganglia with it. Dr. Friedrich Schwab (1878–1946) expressed a similar opinion in *Symbolik* [*Symbolism*] (Lorch i.W., 1932, p. 54): "The spleen, according to occult writings, is the human organ which converts the solar ether into nerve force." Perhaps we might say it condenses the solar ether?

around 1858 paid regular visits in his astral body to the spiritist circle led by Stratil in Mödling near Vienna and revealed his presence through the mediums and by means of the psychograph just as if he were a disembodied spirit (D. Horung: *Neueste spiritualist. Mittheilungen* [*The Latest Spiritist News*] Berlin, 1862).

Marquis Saint Yves d'Alvveydre spent some time in Agarttha while in the state of bilocation. This is supposed to be the subterranean kingdom of the so-called "Lord of this World" in Central Asia (*Mission de l'Inde en Europe* [*The Mission of India in Europe*] Paris, 1910, 1911).

Astral spies were active during the First World War, one of whom was Hofrat H. in Munich, according to Surya. He reports that a German on the western front managed to overhear, from the astral plane, the French Divisional Staff drawing up a plan of attack ("Geistiger Monismus" ["Spiritual Monism"] No. 3, Freiburg i. Br., 1936, pp. 45–47).

However, there is an early precedent for all this. The prophet Elisha (850 B.C.) repeatedly spied on the encampment of Ben-Hadad, King of Syria, by spiritual means, for the benefit of Israel (II Kings 6: 8–12). The prophet described his sorties onto the astral plane as *his heart going on a journey* (II Kings 5: 26). The expression is pregnant with meaning, as a rapid excursion into the history of the esoteric will show.

Confucius (551–478), paid a visit to Lao-Tse (604–?) one day and found him sitting "as stiff as a sturdy tree." On coming out of his trance, his almost inanimate friend explained, "I let my heart go on its travels" (Tschuang-Tsi: *Das wahre Buch vom südl. Blütenland* [*The True Book of the Southern Flower Land*] Jena, 1940, Book XXI, Parable 4).

Jerome Cardan (Geronimo Cardano, 1501–1576) said of his autosomnambulism, "It brings about a certain separation in my heart, as if my soul wishes to depart. A feeling spreads through my whole body as of a door being opened."[28]

The Portuguese nun, Sister Mariana Alcoforado (1640–1723), wrote in the first of her wonderful "Portuguese Letters"

---

[28]Similar pictorial language was employed by the Malayan fakir, Harwouth Dixon (born November 18, 1907) when describing his method to a Hamburg nerve specialist in 1948: "In order to supress all organic activity, I lie down quietly and melt."

addressed to Noel Bouton de Chamilly (1638–1715): "My heart began to move violently so that I felt it was trying to leave me and go to you. I was so overcome with intense excitement that I was bereft of my senses for more than three hours" (Rilke).

August Strindberg (1849–1912) was aware that "Anyone who has ever been in a trance knows the feeling of his heart jumping out of his body and of relinquishing his spirit; it is the memory of a pleasant death."[29] *Ein Neues Blaubuch [A New Blue-book]* Munich, 1920, p. 868).

In the opinion of all ancient peoples and in that of present-day Orientals and "primitive natives," the soul is not immaterial but is a subtle body or, more accurately speaking, is clothed in a subtle body. The Indians know the astral body under the name of *lingasharira*, the Maoris call it *wairua*; the ancient Greeks termed it the *ochēma* (from the root *ochēo* = "I support") and the Apostle Paul writes of the *sōma pneumatikon* (the spiritual body). For him who had been "out of the body" himself (assuming II Cor. 13: 2 describes a personal experience), it was an established fact that "there is a natural body, and there is a spiritual body" (I Cor. 15: 44).

The Church Fathers call this body the "Astroid" (Haenig) and refer to its "antipodes." The Platonists, too, speak of the etheric body as the vehicle of the soul.[30]

Paracelsus refers to it as the "sidereal body," Helmont as the "astral body," Jakob Boehme as the "force body," the "body which arises in the tincture" and the "quintessential body," Jung-Stilling (1740–1817) as the "seed of resurrection," Eckartshausen as the "schema perceptionis" and Baron von Kleeberg (died 1936) as the "veil body," at which point we come to

---

[29]Exteriorization is dangerous and can end in death. Stanislaus de Guaita (1860–1898) is said to have perished from its effects (Anne Osmont). Johann Dürr (J.D. Cinvat) issues a direct warning in his *Experimental-Magie [Experimental Magic]* (Leipzig, 1928, pp. 24, 25) that the astral cable—the "silver cord" spoken of by wise King Solomon (972–932 B.C.) in the person of his "Preacher" (Eccl. 12: 6)!!—is all too easily severed. This is especially true when such foolish methods of "bilocation" are employed as were practiced in the medieval Hanse Guilds which admitted a new member only after he had been strung up in smoke by a cord round his neck to initiate him in a trance state (Hartmann, Hoefler).

[30]Agrippa: *Occult Philosophy* (Book III, c. 36. See also Book III, c. 50).

the idea of *Gespinst* (i.e., "fabric") whence *Gespenst* (i.e., "phantom")! Cf., "phantoms of the living" (Padmore).

In 1908, an English physicist, Fournier d'Albe, prompted by recent microscopic and microchemical examination of the structure of living cells, put forward the suggestion in his *New Light on Immortality* (London) that it might be possible to have a coherent extract of all the elements important to life and that these could form a sort of gaseous body (phantom) in the shape of the human body. The good man evidently favored the idea of a "gaseous vertebrate" (Haeckel) which was briefly hinted at by Carl Buttenstedt in his *Die Übertragung der Nervenkraft* [*The Transmission of Nerve Force*] (published by the author, Berlin-Rüdersdorf, ca. 1898)!

Dr. Baraduc (Paris) has discovered, after weighing this "coherent extract of all the elements in cells which are important to life," that they amounted to 26 grams. Hector Durville (1849–1923) found 30 grams for men, while the "fluidal" for women amounted to only half that weight. Cf. André Maurois: *Le peseur d'âmes* [*The Weigher of Souls*] (Paris, 1931)!

In 1907, Prof. Elmer Gates of the USA, using special rays, made the departing soul of an electrocuted guinea-pig visible on a projection screen (Rhadopsin screen). For those who are not able to see the aura very easily, Dr. Walter Kilner devised the "Kilner Screen" in 1910, as described by Surya in *Okk. Diagnostik und Prognostik* [*Occult Diagnosis and Prognosis*] (Lorch i.W., 1950).

Over in the USA in 1911, Dr. Patrick O'Donell of Chicago claimed to have found a way of making the human aura visible by using a secret fluid he prepared (dicyanin like Kilner's dye?) which he enclosed between two plain glass plates to form a type of light filter. The idea was to make the eyes sensitive to the aura when they viewed it through this filter. By combining it with a cinematograph apparatus, Dr. O'Donell is said to have demonstrated the aura in a large auditorium (*"Die photographierte Seele"* ["The Soul in Photographs] in the *Berliner Tageblatt*, No. 362, July 19, 1911).

THE GREAT WORK

Except a man be born of water and of the Spirit, he
cannot enter into the kingdom of God. That which is
born of the flesh is flesh; and that which is born of the
Spirit is spirit.

—John 3: 5–6

The "Great Work" (in Latin: *magnum opus*) of the Rosicrucians
was of three kinds: chemical-physical (the *lapis philosophorum* =
the philosophers' stone or gold-making stone); medical (preparation of the *tinctura physicorum* = the elixir of life = the radical
tonicum plus something to sharpen the senses) and physiological. The *physiological* Great Work corresponds to the *old Turkish
Freemasonry*,[1] to *kundalini yoga* and to the *circulation of light* of
the esoteric Taoists. No one, in my opinion, has given a better
description of *kundalini yoga* than the Swede Eira Hellberg; it
is short and clear without any trimmings to confuse the issue.
She knows of two varieties, which she explains. The first of
these is "psychogenic" (Greek for "soulmade") and produced
by the imagination, not needing the intervention of anyone else.
For this reason, it may also be termed "autogenic" (Greek for
"produced by oneself") and is in line with the "autogenic training" of the Berlin mental specialist Prof. J.H. Schultz, M.D. The
second variety is "heterogenic" (Greek for "produced by others") and is effected in a purely technical manner by massage.

---

[1]Rudolf Freiherr von Sebottendorf: *Die Praxis der alten türkischen Freimaurerei*
[*The Practice of Old Turkish Freemasonry*] (Leipzig, 1924).

AUTOGENIC KUNDALINI

"After the student (of yoga) has devoted himself to these (previously described) exercises for two months, he proceeds to *nourish the brain*. And here we have the natural cause, the power source of the mysterious oriental hypnotic and telepathic arts. A Buddhist priest who was resident in Europe during the First World War (1914–1918) and had himself performed the exercises, divulged the secret to a westerner. Ever since the days of Zoroaster, it has been known that the secretory products of the sex organs represent an invaluable nutrient for the brain cells and the nervous system, and the really expert magicians of all nations made use of this in a number of different ways.

The yoga adepts employed it brilliantly. During meditation, they persuaded themselves that their thought exercises transferred the seat of consciousness from the brain to the sex organs, i.e., that they had started thinking with the latter. There are diseases in which the patient thinks that his brain has been removed to one of his fingers; they have the same symptoms as found in the yogi: the blood flows to the member in question (heavy brainwork draws blood to the brain, as is well known).

So, as we have seen, the yogi visualizes that he is thinking with his sex organ. He is not permitted to indulge in an overt erotic fantasy, but he does so in a roundabout way by meditating on the eternal growth of living things in nature. After an hour the sex organ becomes engorged with blood. However, this stimulus must not lead to ejaculation but, as soon as the practitioner observes that he has achieved his purpose, he must raise his thought-processes up into the spinal cord and attempt to draw the blood up with them. From there he gradually lifts his consciousness back to the brain. The blood, which carries the secretions of the sex glands with it, serves to sustain the brain cells and the whole body. A strong feeling of release is obtained and the mental output is intensified amazingly.

Foreigners express great surprise at the youthful, vigorous appearance exhibited by Buddhist monks even in old age. *Men of 80 and 90 look as if they were in their 30s and work just as hard.* Here we have the secret; a rejuvenation process known in the

East for thousands of years. This is how the Hindus maintain the fabulous mental powers with which they perform their fakir dislays. The absolute sway exercised by the will over each and every bodily function enables them to accumulate a condensation of power in mind and body."[2]

HETEROGENIC KUNDALINI

The less enterprising folk, such as the Egyptians, Persians and Chaldeans, used to treat men and women with hot compresses over the ovaries or testicles. The compresses were as hot as could be borne by the skin and were continuously changed for a period of fifteen minutes. Following this the body was given a species of massage by kneading and rubbing. This drew the blood down to the lower organs, the secretions of which were absorbed by the blood and exploited by the brain. Those who desired to preserve their mental faculties in good working order underwent this treatment, because they knew how important the sexual substance is to the nervous system in particular. The hot applications were continued for ten days in a row, and then they were used on the back for a further ten days from the neck to the sacrum, since the sympathetic nervous system branches out from the spine. There was a pause of ten days and then the treatment was renewed. It was always followed by a plunge-bath at 40–45 degrees centigrade.

Hence, the basic concept was the same as with the Hindus, but external aids were used.[3]

An approach to a "hydrotherapeutic kundalini yoga" has also been made in the West. Thus, "Louis Kuhne (born 1835), originally a shoemaker, then the first inspired exponent of nature cure in a large German city (Leipzig), who was the originator

---

[2]E. Hellberg: *Telepathie. Okkulte Kräfte* [*Telepathy and Occult Power*] (Prien, 1922, pp. 211, 213).
[3]Hellberg, op. cit., pp. 225, 226.

of a "new science of healing or the doctrine of the unity of disease and the consequent possibility of cure without drugs or operations" (Leipzig in 1914 and on many other occasions) saw in the sex organs "the root of the tree of life" influencing the whole organism through the sympathetic plexus. In order to liberate such a strong action on the whole man and to stir up the life force ("the life force of the whole body is fanned into a flame"), he advised his particularly popular *friction sitz-bath*, "the Kneipp Cure from within." A foot-stool for the patient to sit on was placed in a bathtub. The water in the bath came up to the seat without actually wetting the latter and the external sex organs were gently washed with a coarse linen cloth. The temperature of the water was 10–15° (or naturally cold) and the bath lasted for 10 to 60 minutes (Brauchle).

An improvement on Kuhne's bath was the "new friction sitz bath" of Adolf Just (1859–1936), famous for his "Jungborn Cure," who gave up book-selling to open a sanatorium devoted to nature cure.

The esoteric Taoists (e.g., the *Kin tan kiao* sect—of the golden cinnebar), teach the transmutation (or physiological *metanoia*) of the seminal powers, which are normally used in a straightforward manner for procreation and sensual gratification, so as to build up the spiritual body by reversing their expression (i.e., to produce the "golden flower," the Chinese *Ging Hua*). Not content with raising the "serpent power" or *kundalini* from the sacral plexus to the center in the crown of the head (Sanskrit, *sahasrara*), they rotate the "Light" in the circulation.

Under the Master's guidance, the stream from the sex glands is linked to the front middle of the body by a *thread of thought* from whence it is led in a divided stream round the waist on each side until it reunites with itself at the kidneys. It then travels up the spine, over the head and down the middle of the forehead to the breast and midriff. The *circulation of light* is then closed. The wheel of dharma turns.

On inhalation, the vital power is led, *in imagination*, along the spine and up to the brain, and on exhalation it is returned to its source down the front of the body.

Our immortal essence is *visualized* as rising up in the guise of the *puer aeternus* (the eternal child), bursting open the cranium at the "third eye" and being born with a cry that is echoed by the heavens. The newborn creature is throned as a deathless being in the lotus chakra above the crown of the head.[4]

---

[4]Prof. Erwin Rouselle (1890–1949) in his "Seelische Führung im lebenden Taoismus" ["A Psychic Introduction to Living Taoism"] (*Eranos-Jahrbuch*, 1933, Zürich, 1934, pp. 184, 194, 196). The "newborn creature enthroned as a deathless being in the lotus chakra above the crown of the head" is illustrated in Table III ("The liberation of the spiritual body into an independent existence") of the *Tai I Ging Hua Dsung Dschi*.[5] The preceding diagram in Table II ("Entstehung der Neugeburt im Raum der Kraft"— "The Formation of the new Birth in Space and Power") shows the "puer aeternus" (Latin for the "eternal boy," the child of eternity = immortality) in *statu nascendi* in the mother's womb or solar plexus region as the case may be. This is just like the Table "Ergon and Parergon" in the alleged treatise of the Constance royal physician and tutor to the prince's family mentioned in footnote 6.

What is the reason for these incredible similarities in technical terms and, more extraordinary still, in pictorial representations? The answer may lie in the fact that Rosicrucians fled to China during the Thirty Years' War . . . !

Carl Gustav Jung (born 1875) wrote, "As I have shown in collaboration with Richard Wilhelm (1873–1930), Chinese alchemy advanced the idea that the aim of the Magnum Opus was the 'diamond body' " (*Psychologie und Religion* [*Psychology and Religion*] Leipzig, 1940, p. 183). Details of the crystallization of the so-called ki force (Chinese) in the form of idols in the heart of the believer can be read in the *Amulettes, Talismans et Pantacles* of Jean Marqués-Rivière (Paris, 1938, p. 261). I shall have to be content here with recounting the experience of a modern European student of mantra: "A dear friend of mine, now dead alas, who had a great talent for the so-called 'Kerning' exercises, had the following mystical experience after only one year's practice. He clearly perceived a ball of light forming in his sacral region and becoming larger and larger. And then, in this ball, a boy took shape, who grew week after week. At length, my friend went to see Karel Weinfurter of Prague, who told him that this was quite a common result of the Kerning exercises. He suggested it was the birth of Christ in us, and went on to say that if he persisted faithfully, this 'Christ' would step out of him into objective reality and speak with him!" Thus G. W. Surya (= Demeter Georgiewicz Weitzer; August 23, 1873–January 3, 1949) in the book *Theurgic Methods of Healing* (Lorch i.W., 2nd edition, 1936, p. 242, footnote). The same thought was also voiced

In the instruction manual of a certain sect[5] we encounter "New Testament phraseology" which we may have regarded in the past as no more than stock religious sayings. In their unfamiliar setting, however, they can be very illuminating psychologically: "the Light was the life of men," "the light of the body is the eye," being born of Spirit and (seminal) water (John. 3: 5), the mystic marriage (Matt. 22), oil in the lamps (Matt. 25). The "Old Turkish Freemasonry" is derived from the Arabic "Science of the Balance" or "Science of the Key" (*Ilm el miftach*), which reached Venice in the ninth century. It practiced three finger positions of the right hand "provided" with vowels. These were used to guide the flow of blood (with an objectively measurable rise in temperature), to take up the "water of life" (Latin: *aqua vitae* = Od) in excess of requirements and to incorporate it in the body gradually by means of "grips" starting at the neck and working downward to the abdomen.

We meet one of these hand positions—thumb and index finger spread at right angles to one another—in a Rosicrucian plate of pictures,[6] where it has the key-word *Azoth* over it. This word is composed of the first and last letters of the Latin, Greek and Hebrew alphabets[7] and refers to the inward utterance of

---

by the *Cherubic Wayfarer* (Angelus Silesius, i.e., Johann Scheffler, 1624–1677):

Ich muß Maria sein
Und Gott in mir gebähren;
Soll er mir ewiglich
Die Seligkeit gewähren.

Like Mary I must be
And bear in me my Lord;
Then He eternally
His bliss will me afford.

[5]*Thai I Gin Hua Dsung Dschi* [*The Secret of the Golden Flower*]. Partly translated by Richard Wilhelm (1873–1930), Munich, 1929. Like Rouselle, Wilhelm was initiated into the Taoist Dau De Hüo Sche society at Peking.
[6]The Table "Poculum Pansophiae" in the *Speculum Sophicum Rhodostauroticum* [*The Rosicrucian Mirror of Wisdom*] of 1618 by Theophilus Schweighardt = Konstanz (i.e., Daniel Mögling, physician and tutor to the Landgrave Philipp von Hessen-Butzbach).
[7]*A-Z* (Latin), *Alpha-Omega* (Greek); *Aleph-Tau* (Hebrew). Cf. "I am Alpha and Omega" (Rev. 1: 8); i.e., the whole alphabet!

the vowels together with certain consonants (and hand positions).

And so, the yoga and Taoist methods of which we have been speaking consummate the physiological "Great Work" of bodily regeneration, macrobiotics and the precocious assumption of "occult powers" which will one day become more widespread—powers based on *pure imagination* but involving the transmutation of the seed.

The "science of the key," i.e., the "Old Turkish Freemasonry," on the other hand, is founded on a concentrative technical basis. The attention is focused on the "magnets" of the thumb and index finger of the right hand, thus making them extraordinarily receptive of the cosmic Od, which is assimilated by hand-grips in a purely technical manner.

The *auto-magnetic* procedure is completely *technical* from start to finish: "According to an author of the time of Alexander the Great (356–323), who is borne out by reports of present-day travelers who have taken an interest in such matters, the Brahmins obtain a kind of new life by certain practices. They run their hands up from the epigastrium[8] to the head, professing to raise their soul to the brain and unite it with the Godhead."[9]

This method of raising the "serpent fire," by the use of self-magnetizing passes, was also known to the Rosicrucians of the Middle Ages. The evidence for this is to be found in the so-called "Parabola" which were printed in the *Einfältig ABC-Büchlein für junge Schüler* [*A Simple Little ABC Book for Young Scholars*] which came out under the title *Die geheime Figuren der Rosenkreuzer des 16. und 17. Jahrhunderts* [*The Secret Diagrams of the Rosicrucians of the 16th and 17th Centuries*] published by Herold, at Altona, 1785, 1788 and in a new impression by Hermann Barsdorf at Berlin in 1921. In paragraph 11, the author recounts how he wandered into a rose garden and found there "a great mill . . . in which were no flour bins or other things that pertained to grinding. . . . Then I asked the old miller how many water wheels he had. 'Ten,' answered he. The adventure stuck

---

[8]The epigastrium is the abdominal region near the navel and solar plexus. The Indian name is *manipura*.

[9]Abbé J.B.L(oubert), *Le Magnétisme et le Somnambulisme devant les Corps savants, la Cour de Rome et les Théologiens* [*Magnetism and Somnambulism before learned bodies, the Court of Rome and the Theologians*] (Paris, 1844, p. 448).

in my mind. I should have gladly known what the meaning was."

The meaning is this: man himself is the mill and the ten water wheels are the ten fingers, which draw the "water of life" down from the solar system and impart it to the cerebral system by means of the "several grips" (i.e., hand grips) mentioned in paragraph 6 of the "Parabola," that is to say, by the use of magnetic passes. (Transmutation of the Lights.) The analogy of the mill with its water-powered wheels is also to be found in esoteric Taoism:

> If, when the true power has been accumulated in a large amount, the student refrains from releasing it to the outside in the normal way, but gives it a retrograde motion, it is the *light* of the being. The *turning water wheel* method is used. If you continue to turn, the true power will reach the root drop by drop. Then the water wheel stops, the body is pure, the energies are renewed. First comes purity and then renewal. *When the seed is transformed, the body is fit and well.* There is a popular tradition that the venerable Master, Pong, lived to be 880 years old because he had used servant girls to cherish his body.[10] However, this is a mistake, in actuality his method was the sublimation of spirit and energy.[11]

This secret lore of the creation of the "Golden Flower" (Chinese: *Chin Hua*) or the "Flower of Light" (Chinese: *Chin Huang*) in man, which the Rosicrucians termed the "Glorified Rose," meets us in the Tyrolean legend of the *enchanted rose-mill*. A hero belonging to the retinue of Dietrich von Bern (= Theoderic the Great; 454–526) discovered it in a dell on the age-old Tyrolean *Troj de réses* (= path strewn with roses), which goes from the Karrer Pass northward through the Tierser valley. After he had sung a *song*,[12] "the rose fairy showed the knight into the celler of the *mill*.[13] From there there was a *passage*

---

[10]Shunamitism; cf., I Kings 1: 1–4.
[11]Richard Wilhelm, op. cit., p. 156, 157.
[12]"Song" here mean *mantram*.
[13]"Cellar of the mill" here means the lowest story of the body, the sacral plexus.

leading into the mountain[14] and terminating in the brightest light.[15] And the knight's happy eye[16] beheld King Laurin's paradise garden.[17] He also saw the silk thread which encompasses everything.[18] And the rose paradise[19] opened to admit him— for ever. The knight had stepped into eternity."[20, 21]

The word *Berg* meaning mountain, as used in the original of this German-language story, comes from *bergen* = "to hide." The "Berg des Lichts" ("Mountains of Light"—Bit Nur) is *concealed* in man himself. In the stanzas of the curious Middle High German poem, written by an unknown hand ca. 1260 and entitled "Wartburgkrieg" ["Wartburg Contest"],[22] Wolfram von Eschenbach (1170–1220) makes the dwarf king Laurin say to Dietrich von Bern: "You have yet to live to the fiftieth year, Dietrich. And though you may be a strong hero, death will still overcome you. But you must know that my brother, dwelling in Germany, has power to give a thousand years of life. You need only choose a mountain which is *fiery inside*.[23] The people will imagine that you have descended into great heat, but you will become the companion of earthly gods; you will be like earthly gods." Dietrich answered King Laurin: "That is what I

---

[14]"The passage" here means the spine, back "cross," "Rosy Cross," the Indian *sushumna*.

[15] Cf., *Reise ins Licht* [*Journey into the Light*], Wilhelm, op. cit., p. 155.

[16]"Happy eye" = a trance, the Indian *samadhi*; or ecstasy.

[17]"Paradise" = [the plane of] *Devachan*.

[18]This is the "Homeric Chain," the chain of correspondences and influences (reciprocal effects), the "Aurea Catena."

[19]The "rose paradise" = the Kingdom of Heaven. Heaven in the human body is the upper part, the head and Heaven's "light" is the crown center (the Indian *sahasrara*).

[20]"Stepped into eternity" does not mean dead here, the achievement of "cosmic consciousness." Cf., Dr. Bucke, M.D.: *Cosmic Consciousness* (Philadelphia, 1901).

[21]Otto Rahn (died 1939), *Luzifers Hofgesind* [Lucifer's Servants], Leipzig, 1937, pp. 188–190.

[22]Translater's note: the record of a song contest between certain celebrated poets, which was held on the Wartburg.

[23]The "Serpent Power" is also called the "Serpent *Fire*." Voluntary control of the blood flow always creates heat. Cf., the Tibetan art of *tumo* described by Alexandra David-Neel in her *Mystics and Magicians in Tibet* [*Heilige und Hexer*] (Leipzig, 1932, pp. 212–225). Also the magnetizer of the Abbé Loubert "soon feels a moderate warmth spreading through him."

will do and shall look forward to it with pleasure. Never shall my mouth reveal it to other human beings."[24]

The rose, or its diminutive, the rosette, is used widely nowadays as a description of the female sex organ. "No rose without a thorn," the thorn is the phallus, the male sex organ. *Therefore, "Rosy Cross" carries the idea of sublimating the sexuality and raising the "back cross" (the mystical ladder)*, so that the seven roses (the Indian "lotuses" or "chakras," the "wheels" or centers of the subtle body) are aroused from their "thorn-rose sleep."

In the ancient Greek mysteries (i.e., allegories), the staff of Aesculapius, with a serpent wound round it, signifies healing power derived from an excess of Od obtained by developing the "Serpent Power."

The *caduceus* of Hermes is a wand bearing two entwined snakes and, at its end, a pair of wings. The meaning of this is also clear. Once again it is the *kundalini*, which winds its way up the spine (the Indian *sushumna*) by the two channels, Ida and Pingala. The two wings are the two "lotus petals" between the eyebrows; they correspond to the center of the subtle body known as *ajna*.

Goethe says, "I feel as if my 'I' is squeezed between my eyebrows." The eyebrows have a vague resemblance to a butterfly and it is as a butterfly that, according to legend, the soul escapes from the sleeping body (astral projection). In Greece the butterfly was a symbol of immortality.

When the Rosicrucians speak of the *Magnum Opus* (Latin for Great Work) as the "Chemical Wedding," they are pointing out that the union (or wedding) of the "King's Son" or spirit and the "Bride" or soul is not merely a spiritual affair (in Greek, *hieros gamos*), but also a physical one, operating right inside the bodily mechanism! Thus we read for example, "After approximately two weeks of practice nobody can doubt any longer that *the neck-hold has brought about chemical changes in the neck*. The time has now arrived when one has the poisonous taste of mercury on the tongue if the latter is touched with the forefinger of the hand bent at right angles. Later on the taste of salt develops."[25]

---

[24]Rahn, op.cit., pp. 173, 174.
[25]Rudolf von Sebottendorf: *Die Praxis der alten türkischen Freimaurerei* [*The Practice of Old Turkish Freemasonry*] (Leipzig, 1924, p. 37, also p. 15).

The evangelical prelate of Württemberg, Friedrich Christoph Oetinger (1702–1782), who was both clairvoyant and possessed of great spiritual authority and used to preach to the earthbound spirits in the darkened church late at night, had the right idea when he exclaimed: "Corporality is the end of God's Way!"

DISCUSSION

The spirit is there, but the *spiritual body* has to be made like a garment with which to clothe that spirit. This garment requires a long time for its preparation. A man weaves and shapes this spiritual body every hour of his existence in all his thoughts and activities.

—Oliver Lodge (1851–1922)
in a communication, 1944

The best account of the Taoist Way was given by Prof. Eduard Erkes (of Leipzig) in "Psyche" (1949, Vol. 3, pp. 371 ff) in my considered opinion. Like Professors Richard Wilhelm and Erwin Rouselle (1890–1949), he was an initiated Taoist. A work on "Kundalini Yoga" has recently been written by a Master Y-Kuan (Munich, Planegg, 1952). I have not read it yet, however. The older works of Arthur Avalon (Sir John Woodroffe), for example, are widely available.

Prof. Eduard Erkes was kind enough to answer, on January 3, 1952, a question put to him on the point as follows: "without personal instruction by a master of meditation it is very difficult and not without its dangers to try and learn to meditate. The crucial indications as to whether one has meditated correctly are not given in the literature but only verbally, and wrong training or any disturbances can easily damage the health."

I share this opinion, and can now add nothing more on the subject of this chapter without breaking silence on those things which may be disclosed only by a master (or Guru)!

LIFE STORAGE

Where inroads have been made in the bosom of
Mother Earth, the prophets of the Hidden World and
of the Wisdom of God love to dwell—one has only to
think of the part played by the interior of mountains
in the life of a Paracelsus, Jakob Boehme, Swedenborg,
Novalis, Franz von Baader and so many others.

—Fritsche[1]

In the section on "Human Hibernation" in my *Streifzug ins Ungewohnte [An Excursion into the Unusual]* (Freiburg i. Brs., 1949,
pp. 264 ff), I wrote among other things as follows: "I am morally
certain that the genuine Rosicrucians knew of a *processus vitae
interruptionis* (a method of suspended animation), and this is
borne out by the wealth of old stories concerning old men
dressed in antique costumes or vestments who were found *sleeping* in mountains (caves)."

The oldest and best-known of these accounts of a *prolonged
sleep* is that of the *Seven Sleepers*. "According to the legend, seven
Christian youths, honored as saints (their Saint's Day is on June
27, or, in the Eastern Church, August 4, the so-called 'Magical
Day'), who were shut up in a cave at Ephesus during the per-
secution of the Christians under Decius in A.D. 251, fell asleep
there and were only woken in A.D. 446 under the Emperor
Theodosius II. It is a saying that it will rain for seven weeks, if
it rains on Seven Sleepers' Day (June 27)" (Brockhaus). The

---

[1]Dr. Herbert Fritsche (Bad Pyrmont): *Aus der Gnadengeschichte einer Stätte [Ex-
cerpts from the Religious Annals of a District]* (Pyrmont, 1946, p. 36).

young men were called Maximanus, Malchus, Martianus, Dionysius, Johannes, Serapion and Constantius. After they had had the opportunity of bearing solemn witness to their wonderful deliverance before the Emperor and the Bishop of Ephesus (Kalionsberg), they passed away peacefully. (This is reminiscent of the two survivors of the six "Bunkermen" of Gdynia in the summer of 1951, who had been trapped since 1945 in an underground supply depot due to the collapse of the upper structure!) This legend has been raised to the status of a dogma in Islam (The Koran, Sura XVIII, ajat 3–25; "The Cave").

Other examples are the popular German legends of "Barbarossa's Cave" in the Kyffhaeuser mountain where the Emperor Frederick I (Barbarossa or "Red Beard," 1121–1190) is said to sleep an enchanted sleep, and of the Untersberg at Salzburg, where Charlemagne (768–814) rests in one of the many caves.

For non-Germanic cave stories I will content myself with a reference to Mexico, where there is supposed to be the entrance to a subterranean world in the grotto of Chapultepec, not far from Mexico City, into which King Huemac II disappeared and from which he will emerge one day in order to take back his kingdom (E. Beauvois: *L'Elysée des Mexicains comparé à celui des Celtes* [*The Mexican Elysium compared with that of the Celts*] *Revue Hist. des Relig*, Vol. X: 1884, p. 27).

Dr. A. Krumm-Heller in his *Der Rosenkreuzer aus Mexico* [*The Mexican Rosicrucians*] (Halle a.d.S., 1919, p. 7), writes as follows of the Cerro de Chapultepec: "Hundreds pass it every day without realizing that there is an entrance into the mountain at this point. It is not like the stalactite caves of Europe, which confront the traveler in their natural state; the rockface here has been dressed by the ancient inhabitants of Mexico and remains as an impressive tribute to their immense devotion and skill. No one knows or suspects what lies below. In the days of the Aztecs, this cave where government buildings now stand, was used as a place of initiation. Hernando Cortez (1485–1547), the conqueror of Mexico, never learned what was there, not even from his paramour, although he was always trying to ferret out secrets; nor did that student of Aztec affairs, Father Sagahun, do any better. The fact is that there used to be a temple of initiation in the depths of this mountain, where a white lodge meets today."

Several real-life phenomena spring to mind, when one is looking for analogies to these legends of heroes entombed in a state of suspended animation or is trying to assess the theoretical feasibility of what is usually taken as wishful thinking. These are:

a) Hibernation in animals;

b) The anabiosis of microorganisms;

c) Comas;

d) Apparent death;

e) Fakirs who survive burial alive.

Because examples drawn from the standard works on the subject[2] might seem out-of-date and to have lost their evidential value, we shall present the *latest* data.

HIBERNATION

The old examples of the hibernation of animals are still as useful as ever, but there is a recent instance of human hibernation in the married couple, Gehrke of Wisconsin in the USA. Each year from October 15 to April 15, the Gehrkes never left their bed, took only a little nourishment and were cared for by a daughter. It was the general opinion locally that this practice helped the two "dormice" to preserve their health. This couple was doing what, according to the registrar's office at Pskov (Russia) in 1898, was practiced by the *Leyka* (= those who sleep

---

[2]Dr. G.H. Berndt: *Buch der Wunder und Geheimwissenschaften* [*A Book of Marvels and Occult Sciences*] (Leipzig, n.d., Vol. II, p. 684–691). Dr. Albert Neuberger: *Physik und Chemie* [*Physics and Chemisry*] (Munich, 1924, pp. 128, 129; Collection: "The Marvels of Science"). Arthur Grobe-Wutischky (1884–1928): *Fakirwunder und moderne Wissenschaft* [*Fakir Prodigies and Modern Science*] (Berlin-Pankow, 1923). Albert de Rochas: *La Suspension de la Vie* [*The Suspension of Life*] (Paris, 1914). Prof. Richard Schmidt: *Fakire und Fakirtum in alten und modernen Indien* [*Fakirs and Fakirism in Ancient and Modern India*] (Berlin, 1908).

in). When the head of the family saw that provisions were short at the end of autumn, he reduced the rations and everybody went to sleep for four or five months. People got up only to heat the cabin and to eat a piece of bread dipped in water.

THE ANABIOSIS OF MICROORGANISMS

Plant and animal organisms have been found in the mouths and stomachs of frozen mammoths which have been recovered from the Siberian ice-fields after 20,000 years. These organisms have revived after thawing out.

PROLONGED STATES OF TRANCE (COMAS)

Doreen Shook, a small American girl living in Albany (New Jersey) entered a coma in 1941 at age 7. She remained fast asleep for 770 days and nights. She went to bed after a perfectly normal day at school and failed to wake up again. The doctors who treated the child stated that her general health was good and that she had not lost weight. The patient was kept alive with liquid nourishment (vitamin preparations, etc.) supplied by means of tubes.

Another instance of artificial feeding is that of a man in the Spanish city of Albacete, who fell into a deathlike trance in April, 1942. He returned to consciousness for brief moments only. His cardiac action was normal and there were no other symptoms of disease.

Artificial feeding was also used (through the nose) in 1948 on a man in Cincinnati (Ohio) who had already survived for more than 2,000 days without returning to consciousness and yet remained in good health to all appearances. The doctors in charge of the case said that five-and-a-half years of coma was a record and thought that the patient would remain in the same condition for a great while longer. A heavy object fell on the man's head before he lost consciousness and some of his brain cells had been destroyed by the action of blood clots in his head. Since the accident he had continued to sleep, opening his eyes from time to time but did not respond when addressed.

Twenty-six-year-old employee, J. Windrum of Belfast has been unconscious since she was thrown from a bus on December

6, 1948. The doctors were at a loss what to do because, although her coma was not very deep as far as they could tell, they were unable to wake her out of it. That was how matters stood on January 20, 1949.

On April 11, 1950, there died in an old folk's home in Sweden, 88-year-old Karolina Karlsson, who had at one time aroused worldwide interest by slumbering like the Sleeping Beauty for thirty-three years. This case, too, has remained a medical riddle in spite of all the attempts made by doctors to unravel it. In 1875, when she was still a schoolgirl (cf., the Shook case!), Mrs. Karlsson had gone to bed not feeling well and it was not until April 1908 that she got up again for the first time. While in her lethargic state she often seemed to take notice of what was going on around her. During this time she was fed mainly on milk. On regaining full consciousness, she could still read and write and had not forgotten the names of the King and Queen of Sweden. She made a quick recovery and enjoyed good health right down to old age.

APPARENT DEATH

In the spring of 1943, the Honduras farmer's daughter, Alicia Dobricias, who was 17 years old at the time, was bitten by a poisonous snake. She was carried indoors helpless and was given belated injections by the doctor. For three long weeks, the girl lay unconscious in bed, with her breathing almost non-existent. Her pulse weakened day by day until finally the doctors pronounced her dead. Just before she was to be placed in her coffin, the mother took her daughter by the hand and observed that her arm was quite warm, as warm as that of a living person. The doctor was recalled but could only shrug his shoulders because the girl's heart was not beating and her lungs showed no signs of functioning, even after prolonged examination. On the other hand, *rigor mortis* had not set in. The advice given was to leave Alicia in bed and to take her temperature from time to time. There seemed to be no point in giving injections since the circulation had apparently stopped. After an unbroken sleep or strange catalepsy of the body for 96 months, the seeming corpse was restored to life at the beginning of 1951. The miracle of Trujillo is even more remarkable for the fact that during the whole time the farmer's daughter took no nourishment, did not alter her position in bed and never lost weight.

FAKIRISM

"Pandit Malavija, a yogi, had himself buried alive for 72 days when his mental and physical strength started to fail. On coming out of his 'grave,' he looked more vigorous than he had done for decades. Then, as he started to age again after many years, one of his attendants begged him to renew his energies once more, to which he merely replied 'My time has come,' and departed this life with cheerful resignation in 1950. We conclude that his wisdom was superior to his power."[3]

The question now arises as to what means might be employed to "preserve" living persons. One answer might lie in "deep freezing." Let us take a look at the chronological development of this idea. In his fantastic novel *Atalanta, die Sklavin des Bärensees* [*Atalanta, the Slave of Bear Lake*] (1913), popular writer Robert Kraft (1886–1926) told of a mysterious scientist, Professor Dodd, who froze human beings inside blocks of ice and kept them like statues in a sort of museum until he was ready to thaw them.

Prof. de Lampe of the University of Leyden stated in 1939, on the basis of his experiments, that it would soon be possible to put people into cold storage for fifty years and that this would enable them to live to be 2,000 years old!

Nobel prize-winner, Alexis Carrel (1873–1944) said something similar around the same time in his book, *Man, the Unknown* (p. 89): "Perhaps it would also be possible to prolong human life and cure many diseases, thus giving exceptionally gifted individuals a longer lease, if one could practice *hibernation* from time to time" (retranslated from German, Tr.).

---

[3]In Lord Lytton's *A Strange Story*, Haroun of Aleppo declared "that he had thrice renewed his own life, and had resolved to do so no more. . . . The soul is not meant to inhabit this earth in fleshly tabernacle for more than the period usually assigned to mortals" (Chapter XXXIX, pp. 208, 209). And the same author put these words in the mouth of Zanoni (in the novel of that name): "Mejnour, cast down thy elixir; lay by thy load of years! Wherever the soul can wander, the Eternal Soul of all things protects it still!" (Book The Seventh, Chapter XIV, p. 384).

Professor Paul Bequerel (sic)[4] declared at the Sorbonne in Paris in 1949:

> After numerous experiments, we have succeeded by means of dehydration and low temperatures[5] in suspending the growth of whole plants, bulbs and small animals for an indefinite time without harming their later development. Biologists in other countries to whom I have communicated my findings are improving my methods and are concentrating on stopping the vital processes of animals for a given period. Perhaps *in fifty years* it will be possible for a person to break off his life at a certain point and to resume it in another century.[6]

Taking their cue from the revolting experiments in the infamous *subcooling tests* conducted by the criminal SS scientists on the inmates of concentration camps in Germany during the Second World War, American scientists concluded, after numerous experiments of their own on animals, that a "frozen" man is literally a "suffocated" man!

The point they were trying to make was that every warm-blooded animal is powered by the energy produced when fuel burns in oxygen. And so, as the cold starts to penetrate, the body keeps calling on fresh energy reserves, consuming in the

---

[4]Trans. note: Prof. Bequerel is incorrectly called "another Nobel Prizewinner" perhaps by confusing him with A.H. Becquerel.

[5]As long ago as 1914, de Rochas was saying in his *La Suspension de la Vie* [*The Suspension of Life*] that frogs had been revived after being kept frozen in many degrees of frost. According to a report written in 1919 by Dr. A. Neuburger (*Psych. Stud.*, p. 422), the physiologist Bachmetieff had frozen dogs and cats stiff and then thawed them, using certain precautions to prevent internal injury; whereupon they returned to the normal life of their species.

[6]In Madrid in 1933, a Spaniard managed to enter a state of suspended animation following many years of training under the fakirs of India. "He sat down in a water-filled metal tank under the observation of a panel of doctors. The water, which came up to his mouth, was brought to the freezing point by electrical means and the Spanish fakir was literally frozen into a block of ice, in which he remained for 24 hours. The ice was then thawed and the cold and stiff body was lifted out of the tank. Eventually, after hours of massage, the man was restored to life and vigor" (Dr. Eugen Georg: *Der Mensch und das Geheimnis* [*Man and Mystery*] Berlin, 1934, pp. 255–256).

process immense amounts of oxygen until, when all supplies have been used up, death ensues.

Now if the cold is so intense that combustion in the body is given less time, and torpidity occurs *before* the individual suffocates trying to satisfy the massive oxygen requirement, then the person so treated will be stiff and cold—but not dead. If, then, he is restored by thawing him out as quickly as possible by the action of the greatest possible amount of warmth on the chilled organism, with a view of course to keeping to a minimum the critical time during which there will be an immense consumption of oxygen once more to combat the cold, the frozen individual will live again. The development of the "quick-freeze process" is only a question of time. The idea has been conceived, all that is needed is the "tools" to bring it to birth!

But what would be the object of the exercise? According to Carrel, exceptionally gifted people would have greater scope in which to exercise their abilities. We would have the men of yesterday in the world of tomorrow (and the conquest of time would follow that of space). Such people would be better interpreters of past events than films and books. Also, there is a lot to be said for the suggestion made by Dr. W. Schmidt-Hoepke that, instead of the wholesale slaughter of entire herds of animals when fodder is scarce, they could be frozen alive until crops were plentiful again.

But what might be the disadvantages of "keeping people on ice"? In a modern dictatorship (a human ant colony) it is quite conceivable that millions of soldiers could be put into cold storage ready for a sudden attack, without any possibility of the fact being monitored by an international disarmament commission.[7] The mere thought of such a possibility, shows us where the abuse of scientific knowledge (knowledge which ought to

---

[7]This idea was devised by Bruno Noah in a utopian novel written in 1934, and has still to be proved true! Meanwhile "frozen sleep" has been introduced as a new form of narcosis! Reports from the University of Toronto (Canada) indicate that this is especially useful in serious heart operations. In Philadelphia (USA) in the spring of 1950, Dr. Temple Fay carried out a successful cardiac operation under "frozen sleep." The chief advantage of this method is that it gives the surgeon more time than he has with ordinary anaesthetics.

be used in the service of men) can lead in the hands of evil states and rulers.

I said above that one method of preserving living people is by deep-freezing them. So what is the other one? For the answer, let us turn back to the starting-point of our study—the legendary stories. These say nothing about men frozen in caves of ice but of men sleeping in ordinary caves.[8] Now this plain hint directs us to the highest form of fakirism as the second method of preservation. This method was the only one open to the Rosicrucians, as they would not have had the technical facilities for method number one, and in this they were in the same position as we are today as yet.[9]

I have shown elsewhere that the Rosicrucians were familiar with yoga technique, both that of Patañjali (through Albiruni's translation into Arabic) and the more modern "Steiner-type" meditation (cf., Prof. Nollius, 1620). What is more, Noah[10] knew about putting living beings in "cold storage" too: "In a novel about world war, a description is given of the Chinese training their able-bodied men and causing them to enter a *prolonged sleep* by strange practices. In a way, they convert them into living mummies[11] and keep them in artificial catacombs in the mountains until the time comes for them to be wakened." This awakening of a living mummy in an artificial mountain catacomb was experienced by no less a person than the well-known London mental specialist, the Director of a very famous mental

---

[8]We can see then that the old story-tellers managed to hit the nail on the head without realizing it. The slow action of cold means death with no possibility of restoration to life. Freezing someone to death is not the same as deep freezing them! However, it is possible for someone to awake or be awakened from a prolonged sleep of this sort. Exactly as happens with many patients lying in a coma, old Barbarossa will also stir for a moment and order his attendants to see whether the ravens are still circling round his hidden stronghold in the mountains.

[9]When all is said and done, we may assume that they knew and used electricity! I have discussed this elsewhere.

[10]Bruno Noah: *Die Edda* [*The Edda*] (Berlin-Pankow, 1934, p. 119).

[11]On these "strange practices" cf., Willy Schrödter: *Streifzug ins Ungewohnte* [*An Expedition into the Unusual*] (Freiberg i. Brsg., 1949, pp. 191 ff) and Dr. Albert Gervais, *Im Schatten des Makué* [*In the Shadow of the Makué*] (Leipzig, 1937, pp. 256 ff).

hospital, Dr. Alexander Cannon,[12] who had this to say about his encounter with a Tibetan "immortal" in the cell of a noted master of Yoga:

> The Dalai Lama sat on his throne. Then came a procession of singing monks, one carrying blazing torches. After sitting down in a circle—the room was round—they continued to sing. The Dalai Lama prayed. During the prayer, eight men came in bearing a heavy stone coffin. The coffin lid was lifted to disclose someone who appeared to be dead lying inside.

> I obtained permission to examine the body. There was no perceptible pulse, no sound of a heartbeat. The body was stone cold, and the eyes were like those of a person who has been dead for more than twenty-four hours. I ascertained by means of a mirror, which did not mist over, that there was no breathing. The body lay lifeless—as if in the grave. Then the Dalai Lama said something in a very mysterious-sounding language and stared into the open eyes of the corpse. The latter gradually raised itself in its coffin. Supported by two monks it walked toward the head lama, without for one second removing its gaze from the greatest of all sages. And a few minutes later the body lay there as lifeless as before . . .

> I wondered whether this man really was dead or was only in some sort of trance. The Dalai Lama, reading my thoughts, declared that the man had actually been "dead" for seven years, and that he would not be raised again until another seven years had elapsed. I was further informed that this man was several hundred years old and that he was capable of living for ever— if one could call this sort of thing life. (Retranslated from the German. *Tr.*)

Father Christian Rosencreutz (1378–1484) of blessed memory was laid to rest in a wondrous mausoleum, over the entrance to which were written the following Latin words:

---

[12]*The Invisible Influence* (London, Nov., 1933).

"POST CXX ANNOS PATEBO." That is to say, "After 120 years I shall be opened." One of the fundamental Rosicrucian documents, *Fama Fraternitatis* (Cassel, 1614), goes on to relate how the tomb was found in 1604. With the discovery of this vault and with the speedy publication thereafter of Rosicrucian "kites" flown to gauge public opinion, the above inscription was fulfilled.

When we consider that, when found, the body of our much-loved Father was as unblemished as it had been in life, showing no signs of decomposition, it may occur to us to ask whether this beautifully preserved body of the Impulsor (a Latin title which, in this instance, we may interpret as meaning "a motivator on the spiritual plane"), dressed in his robes of office so we are told, might not have been taken from the yesterday of 1484 into the today of 1604 by his second and third rank successors in much the same way as Cannon's Tibetans treated their "dead" monk?

This would be the fulfillment of the promise "Patebo."

And when will you return to your rest again and when again will you wake? Come back quickly, Father Rosencreutz, for the sun is setting in the West . . . !

DISCUSSION

> I am minded to take a long sleep.
>
> *—Wallenstein's Tod*
> *[The Death of Wallenstein]*

Ever since the spring of 1950, when Dr. Temple successfully preformed a cardiac operation on a "frozen patient" in Philadelphia, further research has been carried out on techniques designed to reduce the body temperature. Probands have been chilled and kept asleep for days at a time without harm.

This latest form of anaesthesia has been found particularly suitable for those with heart defects and, accordingly, surgery was performed in the summer of 1952 on the hearts of 12-year-old Judith Schmidt and 15-year-old Jaqueline Johnston in Cleveland, Ohio, while they were anaesthetized with cold.

Research in the United States, France, and Holland has shown that the application of cold will retard the growth of cancers, halt infections and slow down pathological changes in the lungs and liver.

Hibernation experiments at Professor Seneque's Vaurigard Surgical Clinic have been given the name "potentized anaesthesia." Candidates chosen for these experiments were first relaxed and partly stupefied with narcotics and, when they were too feeble to object, their bodies were clasped between ice-cold rubber cushions which lowered their temperatures to 84–90 degrees Fahrenheit, and they fell into a profound sleep. Those who are dangerously weakened by major operations can be nursed as they lie asleep, covered by cold mackintosh sheets for as long as twelve days, and are much improved when they are thawed out. Similar success has been obtained by Dr. H. Laborit, and Dr. Pierre Hugenard, with over sixty patients, though using more short-term frozen sleep. It is worthy of note that the Rosicrucian, Francis Bacon (Lord Verulam), thought by many people to be the true author of Shakespeare's plays, centuries ago saw a frozen fowl lying in the road. He got down out of his coach, studied it from all points of view, and was struck by the conserving power of ice. Lost in thought, the philosopher himself became chilled through, contracted inflammation of the lungs and died!

Turning now to the possibility of deep hypnosis as a means of producing suspended animation, we are reminded of the legend of the "Maidens of the Dark Angel" (in other words, witches) in whom we partly see the remnant of the heathen Germanic priestesses. The chief Germanic deity, Woden, was known among other things as the one who puts to sleep. Just as Woden, or Odin, put his valkyrie, Brünhilde, to sleep, so the angry fairy cast a spell that eventually sent Sleeping Beauty to sleep for a hundred years! This is a counterpart of the Rosicrucian theme of men lying asleep in their antique costume for hundreds of years somewhere in the mountains.

In his book *Melancholie* [*Melancholy*] (Berlin, 1928, pp. 199 ff), J.E. Porkitzky exploited the idea of "the prolongation of life through hypnosis" in the form of a novel, describing how the 82-year-old grandmother caused her beloved Karin to linger on for years by giving a hypnotic command (!) just as she was about to die.

And he ends, "In fact, if thought was the proven almighty power, should it not be possible to eradicate death from the world or *at least to double the length of human life*" (pp. 210, 211).

TRANSMUTATION

Although the sun never shone on this vault, nevertheless it was enlightened with another sun, which had learned this from the sun . . . a chest, wherein there lay . . . all our books. . . . In another chest were looking-glasses of divers virtues, as also in other places were little bells, burning lamps and chiefly wonderful artificial songs. . . . Concerning Minutum Mundum, we found it kept in another little altar. . . .

—*Fama*

In the summer of 1755, a young man in his twenties carried out a transmutation at Homburg vor der Höhe in the house of the Royal Provincial Commissioner for the Duchy of Hesse-Darmstadt, Siegmund Heinrich Güldenfalk. Thus convinced of the truth of alchemy, Güldenfalk defended it publicly in his *Sammlung von mehr als hundert wahrhaften Transmutationsgeschichten*, etc. [*A Collection of Over One Hundred Genuine Accounts of Transmutation*, etc.] (Frankfurt/Main & Leipzig, Joh. Gg. Fleischer, 1784). He reports his own experience as No. 68 (pp. 120–122) in this book. Schmieder quotes him briefly in his *Geschichte der Alchemie* [*Tales of Alchemy*] on page 549. From the Güldenfalk collection I am taking unabridged No. 79 (pp. 193–204), which has the following title: "A German translation of a Dutch hermetic narrative of Jesse Abraham and Salomon Teelsu, 1731." However, I am citing it here not on account of the "Hermetic" aspect but on account of the magical, which Schmieder did not sanction (pp. 525–526) and therefore did not adduce.

Dear Friend,

You want me to tell you about the life and death, the inheritance and heirs of my blessed master, Benjamin Jesse.

Well then, he was a Jew by birth but a Christian by religion, and he knew that Jesus is the Savior of the World. He professed this both publicly and privately and was a man of exemplary faith, who gave much alms secretly and led a very chaste single life.

As far as I myself am concerned as to how I came to him, you must know that he took me from an orphanage when I was about 10 years old, for I was a foundling.

To begin with, he had me taught Latin and, on the quiet, I also learnt by dint of use and exercise the Rabbinical language. In keeping with my strength and ability, he employed me to help him in his strange laboratory and still-room. He had a very fine understanding of the art of medicine and *cured incurable diseases*. When I reached the age of 25, he summoned me to his dining room and asked me to promise on oath that I would not marry without his knowledge and consent. This promise I made and have piously kept.

As soon as I had entered my 30th year, he called me once more into his dining room, in the early hours of the morning, and said to me in a friendly tone of voice, "My son! The balm of my life is almost consumed (he was about 88 years old at this time), my life is coming to an end and I am near to death. I have made out my will to my cousins and you and placed it on the table in my prayer room, in which neither you nor any other living[1] person has ever been and on the door of which you have never been permitted to knock during my time of prayer."

---

[1]But, it may be inferred, that the dead, i.e. spirits, might enter. We may recall the *theurgic* purpose of the prayer-room in *The Book of Sacred Magic of Abraham of Worms* (1387).

So saying, he led me from the dining room to the double doors of this prayer room and made several applications of some transparent crystal material to the joins or crevices of the doors, manipulating it between his fingers like wax. Having done this, he stamped it with his engraved gold signet, so that his seal was impressed on it. The crystal material immediately hardened in the air and was so brittle that the said seal would immediately break in two at the slightest movement of the doors. He deposited the key of his prayer room inside a small casket, daubing its lid and openings with the same crystal substance and sealing it as before with his signet ring.[2] Then he handed me the sealed casket and ordered me to give it to no one except his cousins, Jesse Abraham and Salomon Teeslu, who at that time were living in Switzerland, and the first of whom was married. After he had returned with me to the dining room and as I stood by watching, he threw the signet he had used into the crystal material and it dissolved in it just as ice melts in warm water,[3] and it precipitated to the bottom of the glass as a white powder, and the crystal water turned the pale red color of French rose. Next he dissolved the glass in the said crystal material and gave me a similar glass together with the keys, with instructions to hand them all to Mr. Jesse.

When all this had been done, he prayed one of the Psalms of David in Hebrew, kneeling as he did so, and then went to sit in his favorite chair, in which he was accustomed to taking an afternoon nap, and asked me to give him a little Malmsey wine[4] such as he used to drink sparingly. After he had taken some wine, I had to stay with him and he laid his head on my shoulder

---

[2]The much-celebrated *sigillum Hermetis* or hermetic seal.
[3]The so-called Alkahest, the universal solvent of alchemy.
[4]Malmsey wine originally came from Monembasia on the east coast of the Peloponnesus and later from the Greek islands. It was a sweet red wine much prized in the Middle Ages. Nowadays it comes from Portugal, Teneriffe, the Azores, the Lipari Islands, Sardinia, Sicily, and Provence.

and dropped into a peaceful slumber. Then, after half an hour had elapsed, he sighed very deeply and, to my great distress, yielded to God his spirit.[5] In accordance with my promise, I then wrote to his cousins in Switzerland, informing them of his death. The following day, I myself received a letter from the said Mr. Jesse asking after my master, and requesting me to let him know whether he was living or dead; *just as if he had been involved in what had happened here.*[6] My astonishment was great as I read it. However, in the sequel I was shown the reason for this, the cause being a special instrument or artifice.

As soon as his cousins arrived, I related everything described above. Mr. Jesse himself, began to smile a little on hearing it, but the other cousin was full of amazement and perplexity.[7] I wanted to give them the key of the casket and the glass containing the sealed transparent material straight away, but they refused until they had recovered from the tiring journey they had just had that day.[8]

But the following day, early in the morning, when all the doors of the house were still locked and we were by ourselves, Mr. Jesse broke the glass over a porcelain dish so that he could use the water inside it. He took some of the water and smeared the seal on the casket with it. The seal immediately melted and he opened the casket, taking from it the key to the prayer room of my blessed master. We then proceeded to the prayer room.

After examining the seal, he smeared it with the crystal water and it softened and melted, and Jesse opened the door, which sprang shut behind us. He fell on his knees and prayed, which we also did. When the prayer

---

[5]This gentle death after a full life is called the "Kiss" by Qabalists.
[6]The events recorded took place in Hamburg (Schmieder).
[7]Salomon Teelsu, in contrast to Abraham Jesse, was not an initiate, as the difference in what they inherited shows.
[8]I see here an indication of rare self-control!

was over, we went from one room into the other, the door closing behind us as before, and there I saw great marvels. In the center of this prayer room stood a table of pure ebony; its top was round with a border of gold plate. In front of this table stood a small kneeling-stool, and in the middle of the table was a wonderfully contrived instrument. The lower part, or foot, was round and of pure gold; the central part was of clear transparent crystal in which was enclosed a perpetual fire that emitted brilliant beams; the upper part was also of pure gold and bowl-shaped.

Directly over this instrument there hung a crystal on a golden chain, artificially shaped like an egg, by which the everlasting fire was enclosed, when it radiated its light.

On the righthand side of this table I saw a golden box with a little spoon inside it. The box held a scarlet red balsam.[9] On the lefthand side of the table there was a small reading desk of pure gold on which lay a book with twelve pages, also of pure beaten gold but so flexible that it looked like paper. Characters and symbols had been drawn in the middles and in the corners of these pages, and it looked as if there were holy prayers at their bottoms. Below this standing reading desk was found the last will and testament of my deceased master. When we were in this room, Mr. Jesse leaned over this desk with great devotion and read some prayers from the golden book and, thus prepared, he took a tiny amount of the above-mentioned balsam in the little spoon and laid it on the instrument standing on the table. At once there was an incomparably fragrant smell, by which we were greatly refreshed and, what was even more wonderful, the vapor so moved in the fire as it ascended and hung above in the crystal egg, that it threw out fearful flashes like lightnings and stars.

---

[9]The red tincture or universal medicine.

After this had been done, Mr. Jesse read the will. The dead man had bequeathed to Mr. Jesse all his instruments and books of knowledge. Otherwise, he had divided his property between his cousins equally. My own legacy, to reward me for my faithful service, was six thousand golden ducats. The two heirs now collected all the instruments and books of knowledge bequeathed in the will. As I have already said, these were on and beside the table in the prayer chamber.

On the right side of this prayer chamber, I saw a small coffer made of ebony and overlaid on the inside with pure gold. Inside it were twelve instruments of fine gold, wonderfully turned and made, and engraved and cut with symbolic letters round about.

We moved on to the next coffer, which was bigger. In this there were twelve mirrors, not of glass, but of some unknown material, very fine and pretty. There were marvelous symbolic letters in the centers of these mirrors. They were set in golden frames. They shone like the mirrors in a palace, with an even reflection, and caught a very true likeness of whatever was put before them.

From there we entered a larger chamber with a very big mirror in it, which Mr. Jesse called the *Mirror of Solomon*. It was one of the world's wonders, because it could be made to show all the pictures in the world. Finally, I saw a well-made cabinet, constructed of ebony, in which there was a globe made of a very wonderful material. Mr. Jesse said that within it were contained both the fire and the soul of this earth, and that that was why it kept moving in the same way and manner as does our earth itself.[10]

What is more, I saw another cupboard suspended over this one. It housed a special instrument made of clockwork, or so it appeared, with a hand or pointer. Instead

---

[10]Perpetual motion or possibly the mundus minutus.

of figures for the hours, it was marked with the letters of the alphabet.

Mr. Jesse said that this instrument worked in the same way as his own, which he had in Switzerland, and that it was by these means that the man now dead had sent warning of his approaching demise. Here was the reason why Mr. Jesse had written me the above-mentioned letter the day after my master had died. He had surmised his death from the pointer of the instrument, and especially when the pointer stood still and no longer moved.

At last we came to the books of knowledge, but these he did not open. Next to the books lay a golden box, in which was a very heavy[11] scarlet red powder, which he picked up joyfully but put the box down again straight away. Next to the prayer room a closet had been made into which we went. There we found four middle-sized chests, in which there were locked up some pure gold bars, and from these the cousins gave me my legacy, twelve gold ducats by weight. But Mr. Jesse would neither take nor accept anything from the remainder, saying, "What I have already been bequeathed, is worth more than all this," for he knew the very arts of my deceased master. Therefore he gave instructions that his share should be distributed among several poor maidens who were without means, to provide them with a respectable dowry. Acting on the advice of these people, I myself got married to a poor but decent girl who had accepted the Christian faith as soon as she had been given part of the above-mentioned treasure for a dowry, and, in God's goodness, she is still alive. As soon as he had packed the things left to him in the will, Mr. Jesse took them away with him. The other cousin, however, being laden with gold, returned home a little later. Because war seemed imminent, Mr. Jesse went to live in more peaceful surroundings in the East Indies, from where he has writ-

---

[11]This is typical of the red tincture or the "Stone."

ten to me *only last year* asking to adopt my eldest son, whom I accordingly have sent to him in the East Indies.

During the time we were in the prayer room, I saw great marvels brought about by the operation and use of the said instruments of wisdom, *which I can not and dare not describe*. I have told you as much as possible, since you are such a very good friend of mine; *more I can not say*. Farewell.

N.B. This letter was dated January 30, 1731.

POSTSCRIPT

I quote below from my files *"Correspondence with Esoterists"* to show what ritual was used by the Hamburg Rosicrucian and Jew by birth, Benjamin Jesse (1642–1730) and to reveal with what degree of success it is still employed today.

My correspondent, to whom I shall merely refer by his initials "AME," was an intimate friend of Gustav Meyrink (1868–1932), by whom he was immortalized as "Baron Müller" in his *Der Engel vom westlichen Fenster* [*The Angel of the Western Window*]. This is what the Hamburg Hermeticist wrote to me on April 3, 1942:

As far as the magical work of this alchemist (i.e., Jesse) who lived a very quiet and retiring life, is concerned, I can disclose to you that he operated according to the Jew, Abraham of Worms, who obtains his knowledge from a hermit and magician dwelling near the town of Arachi in Egypt,[12] and had brought it back with him to Germany. This old magician was called Abra-Melin.[13]

I myself know the book very well[14] not only as regards its contents but—and this may surprise you—also *in*

---

[12]Trans. note: Mather's English translation. Schrödter has "Alkiri."

[13]Abra-Melin was really Ibrahim el-Mu'allim (1281–1412) a hakim of Bit-Nur, encountered by Abraham of Worms in 1400. (See Musalam = Dr. Franz Sättler, Vienna, in *Magie* [*Magic*], Berlin-Weissensee, n.d., p. 76.)

[14]It was mentioned by Prof. Alfred Lehmann in his *Aberglauben und Zauberei* [*Superstition and Sorcery*] (Stuttgart, 1925, pp. 257 ff). Also by Will-Erich

puncto practica (in point of practice) too. Not that I personally have operated with it, but a former acquaintance of mine used this art. He used to keep me informed of his progress, but when the apparitions entered his laboratory (where he used a prayer stool in front of the altar), he lost courage and abandoned the work.[15]

The book was entitled, *The Book of the Sacred Magic of Abra-Melin the Mage, as Delivered by Abraham the Jew unto his Son Lamech, A.D. 1458*.[16] This book was published by Peter Hammer, Cologne, 1725. About twenty-five years ago, a new impression was issued, or so I have been told.[17]

In December 1946, the Hamburg Hermeticist wrote to me again on the same theme:

Shortly before the War, I had the following *astral* experience: I went to see my friend, who at that time was attempting the Abra-Melin working, and asked him whether we might summon *Barbiel*.

Peuckert in his *Von schwarzer und weisser Magie* [*Magic White and Black*] (Berlin, n.d., pp. 15 ff), although he does not seem to have known the title of the book.
[15]Having been made aware of this book by Samuel Liddell MacGregor Mathers in 1899, Aleister Crowley (1875–1947) retired to Boleskin House in Scotland in order to undertake a successful invocation of the so-called "Abra-Melin demons." Before reaching the heart of the operation, he was summoned to Paris by the head of his order (Friedrich Levke in his article, "Leben und Lehre Aleisters Crowleys, des Meister Therion" ["The Life and Doctrines of Aleister Crowley, the Master Therion"] in *Merlin* (Hamburg, March, 1949, p. 3).
[16]Trans. note: the above is the title of the Mathers translation from a French MS version. Schrödter refers to an older version written in German, the title of which is as follows: *The Book of the Jew Abraham of Worms, a Book of True Practice in Divine Magic and Wondrous Things, as Imparted by Elohim and by the Holy Qabalah, Translated into German from a Hebrew Manuscript on Parchment Dated 1387*. For the benefit of researchers wishing to trace the original, the title reads in German: "Das Buch des Juden Abraham von Worms, Buch der Wahren Praktik in der göttlichen Magie und in erstaunlichen Dingen, wie sie durch die heilige Kabbala und durch Elohym mitgeteilt worden, aus einer hebräischen Pergamenthandschrift von 1387 verdeutscht."
[17]This new edition by Scheible-Stuttgart, Bartels, Berlin-Weissensee has long been out of print. But readers should note that this book is available in English.

Suddenly, I was lifted into the air by an invisible force, carried along under the ceiling and propelled through the window into the open air. As I caught a glimpse of the sheer drop beneath me, I was seized with fright and returned to my body with some violence. It was all so real and vivid that I could not have experienced it more clearly in full everyday consciousness.

A form appeared quite plainly to my friend behind the altar in his little prayer room, but he did not have the strength to speak to it.

He expressed himself as follows on the person of Jesse on April 1942:

I am very well informed about the letter re Jesse in question. . . . In the course of my investigations at the Johanneum here . . . I discovered the interesting letter of the unknown individual dated January 20, 1731. I made an original copy of it which I stuck in front of the "Alchemistischen Blättern" ["Alchemical Papers"] for 1927. . . . At that time I was actively engaged in research on Jesse and would have made good progress too but for the difficulties created by the Office for Jewish Affairs, which cast doubt on the purely scientific nature of my investigations. I therefore forebore to pursue the matter any further.

COUSIN ANSELMO

by

**Adalbert Von Chamisso
(1781–1838)**

I

When occult arts were lost elsewhere,
Toledo had retained its share;
And one there, so the story tells,
Was Yglano, master of wisdom and spells.[1]

He was rapt in thought at the close of day
As the sand in the hour-glass ran away,
When a caller came and disturbed his rest—
His cousin Anselmo, a troubled guest.

"Good cousin Anselmo, what brings you here
To visit after so many a year?
You *were* on the right road, I would say,
Is this not slightly out of your way?"

"Your greeting's harsh; unfair as well.
Dear cousin, 'tis the truth I tell:

---

[1] As I have shown elsewhere, he is the prototype of a Rosicrucian.

I took this journey from afar
Because your fame shines like a star.

A sense of pride rose like a flame
On hearing people praise your name.
How I love them to recall
Your good example to us all!

Such speculation there has been:
Folk said the world had never seen
A man with so much skill and power
To rule the shades of the midnight hour!

They said that you were wisdom's gold,
Were precious ore. They called you bold—
A man of steel, they said, but mild
And virtuous as a little child!

And yet, one hostile voice was raised
Against the man whom others praised.
A few words spoken out of spite
Were worms in the apple of delight.

The critic asked could it be true
A lion and eagle such as you
With lamb-like heart so pure within
Would spurn his nearest kith and kin?"—

"And your retort, if I might inquire,
To these reproaches sharp and dire?
I am keen to know how you rescued me
From the force of the fellow's calumny."—

"What could I do? My hands were tied,
My misery could not be denied,
All arguments must surely fail
From one so tattered, starved and pale.

Behold me! Did you ever see
A beggar's corpse that looked like me?

I ask you, wipe out this disgrace
And the sneering smile from the scorner's
　　face.

Procure me a living, a bishop's see
Or anything else in the Devil's fee,
And I'll sign my precious soul away
To him and you till judgment day."

"No, no! My cousin. Perish the thought!
My art was not from Satan bought;[2]
I do not kneel at Satan's throne,
The power comes from God alone."—

"From God! Of course, 'twas what I meant;
My hunger spoke, I am innocent.
From God, dear cousin, fetch me bread,
And I'm your man until I'm dead!"—

"Well, tell me now and tell me true,
May I, in turn, depend on you?
Would you repay what I had done
By showering favors on my son?"—

"Repay you; do you need to ask?
'Twould be a pleasure, not a task;
I am no saint, that I confess,
But gratitude I *do* possess.

Rumor has carried to your ear
Tales of my vices and, I fear,
Whispered of virtues that I lack,
And yet I am not wholly black.

I fail to live the way I should,
I choose the bad, neglect the good;

---

[2] *"Omne perfectum ab Deo, omne imperfectum ab Diabolo"* [Everything perfect comes from God, everything imperfect comes from the Devil] (Paracelsus, 1493–1541).

My sins have made me quite unclean,
Ungrateful, though, I've never been.

O gratitude! Thou duty bright,
Celestial pleasure, heavenly light!
Thine impress is upon my heart;
And thou and I shall never part!

And your dear son so fair and fine,
Could I love him more if he were mine?
What joy is gratitude, I say;
Your kindness I would well repay!"—

"Come, come! We look too far ahead,
Your wants concern us first instead.
Dame Martha says it's time to sup
And waits to fill my plate and cup.

Well, she shall bring you of the best,
An offering worthy of our guest;
We have two hens, and they at least
Shall give us something of a feast.

Martha, that flask there, if you will!
A warming beaker you can fill.
Pour the wine slowly from on high
And let the droplets foam and fly![3]

You cousin, leave, I pray, the door;
Stand in this circle on the floor.
There, take the hour-glass in your hand
And concentrate on the running sand!

To test a theory I intend;
You know the start, and I the end.

---

[3]"Even in his times, Caelius Aurelianus (2nd or 3rd century) made use of the monotonous sound of falling drops to lull a sick person to sleep. . . ." Kraepschin in *Unsere Zeit* (September, 1890, p. 210).

Sic hocus pocus, abracadabra so!
In body we're here but in spirit we go!"

He muttered the words he had to say
And breathed on him, too, in a secret way;
With eyes rolled up, Anselmo stood
As stiff as an image made of wood.[4]

II

The appointment is made and Anselmo
    you
Are now a bishop. It is true.
Bishop d'you hear? Then play the part,
With swelling breast and beating heart.

Quickly discard those rags so worn,
So black with age, so poor and torn;
In silk and purple you must dress
And learn the proper way to bless.

This cross for your breast, a shining thing,
And for your finger the signet ring,
Put on, Anselmo, with vestments fine,
And show yourself a proud divine!

So, soon at ease in the palace halls,
He strode between their gleaming walls
And, lit by the reflected glow,
Flung wide the windows and looked below.

How much he longed to cry aloud,
"Behold me here, you common crowd,
This splendid palace that you see
Surely befits a man like me!"

---

[4]Catalepsy.

Yet all was desolate and bare,
With none to enjoy what he had to share
Until one day inside there walked
A . . . niece of whom they both had talked.

The girl was vain, too rude by far,
As certain nieces sometimes are,
And now she dressed in silk attire
With pearls and jewels that shone like fire.

Rule over him, as might be guessed,
Was hers. He was by her possessed.
On house and church she sent the rain;
She 'brought the sunshine back' again.

So changeable she was, I fear,
He fretted, yet he loved her dear.
She petted him, then was unkind—
Yglano passed quite from his mind.

Until, one Vespers strange as rare,
For happiness was in the air,
The door swung open and His Grace
Beheld once more Yglano's face.

"Good evening cousin, it is good
To see you flourishing. I could
Never regret what I have done
To make your lot an easier one.

But time has kept on turning round,
And now as suppliant *I* am found.
To help my son you promised me—
Do so and I'll rewarded be.

The little living that is free,
Bestow it on my son for me;
It is not much but it will do—
The least I could expect of you."

"Excuse me," interposed the maid
In a voice the bishop now obeyed,
"My brother has the prior claim,
His is that living, do not blame.

Some day, perhaps, your son will find
The living that you have in mind:
But not today, we much regret.
Cousin, bide in patience yet!"

"In patience yet!" The bishop tame
Preached his sermon on the same,
"Brother . . . nephew. . . . What's to do?
Pray heed the words she speaks to you.

A bishop's is no kingly state,
And beggars swarm outside his gate;
Although a press of suppliants call,
The help he can afford is small.

There are so few whom I can bless.
Truly it fills me with distress
To turn the others from my door—
A cardinal could do much more.

Elevate me through your knowledge,
Cousin, to the Sacred College.
Your son and you, I'd help you both,
Verily, upon my oath!"

Questioningly, Yglano said,
"A red hat, then, upon your head
And on your foot the ruby shoe,
Would help in what you'd like to do?"

Eager, his grace with sparkling eye
Blurted, "I swear, I do not lie:
Use once again your magic art,
And you shall see me do my part."

The wonder-worker cut him short:
"No need for oaths of any sort:
By all means, let's repeat the test
with you in robes of scarlet dressed."

His hand raised almost threatening there
Traced rapid circles in the air.[5]
"Sic hocus pocus Shibboleth!
Day dawns not before night's last breath!"

The staring prelate did not seem
To breathe, but stood as in a dream.
The word was spoken, the rite was done;
He rubbed his eyes—and still no sun.

III

The news has reached the bishop's home,

The wearer of the triple crown
Bestows on him a cardinal's gown.

Fresh favorite among the old,
He enters now the papal fold;
Where the false sun's glittering light
Hides the pitfalls from men's sight.

---

[5]Bernhard Richter, Kassel-Wilhelmshöhe (Berica; died August 12, 1923) wrote in his *Die neue biomagnetische Schule* [*The New Biomagnetic School*] (Kassel-Wilhelmshöhe, 1920, p. 101, 102) on the so-called Biomagnetic vortex: "This form of application is new. I discovered it on the occasion of an occult experiment, and recommend it when strong influences are desired. The passes just described, becoming shorter but increasingly rapid, lead gradually to a more concentrated motion of the magnetizer's arms and, eventually, with the most energetic possible rotation of the arms, produce a true fluid vortex. By this means, I once obtained within a few minutes (purely by way of experiment) such a rotation in the aura that the subject became almost unconscious. The circles must be as small as they can be, and the smaller they are the more quickly must they be made, etc."

Selfish ambition in him burns,
He follows intrigues, twists and turns.
Yglano is not in his head:
He dwells on pleasure and fame instead.

Alone, one hour as the sunset died,
He sat with the casement opened wide.
And stared, in a sudden fit of gloom,
At the 'blood-stained' sky outside his room.

A footfall sounds in the colonnade,
As the colors into shadows fade;
And, just where the patterns melt away,
Yglano steps out at the edge of the day.

The prelate meets Yglano's eye;
He trembles and his mouth is dry.
The sun sinks, and a fatal star
(He fears) is rising from afar.

Just as a gambler tries to throw
To save his stake in one last go,
Persuasive words he starts to say
The dark suspicions to allay:

"You're here to speak about your son,
To chide for what I have not done.
Such hastiness is quite absurd—
D'you think I'd go back on my word?

All I've become to you I owe,
I am your minion as you know;
I say it loud, I say it free—
And you doubt gratitude in me?

To you I owe encouragement
And gifts bestowed with good intent;
But how I wish your helping hand
Could have done everything you planned!

You hoped to see me dedicate
My energies to Church and State—
A cardinal sounds great to you;
But how much can he really do?

O cousin! Don't you comprehend
How tight the yoke in which I bend?
Wherever I may twist and turn,
The eyes of envy on me burn.

Each mask-like face that "Trust me!" cries,
Is hollow as its hollow eyes.
And he who gives a friendly warning
Traps me himself tomorrow morning.

Forces of darkness (to our shame)
Have now achieved their fearful aim:
Christendom's ruled by robber bands
And harlots thrive within its lands.

And yet, I see, your thoughts still run
On how I should advance your son;
But what, in Rome, can *I* secure
Who try to keep my actions pure?

As bishop, I could pick and choose,
Assent to this, or that refuse;
In villages a man walks tall,
At Rome he's in a free-for-all.

The Holy Father's weak and old,
And finds the Church too hard to hold;
He's ill, his sufferings are severe,
And feels perhaps the end is near.

He could . . . well . . . die, oldest of men.
He could, dear cousin, yes, and then . . .
Not that I wish it, no, not I;
But nature fails, and he could die.

You've helped, but left me powerless still,
Why not your good intent fulfill?
Remove me from this serpents' lair
And clear my way to Peter's chair!

Then will arrive the longed-for day
When all I've promised I will pay.
Your son?. . . . Command! It shall be done,
My Rescuer, my godlike one!"

"Silence!" Yglano cried, "My ear
So many words is made to hear;
But what they mean, what lies behind,
Is something that I mean to find.

As cardinal, your hands are tied;
As Pope, you could not be defied?
Well, we shall see—well, we shall see,
If you have faith, so shall it be."

His hand raised almost threatening there
Traced rapid circles in the air.
"Sic hocus pocus Shibboleth!
Day dawns not before night's last breath!"

The staring cardinal did not seem
To breathe, but stood as in a dream.
The word was spoken, the rite was done;
He rubbed his eyes—and still no sun.

IV

Thrown open was the guarded gate,
And Pope Anselmo emerged in state
To be enthroned 'neath St. Peter's dome,
Acclaimed by all in holy Rome.

He looked down on the cheering crowd
And blessed with "Urbi et orbi" aloud.

The Christian world before him bent;
His holiness was well content.

There pressed on him from every side
Ambassadors from far and wide.
He wore the triple crown to show
He ruled the world; they kissed his toe.

Taking his ease in the papal chair,
Untouched by the smallest hint of care,
He did not feel, important man,
Imprisoned in the Vatican.

The fare was good, the pillow fine,
His steward served the choicest wine;
And any Latin to indite
He gave a cardinal to write.

As for those folk who hoped to come
And in his ears some topic drum
That he was unconcerned about—
The porter used to keep them out.

When morning came the sun arose,
And sand to rest at evening's close;
Day followed night, night followed day,
And time went its unruffled way.

The spring was mild, the summer gold,
The fall was rich, the winter cold;
Day followed night, night followed day,
And time went its unruffled way.

The Holy Father shook his head,
"Never would I have thought," he said,
"Until its rule belonged to me,
How easy ruling earth would be."

Now, as in dream, some form appears,
Thought to be dead-and-gone for years,

A slighted claimant meets his eye,
Who says with a soft uncanny sigh:

"I am Yglano, and I can tell
You know me, cousin, you know me well;
I gave you time, had patience yet,
But now I insist you pay your debt."

Flushing red, then turning pale,
The Pope springs up and starts to rail:
"Out of my sight, you nameless blot,
Know you? Forsooth, I know you not!"

Forward two steps Yglano paced,
And then he mockingly grimaced;
As if for Anselmo's ears alone,
He said in a ghastly whispering tone:

"O gratitude! Thou duty bright,
Celestial pleasure, heavenly light!
Is thine impress on his heart,
Wilt thou and he not ever part?

You worm! I drew you from the mire,
And fattened you with the Church's hire;
I gave you wings for your giddy flight,
But nothing was good enough in your sight.

I did what you wanted me to do,
I made you a bishop and cardinal too,
Then filled your maw with the Holy See—
So what has become of your promise to me?"

The Holy Father began to shout,
"Seize this rude fellow and throw him out:
Ho there guards! We are under attack,
Seize the greybeard and haul him back!"

Yglano continued, since nobody heard,
"Keep for me, Pope, your given word.

I am asking you times one, two, and three—
I, who control your destiny."

But the Pope his stern rebuke resented,
And screamed and howled like one demented,
"Foul heretic wizard, the promise I make,
And will keep, is to burn you alive at the stake!"

Yglano replied, "Now, cousin, you know,
From experience, how the matter would go:
Each for himself—what good would it do
For me to involve myself with you?"

Yglano approached at a rapid pace,
And flicked his hand across the face
Of Anselmo, to make his senses clear
While the dire words echoed in his ear.

He awoke in rags, and still held in his hand
An hourglass starting to trickle sand;
And there was Yglano near the door
Of a bookcase, much as he stood before.

Dame Martha still poured a thread of wine
Into the waiting goblet fine.
And now the wine came to the brim,
And she turned to the host and gave to him.

Yglano took and drank it up,
He thanked her and returned the cup.
He detached the glass from his cousin's hand
And deposited it on a nearby stand.

"I am sorry," he said, "that you cannot share
A morsel of our humble fare;
Such a queer bird you seem to be,
As I think Dame Martha will agree.

And now goodbye! We'll light the hall
In case our cousin has a fall

And breaks his neck; so, Martha, mind him,
But see you bolt the door behind him."

•   •   •

COMMENTS

In the various old texts, different towns or cities are named in
our ballad (*Der Sängerkrieg auf der Wartburg*) as having schools
of astronomy, astrology, natural philosophy, etc. All agree, however, in assigning the origin of these schools—known as schools
of magic—to the Orient. Those that were founded in Spain
later on, undoubtedly owe their existence to the Arabs (Moors).
It cannot be denied that, in those days, the Arabs were more
advanced than the Christians; and many youths from the higher
ranks of society put aside religious prejudice in order to enter
the schools of the "heathen" Mahometans. Certainly, Christians
acquired the above-mentioned sciences from them, and also the
art of magic; and, as the initial contact was made before the
Inquisition had been set up to enforce a mindless uniformity,
magic could be studied without fear of repercussions. Jews in
those days, especially in Spain, transmitted the knowledge and
science of North Africa and Asia to the Europeans. One example is Ibn Ezra or Abraham ben Meir (1093–1167) (Ludwig
Ettmüller: *Der Singerkriec uf Wartburc*, Ilmenau, 1830, pp. 172,
173). The wealth gained by the Jews in medieval Toledo was
expended on two magnificent buildings erected in the Moorish
style. Built in the 13th century, and renamed Santa Maria de
la Blanca and El Transito on being consecrated as churches
after the expulsion of the Jews, the walls of these synagogues
still bear quotations from the Psalms of David in Hebrew concerning prosperity and happiness. On the tiles of El Transito,
a few plain memorials recall the military order of Calatrava to
which the synagogue was surrendered in 1494.

There is a building in Toledo associated with El Greco,
which was erected by the powerful treasurer of Peter the Cruel
(1334/1350/1369) Samuel ben Mirr Ha Levi. It is backed by a
small adjoining edifice. The older part of this dwelling retains
something of its original form, with the little pillared court, and
tiny kitchen, used by the celebrated artist (Domenico Theoto-